THE ROYAL MINORITIES OF MEDIEVAL AND EARLY MODERN ENGLAND

THE ROYAL MINORITIES OF MEDIEVAL AND EARLY MODERN ENGLAND

Edited by Charles Beem

palgrave
macmillan

First published in 2008 by PALGRAVE MACMILLAN® in the
United States - a division of St. Martin's Press LLC, 175 Fifth
Avenue, New York, NY 10010.

Where this book is distributed in the UK, Europe and the rest of
the world, this is by Palgrave Macmillan, a division of Macmillan
Publishers Limited, registered in England, company number 785998,
of Houndmills, Basingstoke, Hampshire RG21 6XS.

Palgrave Macmillan is the global academic imprint of the above companies and has companies and representatives throughout the world.

Palgrave® and Macmillan® are registered trademarks in the United
States, the United Kingdom, Europe and other countries.

ISBN-13: 978-0-230-60866-5
ISBN-10: 0-230-60866-3

Library of Congress Cataloging-in-Publication Data

The royal minorities of medieval and early modern England / edited by
Charles Beem.
    p. cm.
    Includes bibliographical references and index.
    ISBN 0-230-60866-3
1. Great Britain—Kings and rulers—Biography.   2. Children—
Great Britain—History.   3. Great Britain—Kings and rulers—
Children.   4. Great Britain—Politics and government—History.
5. Monarchy—England—History.   I. Beem, Charles.
    DA28.1.R6767   2008
    942.03092'2—dc22   2008013436

A catalogue record of the book is available from the British Library.

Design by Westchester Book Group.

First edition: November 2008

10 9 8 7 6 5 4 3 2 1

Printed in the United States of America.

For Jay

Contents

ACKNOWLEDGMENTS

While an M.A. student at Northern Arizona University during the late 1980s, I wrote an overly long and amateurish history of England's six boy kings, entitled *The Royal Minorities of Medieval and Early Modern England*. Since that time, I have been intrigued by the possibilities arising from a *longue duree* approach to understanding the historical evolution of the English monarchy. In my doctoral dissertation, and subsequent first book, I undertook the task of digesting and analyzing multiple historiographies describing several periods of English history, in order to explore and interpret the collective impact of regnant queenship upon English historical development. Older and wiser now, this volume represents the efforts of seven scholars, all specialists of specific periods of English history, to offer a comprehensive analysis of the collective historical impact of six royal minorities on English political development. Accordingly, I wish to thank the contributors, Frank Wiswall, Christian Hillen, J. S. Bothwell, Gwilym Dodd, R. A. Griffiths, and Michael Hicks, all gentlemen as well as scholars, for making time in their busy schedules to contribute their essays. Thanks also to our editor at Palgrave, Chris Chappell, for his advice and support, and my colleagues Carole Levin, Robert Bucholz, and Richard Cosgrove, for the unflagging enthusiasm they have offered this project.

Notes on Contributors

Frank Wiswall wrote his thesis at the University of St. Andrews on the royal minorities of medieval and early modern England. He published a chapter on the minority of Edward III in *The Age of Richard II*, ed. James Gillespie (Sutton, 1997), and is currently writing a full-length comparative monograph on the royal minorities in England. Since 1998, he has taught history at Cranbrook Kingswood School in Bloomfield Hills, Michigan.

Christian Hillen has studied medieval European History at Washington State University and The Rheinische Friedrich-Wilhelms University in Bonn Germany. He received his Ph.D. in 1999, writing his thesis on the Holy Roman Emperor Henry VII, entitled *Curia Regis*. He is currently a research assistant at The Stiftung Rheinisch-Westfallisches in Cologne, Germany.

J. S. Bothwell is a Lecturer in Later Medieval English History in the School of Historical Studies at the University of Leicester. He is the author of *Edward III and the English Peerage: Royal Patronage, Social Mobility and Political Control in Fourteenth-Century England* (Boydell and Brewer, 2004). His latest monograph is *Falling from Grace: Reversal of Fortune, Exile and Redemption in Later Medieval England 1075–1455* (Manchester University Press, 2007).

Gwilym Dodd is associate professor in medieval History at the University of Nottingham. He is the author of *Justice and Grace: Private Petitioning and the English Parliament in the Late Middle Ages* (OUP, 2007), and the editor of *The Reign of Richard II* (Stroud, 2000). Dodd has also written numerous essays and articles on several aspects of late medieval English history, particularly the history of parliament.

R. A. Griffiths is Professor Emeritus of the University of Wales, Swansea. For the past thirty years, he has published widely on many aspects of the political history of late medieval England, including *The Reign of Henry VI*, which has been published in three editions, and is widely recognized as the definitive work on Henry VI.

Michael Hicks has taught for the past thirty years at the University of Winchester, where he is Head of History and Professor of Medieval History. He has written extensively on the later middle ages, especially the fifteenth century, and has published books on Edward IV, Edward V, and Richard III and his queen Anne Neville. He is currently working on *The Wars of the Roses* for Yale University Press.

Charles Beem is an Assistant Professor of History at the University of North Carolina, Pembroke. He is the author of *The Lioness Roared: The Problems of Female Rule in English History,* and is currently at work on a study of the colorful English Renaissance figure George Ferrers.

WOE TO THEE, O LAND!
THE INTRODUCTION

Charles Beem

Woe to thee, O land, when thy king is a child. . . .

Ecclesiastes, 10:16

Within the manuscript collection at the British Library in London is a curious document entitled "Notes concerning the minority of a king and the administration of government during a king's minority."[1] The anonymous author, who probably composed this work early in the year 1751, consulted a significant body of primary and secondary sources to fashion a narrative that unmistakably identified the significance of minority reigns in English history. Indeed, the author duly recounted the major historical developments of England's six minority reigns: the successive confirmations of Magna Carta by Henry III, the growth of councils and parliaments as consultative and administrative bodies under Richard II and Henry VI, the historical evolution of the office of Lord Protector of England, and the recognition of kingship as an abstract entity in political theory. This history of English royal minorities was compiled to serve an immediate political purpose. Frederick, Prince of Wales and heir apparent to the British throne, had recently died (31 March 1751), leaving his thirteen-year-old son, the future George III, as the elderly George II's heir apparent. Quite suddenly, the dusty precedents of England's medieval and early modern past became all too relevant to the possible contingency of a mid-eighteenth-century royal minority.[2]

As was done during the final years of Henry VIII's sixteenth-century reign, parliament drafted legislation to prescribe a form of minority government. In the Regency Act of 1751, enacted in case George II died before his grandson achieved his majority, parliament struck a balance between precedents prescribing both conciliar forms and sole regencies. Indeed, the statute mandated that the still formidable royal prerogative was to be exercised by the widowed princess of Wales as regent, assisted by a council headed by her brother-in-law, the duke of Cumberland, should George II die before his grandson achieved his majority. Such compromises represented a serious attempt to create the conditions for consensus building between opposing political factions, the most positive historical legacy of English minority reigns.[3] These arrangements, which attempted to mediate the fierce animosity between the mother and the uncle of the future king, reflected more than just a cursory glance at the history of English royal minorities.

Invariably, the second Hanoverian king lived long enough for his grandson and heir to achieve his majority. However, the threat of a possible royal minority appeared once more in 1765, when George III himself was struck down by a serious illness, perhaps the first signs of porphyria, necessitating another constitutional crisis over the possible regency of his three-year-old son. On this occasion, as in 1751, the strife of party politics was the modernizing trend that updated the perennial political power plays that always presaged the possibility of a royal minority.[4] George III's recovery, however, prevented the accession of what might have been the first infant king since the fifteenth-century Henry VI.

The legislators responsible for the drafting of the Regency Act, the obvious target audience for the "Notes concerning the minority of a king" manuscript, invariably came across a number of options to choose from concerning the form and function of a minority government. Nevertheless, the unavoidable conclusion to be drawn was that, even under the most stable of English royal minorities, political instability was unavoidable within the evolution of a system that never developed any permanent constitutional mechanisms to deal with this anomalous manifestation of kingly sovereignty. At their worst, however, minority reigns resulted in the most spectacularly violent political upheavals in medieval English history.

Minority reigns dot the landscape of medieval and early modern English history with astonishing regularity, as they applied periodic tests through time upon the durability of the English body politic. These minority reigns included those of Henry III (1216–27), Edward III (1327–30), Richard II (1377–89), Henry VI (1422–37), Edward V (April-June 1483), and Edward VI (1547–53).[5] While no further royal minorities have occurred since the untimely death of Edward VI, there have been a few near misses. In the aftermath of the Glorious Revolution (1688–89), to an indeterminate number of Jacobites, James Stuart, son of the deposed James II (known later in life as "The Old Pretender"), made an attractive Catholic alternative to William III and later Queen Anne, following his father's death in 1701, when he was thirteen. As the Act of Settlement (1701) attempted to preserve the hereditary principle within a parliamentary mandated Protestant succession, royal minorities were a distinct possibility during the 1750s and 1760s, and during much of the reign of William IV (1830–37), whose underage heir was his niece Victoria.

MINORITIES AS A DISTINCT FORM OF KINGSHIP

Royal minorities changed the way England was governed, as it altered the way English subjects perceived their king and his relationship to God, war, and the maintenance of law and order. Examined collectively, it becomes clear that the events and consequences of English minority reigns significantly affected the course of English medieval and early modern political development. As the study of female rule provides a particular perspective upon the historical evolution of English political theory and structure, so does that of the royal minority.[6] The means by which regents, protectors, and various forms of royal councils attempted to legitimize their exercise of political authority through time altered the political and constitutional development of the English monarchy, as did the actions of certain royal minors themselves, in their adult reactions against the constraints placed upon them during their underage. Uncovering the collective historical impact of these minority reigns and explaining their historical relationship to each other is a historical task that is well worth investigating.

The accessions of England's six minority kings required ad hoc innovations to one basic political problem, the theoretical clash between the right of inheritance to the estate of kingship and the exercise of the political, sarcedotal, military, and juridical prerogatives attached to the office of king. While precedents derived from inheritance practices provided the closest analogies for the disposition of the *estate* of kingship, the *office* of king was no ordinary feudal tenure. As Henry VI's lord chief justice John Fortescue observed, "though the king's estate be the highest estate temporal in the erthe, yet it is an office in wich he mynestrith to his reaume defence and justice."[7] Minor kings were always recognized as possessing the *estate* of kingship, which could be "farmed out" to a regent, protector, or council, and a "body natural," which, subsumed by the immortal "body politic" of kingship, could be possessed as a legitimizing agent for exercising royal authority.[8] The crown, however, transcended the obvious analogies to feudal inheritance rights. Like their adult male counterparts, under-age male kings came to be considered through time as *persona pub-lica,* or a "corporation sole," in full possession of the seemingly indivisible sovereignty vested in the "body politic" of kingship, which was not so easily farmed out or possessed by either an individual or a group of individuals acting collectively. In all cases, it was recognized that the minority king possessed full kingly sovereignty, whether or not he was recognized in law as a minor, allowing him to legitimize the acts of his government by "consenting" to their policies that offi-cially were his own.[9] Even when the king was an infant, such as the fifteenth-century Henry VI, who became king at the age of nine months, means were devised to discern his royal consent to the ac-tions taken on his behalf.

Despite the various fictional devices designed to create the percep-tion that a capable adult king was ruling, the practical and necessary cleavage between the wardship of the minor king and the use of his royal prerogative constituted an exercise of royal authority lacking the full legitimacy conferred upon it by the actual participation of the king himself. Such delegated power inevitably fractured the wholeness of kingship, as represented by the medieval theory of the king's two bod-ies; while the minor possessed the eternal "body politic" of kingship from the moment of his accession, his "body natural," while possessing the kingly estate, did not initially rule, the lives of England's minority kings were consumed by "on the job training," turning fiction into re-ality as they spent their youths moving steadily toward the ultimate goal of attaining their full majority, unless death or deposition stopped them in their tracks.

For those minors who did achieve their majorities, their kingly ap-prenticeship involved negotiating a symbiotic political relationship between themselves and those who governed on their behalf, as royal power slowly but inevitably transferred to the maturing king. In the history of English royal minorities, this process was often traumatic, especially when those in control of the minority attempted to modify or simply resisted the expressed will of the boy king. Henry III, Edward III, and Richard II sought majority retribution against those who had imposed minority constraints, resulting in significant consti-tutional ramifications for barons, kings, and the evolutionary develop-ment of the king's inner council as well as great councils and the representative institution of parliament. The most astute of men who exercised authority in minority governments, such as the fourteenth-century John of Gaunt, duke of Lancaster, and the sixteenth-century John Dudley, duke of Northumberland, kept an eye on both the present as well as the future, when the minority king would rule in his own right. Explaining how the multiple processes at work during minority reigns were negotiated and accomplished through time is the primary goal of this volume of essays. The historical examination of the collective impact of English minority reigns brings into focus a significant facet of English political and constitutional development from a unique perspective, as each succeeding minority reign brought a periodic test to the strength and durability of a constantly evolving system of government over nearly a three-hundred-and-fifty-year period. The triumph of primogeniture, the growth of conciliar government, and rapid bursts of increasing legitimacy for parliament as a representative and administrative force all occurred within the historical context of English minority reigns.

The editor has not attempted to impose any interpretive framework upon this project other than to request that the contributors consider the question of whether these six reigns, spread out over the course of four centuries, have any substantive historical relationship to one another. These scholars have brought an eclectic approach to their thoughts concerning the concept of royal minorities as a *particular* type of historical epoch in English history. Frank Wiswall has crafted a solid and lucid study of the construction and maintenance of England's first postconquest royal minority of Henry III. As Henry's minority had no substantive English historical antecedents to compare to, Christian Hillen has embellished Wiswall's survey with a discussion of royal minorities in the larger context of thirteenth-century Europe, employing the reigns of French, German, Aragonese, and Hungarian minority kings as a comparative model to measure the form and function of Henry III's minority against the progression of European-wide political structures.

The remaining chapters focus exclusively on the history of English minority reigns themselves. In chapter 2, J. S. Bothwell has subjected England's greatest medieval royal scandal, the de facto regency of Isabella, the "she-wolf of France," to a rigorous historical analysis that uncovers a startling amount of continuity in the forms and functions of royal administration between the reigns of Edward II and Edward III's minority and early majority reign. Like Bothwell, Gwilym Dodd challenges the conventional historiography of Richard II's minority to offer a number of fresh historical perspectives on both the political theory and the forms behind this watershed minority reign, which in turn provided a powerful model for the succeeding minority reign of Henry VI. In chapter 4, R. A. Griffiths looks both backward and forward through time to offer a thorough distillation of his fruitful career studying the Lancastrian monarchy on the significance of Henry VI's long minority, as does Michael Hicks for the succeeding House of York in chapter 5. In this chapter on the tragic minority of Edward V, Hicks offers a direct and succinct account that provides the crucial historical link between the medieval minorities and that of Edward VI. In his final chapter, Charles Beem examines Edward VI's royal minority against the collective impact of the five previous ones, to provide a thoughtful interpretation of Henry VIII's attempts to create the ideal scenario for an anticipated minority succession and a fresh perspective on the historical agency of England's final minority king.

THE BOY KING IN HISTORY

The role heredity has played within political structures throughout history has been subject to the luck of the draw. For instance, one of the worst-case scenarios for minority successions occurred in sixteenth-century Scotland, where *all four reigning monarchs* succeeded as minors. Since the dawn of recorded history, minority reigns have occurred whenever monarchical governmental systems, usually in male-dominant political societies, were stable enough to impose a system of hereditary succession. Royal minorities, from Tutankhamen of Egypt to P'u Yi, the last emperor of China, constituted occasional inconveniences as well as opportunities for various forms of monarchical government.

Old Testament kingship, which cast a powerful historical influence upon Christian medieval Europe, offers a number of archetypal models for the forms and functions of royal minorities. As the Tribes of Israel developed more complex political structures, their first king, Saul, owed his elevation to both election, which recognized his abilities as a charismatic war leader, and his covenant with Yahweh, symbolized by his ritual anointment by the prophet Samuel.[10] The dynastic principle, however, only came into effect with the rise of the Davidic royal house, commencing with the accession of Solomon, one of David's younger sons, due to the efforts of a cabal headed by his mother, Bathsheba, and the prophet Nathan (1 Kings 1–3).[11]

Following the division of Solomon's empire into the separate kingdoms of Israel and Judah, only Judah adhered to a strict dynastic principle, keeping the royal line of David on the throne until the kingdom's destruction in 586 B.C. Not surprisingly, Judah experienced a number of royal minorities. In one case, the accession of a minor was the only recourse to preserve the Davidic royal line, as when Queen Athaliah "destroyed all the seed royal" of Judah except for the youth Jehoash, who was hidden away for six years while Judah experienced the rule of what was essentially a regnant queen noted for her wickedness (2 Kings 11–12). Athaliah was eventually toppled by a palace coup led by the high priest Jehoiada, who placed seven-year-old Jehoash on the throne, employing his youthful sovereignty to provide legitimacy for Athaliah's murder and the destruction of the cult of Baal in Judah. Like Jehoash, Henry III, England's first post-conquest minority king, did not have to compete with any formidable adult male challengers within his family to achieve his succession, as did his cousin, Arthur of Brittany, and his fifteenth-century descendant Edward V. The accessions of Richard II and Edward VI also represented "Jehoash-like" new beginnings, as these youths were perceived as providentially provided kings, "God's elect," whom God had unmistakably chosen to succeed even as youths. The story of Athalia and Jehoash was both a positive and a potent example of the opportunities provided by the accession of a child. Indeed, the episode was reproduced during Henry VI's fifteenth-century minority in John Lydgate's *The Fall of Princes,* a didactic poetic history derived from Boccaccio and commissioned by the Lancastrian prince Humphrey, duke of Gloucester.[12]

The Old Testament provided other examples to medieval and early modern English political society of God providentially providing a child to do "what was right in the eyes of the Lord." The career of Josiah, the most distinguished boy king of Ancient Judah, provided a powerful historical analogy for the reforming kingship of the sixteenth-century Edward VI of England. Like Edward VI, Josiah owed his elevation to direct primogeniture, as the son of Amon, a king who did "that which is evil in the sight of the Lord" (2 Kings 21:20). In contrast, the youthful Josiah walked the straight line of the God of Israel, eventually instituting reforms that restored the observance of Deuteronomic law as he banished the forces of idolatry (2 Kings 22–23). Old Testament kingship, as it was incorporated into the historical tradition of medieval and early modern Christian Europe, provided a striking justification for minority reigns, as the Church conferred spiritual legitimacy on hereditary kingship, which endowed primogeniture as a mechanism for recognizing the accession of "God's elect," even when he was a child.[13]

God's elect still needed to be trained for their future roles as adult kings, a crucial task for all minority regimes. In this regard, the success rate was hardly encouraging. In fact, of all England's boy kings, only

Edward III went on to a truly successful majority reign, although Edward VI had all the makings of a successful adult king, had he lived longer. Nevertheless, throughout the middle ages and into the sixteenth century, contemporaries had little choice but to contemplate the meaning of minority kingship. Early in the fourteenth century, William of Pagula wrote "The Mirror of Edward III" soon after the still youthful and presumably impressionable Edward achieved his majority, while later in the century John Wyclif composed "On the duty of a King"—works inspired by the occasion of a royal minority to set down clear guidelines for the proper training of kings.[14] During the minority of Richard II, John Gower, the contemporary and friend of Geoffrey Chaucer, on the prompting of the youthful king, composed the *Vox Clamantis* in Latin, and later the *Confessio Amantis* in English, poems long and didactic, containing sections on the proper training for a king, the ideal (in book VII of the *Confessio*) being Aristotle's tutoring of Alexander.[15] Over the course of Richard II's reign, as youthful promise progressed into the violence of his later minority and the tyranny of his adult kingship, chronicler Thomas of Walsingham blamed Richard's failure as an adult king on a lack of proper princely training.[16] By the later sixteenth century, chronicler John Stow quoted from a later version of Gower's *Vox Clamantis*, "the foolish counsel of the lewde and yong he [King Richard] did receive, and grave advise of aged heads, he did reject and leave. . . ."[17] As we shall see, Henry VIII, the father of England's final minority king, made sure that the future Edward VI avoided the pitfalls of Richard II's misguided youth to become the most rigorously trained of all minority kings.

ANGLO-SAXON AND NORMAN KINGSHIP

Edward VI's sixteenth-century minority was the end product of nearly a millennium of precedents relating to royal minorities in English history. Like the ancient Israelites, who evolved from tribal confederations to charismatic and finally hereditary kingship, Anglo-Saxon kingship evolved from the first arrival of these barbaric Germanic tribes, in the fifth and sixth centuries A.D., until the Norman conquest of 1066. The first Anglo-Saxon political leaders were the products of two developmental trajectories: kings (*reges*), based upon birthright, and military leaders (*duces*), based upon leadership ability.[18] In both cases, however, the maintenance of a position of authority depended upon widespread recognition of charismatic military prowess.[19] As the Anglo-Saxons established kingdoms in the centuries following their initial invasion and settlement, as they subdued the Romano-Celtic populations, and as they battled Picts, Vikings, and each other, the kings of the heptarchy owed their elevations primarily to military competence, rather than primogeniture, even after their conversion to Christianity. While royal blood was undoubtedly a major factor in their elevations, designating kings was primarily an elective process.[20] Consequently, minority reigns were virtually unknown in early Anglo-Saxon England as royal uncles, cousins, younger brothers, or other adult male kinsmen often succeeded in place of underage eldest sons.

During the seventh century, as Northumbria emerged as the dominant Anglo-Saxon kingdom, the first English royal minorities made their appearance. In his work *Ecclesiastical History of the English People*, the venerable Bede tersely described the accession of eight-year-old king Osred, the son of Aldfrid, in the year 705, who reigned for eight years. These kings were the successors of Oswy, the powerful *bretwalda* who summoned and decided the fate of the English church at the Synod of Whitby in 664.[21] Although Bede did not explain *why* a child became king at this time, it can be inferred that Osred's accession reflected the strength and legitimacy of Oswy's dynasty.[22] During the eighth century, as Northumbrian predominance gave way to Mercian, and during the ninth, as Wessex held out under the Viking invasions, royal minorities disappear from the historical record, as the "job description" of successful kingship demanded formidable military and leadership abilities, relegating primogeniture as a secondary determinant for the succession.

Only with the triumph of the royal House of Wessex, which had absorbed the rest of the Heptarchy kingdoms and the Danelaw by the tenth century, did instances of primogeniture and royal minorities reappear within Anglo-Saxon succession patterns. The Wessex king Edward the Elder (899–924) succeeded his father Alfred the Great (871–899) as his eldest living son, but Edward was also a capable adult possessed of superior military ability. Edward, however, was succeeded in turn by a procession of his adult sons, Aethelstan (924–939), Edmund the Elder (939–946), and Eadred (946–955). With Eadred's death, however, Edmund the Elder's fourteen-year-old son Eadwig (955–959) was recognized as king of Wessex, while his younger brother Edgar was elected king of Mercia and Northumbria, even though he was only twelve. In both instances, regal power was exercised by councils; in the case of Wessex, dominated by Dunstan, Abbot of Glastonbury. Eadwig was apparently a difficult child monarch, and, following his untimely death, Edgar, now fifteen, was elevated to the kingship of Wessex. In 973, Dunstan, now archbishop of Canterbury, crowned the adult and energetic Edgar as king of all the English.

Edgar's reign provided a positive historical example of the transition from underage to adult king, as it witnessed the continuing evolution of Anglo-Saxon kingship as the font of justice.[23] Edgar's success in emulating the now varied responsibilities of kingship allowed contemporaries to view his youthful accession as the providential work of God, echoing the achievements of the biblical Josiah:

He became greatly honored wide throughout the land of the nation, for he readily honoured God's name, and deliberated God's law over and again, and promoted God's praise far and wide, and counseled all his nation wisely, very often, always continuously, for God and for the world.[24]

Edgar's various marriages, however, produced dynastic instability. By his first wife Aethelfleda, Edgar had a son, Edward the Martyr (975–978), whom the Witan elected to succeed his father at the age of thirteen. Edward's elevation was not unanimous, however. The child king Edward, who suffered from bouts of uncontrollable rage, was hard to handle, which resulted in the advocacy within the Wessex Witan for the candidacy of his younger half brother Aethelred, the son of Edgar's second wife Aelfrida. In 978, as Edward entered Corfe Castle in Dorset to visit his stepmother and younger brother, he was stabbed to death by Aethelred's household men, while Aethelred succeeded him as king at the age of ten.[25] For the rest of Aethelred's minority, his mother Aefrida, in conjunction with the Mercian ealdorman Alhere, dominated the government.

In marked contrast to Edgar's, Aethelred's early kingship created a powerful historical model for the undesirability of minority reigns.[26] Writing well over a century later, historian William of Malmesbury reported that during his christening, Aethelred "interrupted the sacrament by opening his bowels," causing Archbishop Dunstan to predict that he would be "a wastrel when he becomes a man."[27] Aethelred was also saddled with guilt over the murder of his martyred half-brother, although, as a child, he played no part in this crime.[28] But he also inherited a growing conflict between monastic and secular aristocratic power that rendered him a flesh and blood pawn for rival factions during the course of minority reign. At the same time, renewed Viking invasions also cast a pall over his reign, which, the *Anglo-Saxon Chronicle* reported, began with the appearance of "a bloody cloud . . . many times in the likeness of fire," and which contemporaries perceived as an ill-omen for an ultimately disastrous reign.[29]

Two centuries later, the verdict on Aethelred's minority reign was summed up in verse, highly reminiscent of the extract from *Ecclesiastes:* "When a child is king, and a ceorl bishop and a slave ealdorman, its bad news for the people."[30] From Aethelred's majority to the Norman Conquest there were no more royal minorities, as the English succession was determined by a plethora of mechanisms that remained intact for the duration of English medieval history: primogeniture, election based upon royal descent, and conquest.[31] From the death of the Danish interloper Canute in 1035 until William of Normandy's invasion of 1066, election emerged as the dominant mechanism for determining the succession, as royal claimants were constrained to defend their rights against a literal procession of vigorous adult male challengers.

With the death of Edward the Confessor in January 1066, an intense competition ensued between members of the Godwin family, the king of Norway, and William, duke of Normandy, for the English crown. All of these claimants, Harold Godwin (who was elected Edward's successor), his brother Tostig, Harold Hardratha, and William of Normandy, could claim some tangential kinship relationship to Edward the Confessor; but when the dust had settled, following William's victory at Hastings (14 October 1066), it was force of arms that had decided the English succession, which carried with it, in the medieval worldview, the blessing of God, the ultimate form of legitimacy.

Nevertheless, in desperation, the Anglo-Saxon Witan hastily elected thirteen-year-old Edgar *Aetheling,* the only surviving grandson of Edmund Ironside, as king. Edward the Confessor had in fact toyed with the idea of designating Edgar's elder brother Edward as his successor in 1056, but the prince died soon after his arrival in England. There was no discussion whatsoever of Edgar's candidacy when Edward the Confessor died in January 1066, when Harold was swiftly elected king. In October of 1066, however, when all the other adult male challengers to William (Harold, Tostig, and Hardratha) were in their graves, young Edgar presented the only possible dynastic alternative to William, a scenario remarkably similar to that of 1216, when nine-year-old Henry III was hastily crowned John's successor. Edgar, however, was not so fortunate. His "minority" reign was short-lived, following his submission to William in late 1066, who treated the youth rather generously, despite Edgar's periodic interventions in the dynastic squabbles of the Norman royal house.

The succession patterns of the Norman and Plantagenet kings hardly appeared to have paved the way for the advent of English royal minorities. On his deathbed in 1087, William the Conqueror split his patrimony between his two eldest sons, Robert Curthose, who received Normandy, and William Rufus, the second son, who received England. When William Rufus died in 1100, his younger brother Henry acted swiftly, seizing the royal treasure at Winchester and securing his elevation as king of England. Henry I's accession represents the continuity of a basic Anglo-Saxon model; his close blood relationship to the Norman royal house rendered him "king-worthy," but his decisiveness, ruthlessness, and leadership ability ultimately secured for him both the English kingdom as well as the duchy of Normandy.

While heredity played only a supporting role in what was still essentially a charismatic and elective kingship, Henry I attempted to impose a system of primogeniture to secure the succession of his own heirs, a major step toward creating the conditions for the rise of minority kings, as he secured solemn oaths from his spiritual and temporal tenants-in-chief to recognize and support his daughter Matilda as his successor.[32] When Henry I died in 1135, however, his nephew, Stephen of Blois, ascended the English throne in a manner remarkably similar to that of Henry I himself in 1100. Matilda subsequently challenged Stephen's right to the throne, a struggle she bequeathed to her eldest son, Henry Plantagenet, in 1148.[33] By 1153, Henry's armed might and widespread acknowledgment of his hereditary right forced Stephen to recognize Henry as his successor. While Henry II's dynastic legitimacy was based upon a theory of female inclusive primogeniture, the theory was only put into practice by a combination of charismatic leadership and military muscle.

Henry II's subsequent thirty-five-year reign (1154–89) was blessed (or cursed!) by a plethora of adult male heirs, whose machinations complicated the development of primogeniture as a means to order the Anglo-Norman succession, a concept that already had begun to determine twelfth-century inheritance practices.[34] The contemporary Gerald of Wales may not have been too off the mark when he described Henry's sons as "princes who did not succeed one another in regular hereditary order but required violent domination through an inversion of order by killing and slaughtering their own."[35] When Henry II died in 1189, he was succeeded in turn by his eldest adult son, Richard I, who died childless ten years later. Richard had two younger brothers, however, Geoffrey, count of Brittany, and John. Geoffrey had predeceased Richard but had a son, Arthur, who was twelve at the time of Richard I's death. Earlier in his reign, Richard had designated Arthur as his heir instead of his adult brother John.[36]

However, on his deathbed, Richard apparently changed his mind, naming his brother John as his successor.[37] At this juncture of English history, there were not any clearly defined legal or constitutional principles governing the succession. There was, in fact, considerable difference of opinion concerning who should be Richard's rightful heir. In his biography of William the Marshal, earl of Pembroke, the loyal supporter of the first four Plantagenet kings, Sidney Painter described the essential differences of interpretation between Marshal and archbishop of Canterbury Hubert Walter. While Marshal argued on behalf of Norman custom, "the younger son is the nearer heir to the inheritance of his father than the child of the elder brother who died before his brother," Walter argued for a succession based on the principle of primogeniture. Inevitably, Marshal swayed Walter, as both men moved swiftly to secure John's rights in England.[38] Worldly and astute, Walter nevertheless had serious misgivings about John's candidacy, as Roger of Wendover recorded:

He [Walter] knew John would one day or the other bring the kingdom into great confusion, wherefore he determined that he [John] should owe his elevation to election and not hereditary right.[39]

The barons of Anjou, Maine, and Tours, however, leaned toward Arthur, as did king Philip Augustus of France, the feudal overlord of the continental Angevin territories, who assumed the role of Arthur's protector.[40] Inevitably, it was the adult John's political and military power that decided the issue; which the resources of the youthful Arthur were no match for. After a six-week interregnum, John was elected and crowned king of England and swiftly moved to secure control over Normandy and Anjou. In 1202, during the conflict between John and Philip Augustus, Arthur fell into John's custody and he disappeared from view, probably murdered at John's express command, or, as some sources claimed, by John's own hand.[41]

Arthur's mysterious and tragic fate seemed to offer ample testimony to the fact that to be king in England at the dawn of the thirteenth century required much more than a hereditary right. To ascend the throne required positive military action, the backing of the baronage and church hierarchy, and the stamina and charisma to push through to completion what was still an essentially elective process.[42] Inevitably, since the death of William the Conqueror in 1087, the victor was invariably an energetic, powerful, adult male claimant, as both the empress Matilda and Arthur of Brittany found to their cost.

Given these circumstances, even the most astute of political observers during John's reign would hardly have envisioned that John would be succeeded by a minority king. However, Arthur's failure to succeed Richard I was the last gasp of an elective monarchy in England. When John himself died in 1216, amid a civil war that sought to place a French prince on the English throne, he was succeeded by his nine-year-old son Henry III. This development, however, which ushered in the first postconquest royal minority, was hardly inevitable.

NOTES

1. British Library (afterward BL) Add 36085 ("the "Hardwicke Papers" vol. 737).
2. See Derek Jarrett, "The Regency Crisis of 1765," *English Historical Review* 85, no. 335 (April 1970): 282–315.
3. J. S. Roskell, "The Office and Dignity of Protector of England, with Special Reference to its Origins," *English Historical Review* 68 (April 1953): 193–233.
4. Ibid., 283.
5. The date of 1389 for the conclusion of Richard II's minority signifies the king's own determination that he had achieved his full majority.
6. See Charles Beem, *The Lioness Roared: The Problems of Female Rule in English History* (New York: Palgrave Macmillan, 2006).
7. Cited in S. B. Chrimes, *English Constitutional Ideas in the Fifteenth Century* (London: Cambridge University Press, 1936), 14.
8. For the classic study on the medieval theory of the "king's two bodies," see Ernst Kantorwicz, *The King's Two Bodies: A Study in Medieval Theology* (Princeton: Princeton University Press, 1957). See also F. W. Maitland, "The Crown as Corporation," in *Collected Papers of Frederic William Maitland* (3 vols.), ed. H. A. L. Fisher, 3: iii, 245–49 (Cambridge: Cambridge University Press, 1911).
9. BL 36085, n. 1. This manuscript notes how Edward III, king at age 14 in 1327, was recognized as an adult king, which the anonymous author identifies within the theory of the "king's two bodies," noting that "the king, as king, is always of full age, that his acts cannot be voided by his non-age."
10. See Tomoo Ishida, *The Royal Dynasties in Ancient Israel* (Berlin and New York: Walter de Gruyter, 1977), 40–52.
11. John Rogerson, *Chronicles of the Old Testament Kings* (London and New York: Thames and Hudson, 1999), 80–85.
12. John Lydgate, *Lydgate's Fall of Princes, pt. 1, books I and II*, ed. Henry Bergen (Washington, DC: The Carnegie Institution, 1923), 249–52.
13. See Henry A. Myers, *Medieval Kingship* (Chicago: Nelson-Hall, 1982), 15–35.

14. "William of Pagula, Mirror of Edward III," *Medieval Renaissance Texts and Studies*, no. 225 (New York: University of New York, 2002), 64–140. For Wyclif, see *Medieval Political Theory—A Reader: The Quest for a Body Politic, 1100–1400*, ed. Cary J. Nederman and Kate Langon Farhan (London and New York: Routledge, 1993), 221–29.
15. John Gower, *The Works of John Gower* (3 vols.), ed. G. C. Macaulay, 3: 33–385 (Oxford: Clarendon Press, 1901). For more recent textual analysis of Gower's work, see Russell A. Peck, *Kingship and Common Profit in Gower's Confessio Amantis* (Carbondale, IL: Southern Illinois University Press, 1978), passim.
16. Thomas Walsingham, *The Chronica Maiora of Thomas Walsingham 1376–1422*, trans. David Preest (Woodbridge, Suffolk: Boydell Press, 2005), 242–45, 254–63, 300–311.
17. John Stow, *The Chronicles of England, from Brute, unto this Present Year of Christ 1580* (London: Ralphe Newberie, 1580), 470.
18. See Martyn J. Whitlock, *The Origins of England, 410–600* (Totowa, NJ: Barnes and Noble, 1986), 5, 113, and Barbara York, *Kings and Kingdoms of Early Anglo-Saxon England* (London and New York: Routledge, 1990), 156–78.
19. Fritz Kern, *Kingship and Law (Studies in Mediaeval History IV)*, trans. S. B. Chrimes (Oxford: Basil Blackwell, 1968), 12.
20. Frederick Pollard and Frederic William Maitland, *The History of English Law Before the Time of Edward I*. 2 vols. (Cambridge: Cambridge University Press, 1878), 2:263.
21. Bede, *Ecclesiastical History of the English People*, ed. D. H. Farmer (New York: Penguin, 1991), 187–92.
22. Bede, *Ecclesiastical History*, 298.
23. Frederic William Maitland, *The Constitutional History of England* (Cambridge: Cambridge University Press, 1946), 59–60.
24. *The Anglo-Saxon Chronicle*, ed. and trans. Michael Swanton (New York: Routledge, 1998), 115.
25. Frank Stenton, *Anglo-Saxon England* (Oxford: Oxford University Press, 1971), 373–74.
26. Ann Williams, *Kingship and Government in Pre-Conquest England, c. 500–1066* (New York: St. Martin's Press, 1999), 107.
27. William of Malmesbury, *Gesta Regum Anglorum: The History of the English Kings*, vol. 1, ed. and trans. R.A.B. Mynors, R. M. Thomson, and M. Winterbottom (Oxford: Oxford University Press, 1999), 269.
28. Stenton, *Anglo-Saxon England*, 374.
29. *Anglo-Saxon Chronicle*, 122.
30. Simon Keynes, "The Declining Reputation of King Aethelred the Unready," in *Ethelred the Unready: Papers from the Millenary Conference*, ed. David Hill, 27 (Oxford: British Archaeological Reports, 1978).
31. Maitland, *Constitutional History*, 59–60, 97–98.
32. Karl Leyser, "The Anglo-Norman Succession, 1120–1125," in *Anglo-Norman Studies* xiii, ed. Marjorie Chibnall (Woodbridge, Suffolk: Boy-

dell Press, 1991), 13:225–41 and C. Warren Hollister, "The Anglo-Norman Succession Debate of 1126: Prelude to Stephen's Anarchy," *Journal of Medieval History* 1 (April 1975): 19–35.

33. Marjorie Chibnall, *The Empress Matilda* (Oxford: Basil Blackwell, 1991), 80–115.

34. John Hudson, *Land, Law, and Lordship in Anglo-Norman England* (Oxford: Clarendon Press, 1994), 65–111.

35. Cited in Robert Bartlett, *England Under the Norman and Angevin Kings, 1075–1225* (Oxford: Clarendon Press, 2000), 7.

36. Roger of Wendover, *The Flowers of History,* trans. J. A. Giles (New York: AMS press, 1968), 68.

37. Sidney Painter, *William Marshal* (London: John Hopkins Press, 1933), 118–19. Also William Stubbs, *The Constitutional History of England.* 3 vols. (Oxford: Oxford University Press, 1873), 1:551.

38. Painter, *William Marshal,* 119.

39. Wendover, *Flowers of History,* 181.

40. Wendover, *Flowers of History,* 179–80; Matthew of Westminster, *The Flowers of History,* trans. C. P. Yonge (New York: MS Press, 1968), 95.

41. For a detailed explanation for the sources regarding John's probable murder of Arthur, see F. M. Powicke, "King John and Arthur of Brittany," *English Historical Review* 24, no. 96 (Oct. 1909): 659–74, and Dominica Legge, "William Marshal and Arthur of Brittany," *Bulletin of the Institute of Historical Research* 55 (May 1982): 18–25.

42. Stubbs, *Constitutional History,* 1:535. Stubbs argued that Richard's 1189 accession was also partly an elective process.

CHAPTER 1

THE MINORITY OF HENRY III
IN THE CONTEXT OF EUROPE

Christian Hillen and Frank Wiswall

On 28 October 1216, nine days after the death of his father, nine-year-old Henry III was hastily crowned king of England in Gloucester Cathedral by the bishop of Winchester, assisted by a papal legate. As England had not experienced a royal minority since the tenth-century Aethelred "the Unready," the nobles loyal to the Plantagenet succession had to create procedures and practices that were for the most part entirely new. Legal customs had established procedures regarding the minorities of noble heirs, in terms of wardship and guardianship of property. But the extent to which these guidelines could be applied to the minority of a king was unknown and probably extremely limited. Moreover, there was very little time or opportunity for the careful consideration of constitutional problems. There was not even any assurance in 1216 that Henry III would remain king of England, since his father, King John, had died at Newark on the night of 18–19 October while losing a civil war against some of his own magnates, who sought not merely to sweep away John but his dynasty with him.

As we shall see, Henry III's minority succession was much more a crisis management response, rather than the articulation of any long-term constitutional principles. While royal minorities had occurred in hereditary monarchies since the dawn of history and would continue to do so for the remainder of the European Middle Ages, the thirteenth century provided a number of minority regimes that have allowed us to position England's first postconquest royal minority against a wider European background. As indeed, many of the factors that allowed Henry III to succeed in England in 1216 were present in other European states, with remarkably different results.

As David Carpenter has aptly put it, "No king of England came to the throne in a more desperate situation than Henry III."[1] The rival, Prince Louis of France, had been invited by the majority of John's barons to mount the English throne in John's place—assuming, of course, that he could successfully wrest the kingdom from the grip of those few magnates who remained loyal to Henry III. Indeed, as soon as word spread of the death of John, the rebel William Longsword, earl of Salisbury, wrote to Hubert de Burgh, John's justiciar and the castellan of Dover, encouraging him to surrender the castle to Louis, as the cause of John's young son was now hopeless.[2]

THE WAR WITH LOUIS, 1216–1217

The situation at John's death was therefore dangerous for the Plantagenet dynasty; it was also somewhat bizarre. One of the rebel barons' grievances against John, as expressed in Magna Carta, was his perceived overreliance on foreigners, specifically French foreigners, for domestic support. The faction of barons who had offered the crown to Louis had therefore appealed to a foreigner with no defensible claim to the English throne in an effort to rid themselves of an English king who promoted foreigners in his service and had pursued what they saw as foreign interests. Nonetheless, the death of John probably proved crucial to the eventual salvation of his dynasty, since the undoubted transgressions he had committed could hardly be laid at the feet of his young son. Henry III himself recognized this. In a royal letter soon after his accession, he declared that "a quarrel arose between our father and certain nobles of our kingdom," but that "it has nothing to do with us."[3] Pope Honorius III confirmed this in a letter of 1 December in which he ordered all of the rebels to return to allegiance to the young king, "whose age proves him innocent."[4] A growing number of those who had rebelled against his father were eventually to agree.

In the meantime, Prince Louis controlled more than half of England, including London and the southeast. He also commanded the allegiance of ninety-seven barons, including nineteen of the twenty-seven greatest barons of the realm.[5] Of those who remained loyal to Henry, however, the two greatest magnates had the ability to turn events to the young king's favor. They were William the Marshal, earl of Pembroke and Striguil, renowned as the greatest knight of the age; and Ranulf, earl of Chester. Both commanded the respect of nobles on both sides of the war, although the Marshal had the edge, being by far the older of the two. He was also close to the young king at the time of John's death, since Ranulf of Chester was campaigning in the northern marches of Wales. The other source of support for Henry came from the Church, and here the advantage for the young king was eventually to prove decisive.

The papacy made no pretence of playing the part of an honest broker in the conflict, as John had surrendered England to the Holy See in 1213 and received it back as a fief, part of the price John paid for his prolonged confrontation with the papacy over the appointment of Stephen Langton as archbishop of Canterbury. This had already proved crucial to the events leading to Henry's accession, as Pope Innocent III's annulment of Magna Carta in the autumn of 1215 had exacerbated the conflict that had created the document. Innocent had annulled the Charter on the grounds that it had been extorted from his vassals, and the barons, despairing of ever being able to hold John accountable for the concessions in the Charter, had determined to rid themselves of the Plantagenets entirely, offering the throne instead to Louis. The French pretender therefore had plenty of military backing, but his moral standing, in the view of the Church, was utterly lacking. This was later to prove vital to the cause of those who supported or who returned their support to Henry III.

King John was buried at Worcester, and the Marshal and his men met the young king and his entourage on the road to Gloucester, where a moving scene ensued in which the Marshal swore to defend the royal boy and his inheritance.[6] The first item of business was to grant greater recognition to the young king, in order to prevent Louis from claiming the throne outright. The royalists could claim to have elected him, but since this was the sort of claim that Louis was making, the result would merely have been a political stalemate. The obvious alternative was therefore to proceed with a coronation.[7] This posed its own problems, as the fact that London was in revolt made Westminster Abbey, the usual site for royal coronations, inaccessible. Archbishop Langton, whose prerogative it was to crown the king, was also absent in Rome.

The ceremony was nevertheless carried out at Gloucester, under the leadership of the papal legate Guala and the bishop of Winchester, Peter des Roches.[8] Prior to the coronation the king was knighted by William the Marshal in a ceremony that foreshadowed the authority that was soon to be demanded of the old nobleman.[9] Indeed,

October 28 proved to be a very event-filled day, as it saw the knighting and coronation of Henry III, and a meeting that evening at which the young king's supporters considered their next move. The French king, Philip Augustus, had been crowned in 1179 at the age of fourteen, and after the death of his father, Louis VII, in the following year, he had ruled in his own name from the age of fifteen. Henry III, however, was only nine years old, and maintaining even the fiction of a fully competent king was clearly impossible.

The royal authority thus devolved, in one way or another, onto those magnates who remained loyal to the royalist cause; but exactly how it did so, and who was to wield it in the king's place, was undecided. The legate, Guala Bicchieri, might have had the clearest claim to the authority of a regent, especially given the fact that, as part of the coronation ceremony, Henry III had offered feudal homage to the papacy, reinforcing the position of Honorius III as the overlord of England and the ultimate guardian of the king's interests. However, Guala had no military experience, and the fact that one of the barons' grievances against John had been his perceived overreliance on foreigners made any regency under the leadership of a foreign diplomat, even one so authoritative as the papal representative, unworkable. He therefore made no attempt to assert power, and left the leadership of the royalist party open to others. That left only the Marshal or the earl of Chester, both of whom had their supporters. Some of the Marshal's men argued that he should accept on the grounds that he would be able to use his position to enrich himself and them, a curious argument given the responsibility for safeguarding the royal inheritance. On his arrival the following day, however, Ranulf of Chester joined those who tried to persuade the Marshal to assume responsibility for the king and his inheritance. The Marshal protested, with some exaggeration, that he was too old, claiming that he was over eighty; but the legate's offer of spiritual absolution eventually overcame his doubts, and he accepted the task of guiding the royalist party.[10]

The title that he used, and the actual job the Marshal was supposed to do, was a matter of debate for about two weeks. It appears from the evidence of several early documents issued from Henry III's chancery in the first days of the reign that the Marshal referred to himself (or at least was referred to by the chancery clerks) as justiciar,[11] an understandable assumption given that the justiciar in Angevin England customarily served as regent during the absence of the king abroad.[12] The situation at hand in 1216 was superficially similar, and the justiciarship fit the description of what the Marshal was actually doing, but the office was still formally occupied by another royal supporter, Hubert de Burgh, who had served in this capacity under John since 1214 and who, due to Louis's raising of the siege of Dover, was able to emerge during a truce to attend a council at Bristol, where he protested against what he must have seen as the Marshal's usurpation of his office.[13] The Marshal therefore needed a new title to describe his position, and, by early November at the latest, he had it and was using it in official business. He was known as *rector regis et regni*—that is, "ruler of the king and kingdom," as straightforward a description of a regent as one might ever expect. This title seems to have been bestowed on him by the agreement of the other major supporters of Henry III, although there is some evidence that the earl of Chester's acquiescence was somewhat uncomfortable.[14] The scope of his authority is well described by Sidney Painter, who tells us that "With some self-imposed limitations his will was the king's."[15]

With considerable dispatch and the apparent consensus of the rest of the royalist party, the Marshal used his new authority to reissue Magna Carta on 12 November.[16] This was a fundamental shift in strategy that eventually proved as decisive to the royalist cause as military force, since it reversed the entire royal position on the Charter and thus disposed of many of the objections of John's opponents. While the terms of the original Charter had been prized from John's grip with the threat of force—a threat written explicitly into the final clause of the original document—the new one, with some significant modifications, expressed a willingness to concede to the barons a large measure of their demands. Moreover, since the new charter was issued on the initiative of the royalists, there were no grounds for the Papacy to overturn it. Over the following weeks, the re-issue began to have the desired effect. In the early months of 1217, while Louis was in France seeking further aid from his father Philip Augustus, some notable defections took place, most prominently the younger William Marshal, son of the regent, and the earl of Salisbury, whose quarrel seems to have been primarily a personal one against John, although the regent promised him the counties of Somerset and Devon as well as several coveted castles in exchange for his defection. Their return to the Plantagenet camp was the beginning of a significant shift in the young Henry's favor, which accelerated following the regent's victory at Lincoln on 20 May.[17] In that encounter, the earl of Chester and Falkes de Bréauté joined the regent in driving a French force out of Lincoln, and the regent (nearly forgetting his helmet) personally led the royalist troops into the streets of the town, fighting from horseback in full armor despite being in his seventieth year. A number of prominent magnates who had sided with Louis, such as Nicholas de Stuteville, were taken prisoner, and the only notable death—regretted on both sides—was that of the count of Perche, Louis's commander in Lincoln, speared through the visor on the steps of the cathedral.[18] This decisive victory was made possible in part by Hubert de Burgh's successful defense of Dover, which forced Louis to split his forces to try to capture Lincoln, being held for the young king by the redoubtable dowager Nicola de la Hay. Only three months later, on 24 August, a fleet of reinforcements from France was defeated in the Channel by an English flotilla, under the command of Hubert de Burgh, off Sandwich. The remnants of Louis's forces returned to France, and the pirate Eustace the Monk, who had bedevilled English shipping for some time, was captured and given a stark choice: to lose his head either against the mast or over the rail.[19]

The military victories of Lincoln and Sandwich were vitally important in a number of respects. They marked the end of Louis's hopes for making himself king of England, and thus ensured the security of Henry III's crown. For the same reason, they also made the 1216 version of Magna Carta more or less permanent. According to Robert Stacey, "by their military defeat the former rebels had lost the corporate leverage by which they might have forced major revisions in the terms of the 1216 offer. Provisions which had been dropped in 1216 from the 1215 original therefore remained dropped, preserved only in the popular memory and in the terms of some unofficial versions of the Charter."[20]

THE REGENCY OF THE MARSHAL, 1217–1219

Nonetheless, the Charter was reissued again in 1217, as part of a great council that met at Westminster from late October to early November. The extent of the shift in Henry III's favor is revealed by the significant number of former rebels who were summoned to this council by name, including Robert fitz Walter, the earl of Winchester, Gilbert de Clare and Gilbert de Gant, among others.[21] As a condition of their return to the royal allegiance, they made out charters of fealty, a number of them under threat of disinheritance should they renege on their oaths, and in return they obtained writs of seisin from the chancery.[22] Despite the royalist victory and the departure of Louis for France (in return for the promise of a substantial sum of money), the wishes of many of the former rebels for amendments to the Charter were addressed.

Many of the problems that faced the regent and his assistants from 1217 onward had to do, in one way or another, with aspects of the royal authority and the simple fact that Henry III was a minor. Indeed, the period that followed the civil war began to reveal the political contradictions inherent in a royal minority, and the difficulties they posed for resolving the long-term problem of restoring stable government. That problem had two major, and interrelated, symptoms. The first had to do with finance and the second more broadly with political authority. Financially, the crown was in extremely dire straits. This was due primarily to the utterly disorganized condition of the finances. During the war, collections from the shires had essentially ceased, and getting them started again was a difficult and sluggish process. The exchequer reopened for business in November 1217, although Hubert de Burgh, who as justiciar was supposed to preside over its sessions, was absent. The regent and the bishop of Winchester supervised instead.[23] In short order, it became clear that any general accounting for the period during the war would be impossible. The first exchequer memoranda roll of Henry III's reign, from Michaelmas 1217 to Trinity 1218, shows no sheriffs at all appearing to render accounts. The summons on 12 November 1217 resulted in only four sheriffs turning up, with no cash at all to submit.[24] Accordingly, the royal revenue from 1217 to 1219 averaged only £8,000 per year, only a third of John's annual revenue in the first year of his reign.[25]

Overall, the financial crisis was double edged. Not only did the failure to raise revenue delay some of the rewards that followers of the new king might reasonably expect in exchange for their loyalty, but it may have reflected—it certainly accompanied—a sharp decline in the production of coin. Between mid-November 1217 and early February 1218 the London mint struck about £3,000.[26] This was an astonishingly low figure compared to coin production even three or four years later and especially low compared to levels from the Canterbury mint from the early 1220s.[27] The second major reason for the impotence of Henry III's government stemmed directly from his youth. The kingdom was filled with local officials who had been appointed by King John, many of whom claimed that their appointments could not be rescinded until the young king came of age. Indeed, many of them based this claim on the assertion that they were safeguarding the king's property and could not therefore relinquish it to the custody of the regent. This occurred on a number of occasions, perhaps most notably in the summer of 1218 when Ranulf of Chester, who was sheriff of no less than three counties, prepared to depart on crusade.

Chester mandated that his own *fideles,* not the king or the regency government, should choose a new under-sheriff should one die in the earl's absence. His bailiffs also swore, in the event of the earl's death, to keep his castles on the king's behalf and to hand them over to no one else—a clear reference to the regent.[28] This exemplified the way in which a royal minority revealed a fundamental political contradiction in the nature of monarchy—indeed, in a way the minority of Henry III turned the monarchy inside-out. As John Watts has observed in his study of the reign of Henry VI, the task of the king's councilors was to offer the king their counsel, usually a straightforward process when the king was an adult and was therefore in a position to accept or reject it as he saw fit. During a minority, however, the king had no such option, and the councilors surrounding the king were in the unusual position of offering their advice to the king only in a symbolic fashion, as it was those same councilors who acted on the king's behalf; they thus essentially advised themselves.[29] This was no less true during the minority of Henry III, although the realities of the situation were perhaps treated with more transparency.

In November 1218, the king was finally provided with a new Great Seal. This was clearly a step of major importance, and it was seen as such at the time, being commented on by many of the chroniclers including Ralph of Coggeshall and Matthew Paris.[30] It depicted Henry III as fully grown, and in this it was consistent with the legal fiction that the king was playing an active role in politics. The king, in other words, was and always had been *theoretically* capable of carrying out all of his duties just as if he were an adult. The reality, of course, was very different, and this was reflected in the restrictions placed on the use of the seal. The first letters patent issued under it prohibited any royal grants in perpetuity until the king came of age. This letter was witnessed by most of the prominent magnates, including the legate Guala, the archbishops of Canterbury and York, the regent, and the justiciar Hubert de Burgh. This was done in the presence of twenty prominent churchmen and twenty-three secular magnates, including eight earls. Clearly this laid great emphasis on the principle of preserving the royal estate on behalf of its minor heir.[31]

There are two matters worthy of comment here. The first is the apparent contradiction between image and reality. The official visual symbols of the king and his authority, such as the seals and the coinage, uniformly depict him during his minority as fully adult, and thus theoretically competent to govern his realm. The emphasis on this legal fiction seems to underline the importance of the continuity of government and the unchanging nature of the monarchy. The distinction in medieval political theory between the king's *persona publica*—that is, the king not as an individual but as a public office or trust, what we might term "the Crown"—and the king's *persona privata*, the king in his personal sense, had not emerged yet and would not do so fully until at least the fifteenth century. Yet a royal minority revealed the need to make such a distinction in order to keep the monarchy functioning, and this sort of legal fiction helped to do that. It stood in stark contrast, indeed, to the very unusual step taken by the governors of the young King Alexander III of Scotland from 1249 or 1250, when he was provided with a miniature Great Seal, less than half the size of a normal one, that depicted the king as a youth.[32] Most other royal minorities, not only in England but throughout the various European kingdoms where they occurred, followed the practice of Henry III's councilors in providing a normal Great Seal (if one was in fact made) to emphasize the continuity of government.

The second issue involves the idea of the protection of the king's inheritance that was so boldly set forth in the first letters issued under Henry's new seal. This principle deserves some analysis, as it presented the regent and his administration with a practical problem. Under both English custom and Roman law, the inheritance of the king was being treated in the same way as the inheritance of any other minor heir—that is, it was being protected just as any of the king's subjects would expect their own property to be protected in similar circumstances. Preserving the inheritance of the king reflected the government's commitment to preserve the property of his subjects; indeed, if the king's property was not safe, neither was anyone else's. The fact that Henry III was a vassal of the pope placed additional emphasis on this point. Roman law had long-standing regulations regarding the protection of minors and their property, and Pope Alexander III had decreed that bishops should safeguard the property of their sees according to the Roman laws that ensured guardianship of minors.[33] As noted in detail below, Henry III was not the only royal minor of his generation in which the Papacy took an interest; in the early thirteenth century, the Holy See was playing a similar role in several other kingdoms as guarantor of the rights of royal minors, notably in Aragon, Sicily, the Holy Roman Empire, and, less successfully, Hungary.

Safeguarding the king's inheritance to the point demanded by the restrictions on the Great Seal, however, also meant denying the claims of some of Henry III's supporters to rewards they thought they deserved. Moreover, the government itself and some of its most prominent members, in the form of the regent, the legate, the earl of Chester, and others, had already violated this principle with the reissue of

Magna Carta, the granting of the Charter of the Forest, and a number of lesser grants of property and titles. Chester had made good a claim to the earldom of Lincoln, and the regent himself had secured the castle of Marlborough (possibly his birthplace) and half of the English lands of the count of Perche, the adherent of Prince Louis who had been killed at Lincoln.[34] A line clearly had to be drawn somewhere while there was still a royal estate to preserve. The parlous state of the Crown finances seemed to require the resumption of royal properties held by many who claimed to be loyal to the king but whose behavior suggested more self-centered motives. In the near term, a comprehensive approach to resumption was not possible, although, as we shall see, it eventually became a need too grave to ignore. Meanwhile, a strong statement of principle had to suffice, and it was punctuated by the apparently intentional destruction of the Charter Roll being kept at the time. No new Charter Roll would appear until after Henry III declared his intention to issue charters himself, effectively ending his minority, in January 1227.[35]

The regent lived for another six months, remaining vigorous and actively in control almost until the day he died. In March 1219, he retired to his manor of Caversham, on the Thames near Reading. Early the following month he formally relinquished his office, but not before some disagreement over what sort of arrangement should now ensue regarding both the king and his kingdom. An incident at the Marshal's deathbed foreshadowed some of the difficulties that would shortly arise in the uncertainty over who would be his successor, or whether he should have one at all. When on 8 April the Marshal declared his initial intention to nominate a successor as rector—that is, to oversee both the person of the king and his inheritance—the bishop of Winchester protested that he himself had originally been made Henry III's guardian and that it was not for the regent to grant away. The Marshal responded that he had only granted the custody of the young king to the bishop temporarily, and that he could regrant it if he chose.[36] However, the following day the regent changed his mind, deciding (perhaps as a result of this quarrel) that nominating a successor would only exacerbate tensions and inflame jealousies. Accordingly, he entrusted the cause of the young king and his inheritance in general terms to the care of the legate Pandulf. When he died on 14 May, therefore, the office of *rector regis et regni* lapsed. The office and its precedents would be mentioned in later power struggles, notably in 1422 at the outset of the minority of Henry VI;[37] but no other single person would serve, either in Henry III's minority or in later ones, as regent for a minor king in England.

THE "TRIUMVIRATE" AND THE ASCENDANCY OF HUBERT DE BURGH, 1219–1223

The regent's accomplishments had been truly remarkable. He had driven a foreign invader from English soil, negotiated an end to the civil war, and begun the long and tortuous process of restoring the royal authority along with the good name of the king. The realm remained, however, beset with numerous urgent problems. Financially the crown was still impoverished, as the result of both the shortage of cash and the retention of royal properties by many of the young king's supposedly loyal magnates. Indeed, in April 1219, the same month that the Marshal resigned the regency, the Papacy sent the first letters urging prompt resumptions of royal property.[38] This was easier said than done. The Marshal himself had tried to address the problem of "squatters" unlawfully retaining castles and other lands by driving Robert de Gaugi out of Newark castle in July 1218, restoring it to the custody of the bishop of Lincoln. The successful enforcement of law upon one castellan, however, was far from indicative of a successful program.

More prominent magnates such as Philip of Oldcoates simply ignored orders to restore their ill-gotten gains, effectively waiting until the Marshal was dead, perhaps in the expectation that things would be easier with a more divided leadership. They were probably right, at least in the near term. In the summer of 1219, the three most prominent political figures in the realm were the papal legate Pandulf, the justiciar Hubert de Burgh—who may have felt that the Marshal's passing allowed him a bit more clear sailing in the administration— and the bishop of Winchester, Peter des Roches, whose shady financial dealings with prominent Jews, however, alienated him from Pandulf, who was also bishop-elect of Norwich and responsible for seeing the measures of the Fourth Lateran Council carried through in England.[39] Pandulf was not happy, and chastized the des Roches for defying the decrees of the Lateran Council.[40] Not surprisingly, the surviving royal letters suggest that around the spring of 1219 des Roches had been displaced by Hubert de Burgh as the principal attestor of much of the royal correspondence, although the bishop continued to warrant much chancery correspondence and formally remained guardian of the king.[41]

The governing arrangement that developed between the three leading men has been referred to by a number of historians as a "triumvirate," although this may give the false impression that there were no other influential officials in the government. The keeper of the seal, Ralph de Neville, remained important long after the minority was over, and the principal justice, Martin of Pattishall, worked hard at restoring the administration of law through the general eyre. Clearly, however, there was tension among the three principal administrators of Henry III's government, each perhaps feeling that his authority was being undermined by the other two.[42] The correspondence of the spring and summer of 1219 reveals rapidly emerging tensions; a writ of 23 April from des Roches and de Burgh instructed the sheriff of Yorkshire, the much-embattled Geoffrey de Neville, not to turn the county's revenues over to anyone except directly to the exchequer.[43] Pandulf responded by tightening his own control of the king's Great Seal, issuing orders on his legatine authority to the keeper, Ralph de Neville, to keep the seal at the New Temple.[44]

Government business remained in disarray until a settlement in early June, as a result of which Pandulf sent a writ to the keeper on 11 June instructing him to obey the bishop of Winchester and the justiciar, "as the bishop enjoins you on our behalf."[45] Although the phrase suggests that des Roches may have been closer to the legate than was Hubert, that impression is perhaps misleading; as a result of this writ, Hubert henceforth attested royal letters, the exception being those that dealt directly with the royal household, which were largely left to the oversight of des Roches.[46] The legate was able to make the supremacy of his authority effective, at least in theory, until he left England in 1221; by that time, as we shall see, Hubert had pushed bishop Peter to the sidelines.

This instability at the top was reflected in continued unrest lower on the political ladder. The Marshal, as noted above, had been less effective than he had hoped during his regency in redistributing castles and properties in the name of Henry III. His death, however, exacerbated existing enmities and tensions. His nephew John Marshal was displaced in three locations by Philip de Albini, an associate of des Roches and the tutor of the young king,[47] and the government "was faced with no less than five separate refusals" to relinquish custody of castles to their rightful holders.[48] William de Forz, count of Aumâle, continued to withhold custody of Rockingham and Sauvey from Falkes de Bréauté, despite orders from the regent to turn them over as early as February 1218. For his refusal (as well as for attending a forbidden tournament) he was eventually excommunicated by Pandulf on 30 November 1219, in a document that also alleged him to be fortifying the two castles against the king. The count responded the following year with the rather original expedient of reconciling himself to the Church by taking the Cross—although he continued to hold the two castles until the summer of that year, the offence that had caused his excommunication in the first place.[49] Nor had Aumâle paid any money on the farm of the two manors into the exchequer since he had first received them from King John in 1215—a matter at least as serious as his unlawful retention, since such open defiance of the exchequer continued to erode the royal finances.[50] William Marshal the younger, now hereditary earl Marshal and earl of Pembroke, also defied royal orders by continuing to hold the castles of Fotheringhay and Marlborough.[51]

More serious, however, was the struggle between William Longsword, earl of Salisbury, and Falkes de Bréauté over the custody of Lincoln Castle.[52] In the autumn of 1219, Falkes was ordered to garrison the castle with his own men against the encroachment of Longsword, who had tried since 1217 to evict Nicola de la Hay despite repeated judgments in her favor by the government; the shrievalty and the castle were both held in her family by hereditary custom, and although Longsword had won the office of sheriff for himself in a compromise ruling by the regent, he sought the constableship of the castle as well.[53] Falkes's intervention saved Dame Nicola's custody, but inserted a potentially dangerous and powerful magnate into a dispute that heightened tensions and threatened private war. It is no surprise, however, that Falkes was chosen for such a task. His holdings in the Midlands were formidable, and the government in its continued weakness had little choice but to use him as a blunt instrument as long as he remained loyal to the young king. The most bizarre detail of this affair was that the government, chronically short of cash, ordered Longsword to pay Falkes's expenses.[54] Indeed, the cash shortage became especially acute in April 1220, when the treasury was literally empty, and the Easter audit at the exchequer that year produced only £52.[55]

The first year following the death of the Marshal was thus a frustrating one for Hubert de Burgh, although by the winter of 1219–20 he was attesting many more government letters than was Peter des Roches.[56] One solution to this sluggish progress was to try to bolster the authority of the king, who was now in early adolescence. On 17 May 1220, the feast of Pentecost, he was crowned again at Westminster by archbishop of Canterbury Stephen Langton, this time with scrupulous attention to proper form. Having fulfilled his prerogative at last, Langton left shortly afterward for Rome. Pope Honorius III had urged this ceremony, and in the same month renewed his pressure for a general resumption of Crown lands, writing to Pandulf that "no one should hold more than two royal castles."[57] The pope's correspondence on the issue gave renewed emphasis to Pandulf's authority to impose spiritual sanctions on disobedient barons who still hoarded royal properties. Although such a resumption could not immediately take place, Carpenter observes that the coronation "marked a turning point in the political history of the minority," in that a number of defiant magnates surrendered or were forced from their illicit holdings in the months that followed.[58] One chronicler, the Dunstable annalist, recounts that the day after the coronation the barons in attendance swore that they would surrender their castles on demand of the king and render proper accounts for them, and that they would go to war against anyone who still refused and had been excommunicated.[59]

The king himself called the baron's bluff. In June 1220, young Henry III himself appeared before the walls of Rockingham and demanded entry, catching the garrison ill-prepared and the count of Aumâle absent, and after a brief show of defiance the drawbridge was lowered for him on 28 June.[60] Hugh de Lusignan, count of La Marche, had demanded Rockingham as part of the dower of his wife Isabella of Angoulême, Henry III's mother, who had returned to France to remarry, having apparently decided to forsake parenting for power in her homeland.[61] The chancery promptly issued letters, dated 29 June, proclaiming that Aumâle had surrendered both Rockingham and Sauvey willingly.[62] Considering that another letter, ostensibly from the king but authorized by the justiciar and the bishop of Winchester, absolved Aumâle of the outstanding revenues he owed for the manors and farms he had withheld since the civil war—an amount of more than £335—the government had essentially bought back its own property. In doing so, however, the king's writ could now run in the areas recovered, and eventually the exchequer received £84 in net revenues from properties in the area in 1220–21.[63]

The recovery of Rockingham and Sauvey demonstrated how slowly and carefully the government had to proceed while beginning, finally, to make some headway on rebuilding the royal authority. More important than the revenue issue, perhaps, was the more direct one of the involvement of the king, young though he was. His appearance in person may not have been the decisive issue in the surrender of the two castles, but it was surely not insignificant. Henry III's personal authority and role remained symbolic rather than fully actuated, yet the use of that symbolism marked the beginning of a vital turn in the course of events. For nearly four years, a number of the most important barons had gotten away with defying the king's officials, ministers, and messengers, many by claiming with increasing specious-ness that they were safeguarding the king's property for him until he came of age. To refuse the orders of the king's representatives was one thing; to refuse the commands of the king himself, whether a minor or not, was treason and revealed the hollowness of the magnates' excuses. The general pattern of events throughout 1220–21 therefore saw the authority of the king, through the person and actions of the justiciar, slowly but more and more steadily restored. Indeed, over the course of 1221 a significant shift occurred in the status of the king and, through him, the administration. The approach of Henry's fourteenth birthday on 1 October occasioned a change in the oversight of the king, as fourteen was the traditional age of discretion in Roman and canon law. Earlier in his reign, up to September 1219, concessions had been made on various issues that would terminate when Henry reached his fifteenth year.[64] Moreover, the age of tutelage traditionally ceased at fourteen, and if this were to be followed, Peter des Roches would lose his position as the king's guardian, the most potent authority that bishop Peter still retained in the face of Hubert's growing power. On 26 July, at the behest of Archbishop Langton, who had returned from Rome with instructions from the pope, Pandulf resigned as legate, departing in October for a diplomatic mission to Poitou.[65] This cleared Langton's position as the highest-ranking cleric in England—he had requested that no new legate be appointed—and effectively dissolved the "triumvirate" arrangement that had prevailed since the death of the regent more than two years before. Its dissolution was indeed confirmed when the bishop of Winchester was compelled to resign his position as guardian. By 1221, also, the gulf between English and foreigners in politics that would so bedevil the adult reign of Henry III had begun to assert itself, breaking into open and mutual accusations of treachery, especially between Falkes and John Marshal, the regent's nephew, in the early months of 1222.[66] In the meantime, however, Hubert de Burgh clearly held the upper hand, and for the best part of the next two years he focused on consolidating the royal demesne and boosting the government's power and wealth, without the need to cooperate with either a papal legate or a royal guardian.

Even without a legate, the pope continued to take an active interest in diplomatic and political affairs in England. He reiterated the vassalage of Henry III in October 1221, promising for the moment not to alter the king's status but reserving the right to do so, if he deemed it appropriate, at some time prior to the king's twenty-first birthday.[67] Potentially this gave Hubert important leverage, as he might use a request to the Holy See for a declaration of Henry III's full age of discretion to further undermine specious claims of the "protection" of royal properties by some of the barons. Such a request, however, might also come from someone else, in order to unseat Hubert himself. The status of the king, therefore, while somewhat uncertain, was a vital card in the political deck. It was also a card that could be played only once, and only by one faction in the administration; as the king grew, the more partisan the atmosphere among his administrators became.

Financially the king's position continued to improve over the course of 1221 and 1222, with the recovery of many of the county farms and the consequent increase of reported income into the exchequer. The pipe roll of 1220 recorded £133 coming in from the farms. Since then the exchequer had regained control of the income from eight counties, and the 1222 pipe roll records an income from this source of £1,657, with overall cash revenue from all sources of £10,340, which rose further the following year to £12,180. The Easter exchequer of 1222 produced also an increase of £413 over the prior year from the sheriffs' audit (*Adventus Vicecomitum*) on its first day.[68] The improvement in the finances was also reflected in a major increase in the production of coin. Between July 1220, following the recoronation of the king, and November 1222, the London mint struck £9,013. The output from the Canterbury mint over the same period was altogether more startling, producing £34,026, almost four times as much as London—understandable given that much of the silver being purchased for coin production was coming into the Canterbury mint from across the Channel, making up for the domestic shortfall that had begun as far back as 1194, with the payment of Richard the Lionheart's ransom for release from prison in Austria.[69] The close rolls from this period also demonstrate that the mint at Canterbury brought in exchanges at much higher rates during the summer months, when foreign trade was busier than in winter.[70]

The obvious improvement in the government's financial position emboldened the justiciar to push the resumption program further and raised concerns that a healthier monarchy might lead to a renunciation of the Charters. Archbishop Langton's cooperation with Hubert, however, ensured that these fears were misplaced; there was no stronger supporter of the principles of Magna Carta than Langton, who had helped negotiate the original and who took a strict-interpretation approach to the wording of the document, especially as it concerned the liberties of the Church. This did not, however, prevent unrest breaking out in Northamptonshire and Yorkshire in May and June 1222 over forest eyres and attempts to impose amercements on the county for holding unlicensed perambulations in an attempt to deforest sec-

THE MINORITY OF HENRY III

tions of the county. Brian de Lisle, conducting investigations in the two shires, imposed fines of £209 in Northamptonshire but was able to enforce only a little over £73 in fines in Yorkshire over the next several years, due to the extent of unrest and the fact that the terms of the Charter of the Forest essentially bound the hands of the government in this matter.[71] Nonetheless, one expedient of the justiciar's in the summer of 1222 was to allow a number of holders of resumed properties to retain custody, provided they paid money into the exchequer for them. This applied to tenants such as Falkes de Bréauté and Philip Mark, among many others, although the earl of Derby, William de Ferrers—the brother-in-law of Ranulf of Chester—was ordered to surrender two castles outright.[72]

The success of the resumptions of 1222 reflected a growing attitude that the royal demesne was, or ought to be, inalienable, although such a principle did not become firmly established for more than two centuries. It also led, in part, to an inquiry early in 1223 regarding the rights of the Crown and the privileges lost during the civil war. To allay fears of a potential return to the practices of King John, Roger of Wendover states that Henry III himself verbally confirmed Magna Carta in January 1223 at a great council at Westminster.[73] In April of that year, the government retreated when Henry III, on the advice of his council, confirmed by letters patent his intention not to pursue the rights that the inquiry had revealed.[74] It is clear, however, that despite a number of setbacks, the government under Pandulf and Hubert had done much to restore the authority of the king since the Marshal's death in 1219. Two other trends had become apparent in the process. The first was that the more the justiciar consolidated his control of the administration, the more financially healthy the administration became. The second was that Hubert had alienated a large segment of the magnate class, generally those who were seen by themselves and others as a "foreign" element in English aristocratic society. By April 1223, however, Hubert might face a major shift in power. The king himself was now rapidly approaching the assumption of full regal authority, and events would shortly take a more decisive and eventful turn in that direction than most people could have imagined at the time.

THE EMERGENCE OF THE KING AND THE END OF THE MINORITY, 1223–1227

The increasing involvement of Henry III himself in the affairs of state became more evident throughout 1223, an eventful year for the young king. The events from April to December of that year were dominated, as never before, by foreign affairs, with the seemingly sudden convergence upon the court of important, and in some cases neglected, matters from many directions: Wales, Poitou, and France. This led over the remainder of the year to the most fundamental shift in English politics since the death of John in 1216; and, indeed, in important ways the entire remainder of Henry III's minority was dominated by foreign affairs, and laid the foundation for many of the developments of his adult reign.

For the better part of two years the approaching maturity of Henry III, and his increasing involvement in government affairs, had lurked like an unexploded bomb beneath the foundations of the administration. During much of that period the concern for Hubert, bishop Peter, and others had been the timing of the king's emergence; whoever could initiate and control it would be in a strong position to continue to dominate matters at court well into Henry III's adult rule. Since the summer of 1222, Hubert had taken tentative steps in this direction, when on a tour of Wales with the king he encouraged Henry III to begin the dispensation of personal gifts, such as wine, game, and timber, to some of his servants and clerics.[75] In mid-April 1223, however, letters unexpectedly arrived in England from Pope Honorius III that effectively set the bomb off and exploded the equilibrium at court.[76] In separate letters, the pope addressed the justiciar and the bishop of Winchester, the earls and barons more generally, and the keeper of the Great Seal, Ralph de Neville. On the grounds that he believed Henry III to possess discretion beyond his years, the pontiff instructed them to "deliver to [the king] the free and undisturbed disposition of his kingdom, and to resign to him . . . the lands and castles" which they withheld from him.[77] By themselves, these letters were not altogether different from the ones that Honorius had issued before; a bull of 29 April 1221, for instance, had been similarly addressed, and gave much the same instruction.[78]

What *was* new about these letters was the stress they laid on the discretion of the king. Moreover, they instructed three officials— Hubert, Bishop Peter, and William Brewer—to set an example for the others by resigning their custodies first. Together with testimony given in 1239 by Hubert, this indicates strongly that the initiative for these instructions originated with Peter des Roches, who knew very well that the justiciar had the most to lose from having to give up his custodies and authority to the king. In terms of properties, the change would be felt hardest by Falkes de Bréauté, who still held the shrievalties of six counties; but the letter to the keeper, Neville, instructed him to follow the orders of the king alone, "causing no letters henceforth to be sealed with the king's seal save at his will."[79] This would deprive the justiciar of his prime function, the attestation of royal letters. The arrival of the papal instructions, however, did not mean that the justiciar had to implement them immediately. Hubert would have to give the king a greater share of power sooner rather than later, but events were to show that it was the justiciar, not the bishop, who for the time being still retained the initiative.

With partisanship at court now firmly in the open, more unsettling news arrived in July, while the earl of Pembroke campaigned in south Wales: Philip Augustus was dead. This necessitated some delicate diplomacy, for it heralded the succession to the French throne of Philip's son Prince Louis, who remained implacably hostile to Henry III and the Plantagenet house. It also seemed to raise possibilities, for Louis may have promised, as part of the agreement which ended the civil war, to restore Normandy to the English throne.[80] If Louis had indeed promised this, he chose to ignore it now; by the time Archbishop Langton had reached him in France he had already been crowned as Louis VIII and replied, in November, to Langton's entreaties regarding Normandy by declaring contemptuously that "in due course and with equal justice he would again seek his own in England."[81] Nor were the magnates of Normandy inclined to rebel against their new French king, who was an adult, on behalf of an English boy. The situation in Poitou was not much brighter, where negotiations over the return of the dowry of Henry's sister from Hugh de Lusignan had been pending for some time.[82] Savari de Mauléon, the seneschal of Poitou, had alienated many of Henry's Poitevin vassals with his heavy-handed tactics.

That factor, combined with the need for Hugh's neutrality (at least) in the situation with Louis VIII, postponed any progress on the dowry issue even further. Much of the fall was taken up with a successful campaign in Wales against Llywelyn the Great, in the course of which Hubert supervised the construction of a castle at Montgomery. The success of the campaign there gave Hubert sufficient leverage to attempt to implement the papal letters and empower the king on his terms rather than those of Peter des Roches. October and November, however, nearly witnessed a renewal of civil war as, according to one account, Hubert narrowly avoided being arrested—perhaps by Ranulf of Chester—by fleeing London with the king and staying in Gloucester for much of November along with Brewer and Salisbury. On their return to London at the end of that month, a meeting was arranged by Archbishop Langton at the New Temple between the two factions, and the letter summoning the dissidents identifies them as the earls of Chester and Gloucester, the count of Aumâle, Falkes de Bréauté, Engelard de Cigogné, and others.[83] These were clearly the major opponents of Hubert and his program. Des Roches was present as well, for (according to the Dunstable annalist) the meeting, on 3 December, broke down in a shouting match between him and Hubert, each loudly accusing the other of treason against the king, whereupon Des Roches and his adherents stormed out.[84] Langton and Hubert responded by taking the final initiative they could: They gave Henry III control of his seal. On 8 December, the king authorized the custody of Colchester castle to the bishop of London by letters patent, attested by Hubert.[85] Two days later, however, a more momentous change took place when Henry himself began to attest royal letters directly. Rather than the formula *teste H. de Burgo* or some other administrator, the attestation on the close roll read *teste me ipso* and continued to do so regularly henceforth.[86]

This may suggest, as it did to Powicke, that the king's minority was now over.[87] However, the release of the seal to the king did not lift the ban on permanent alienations that had existed since 1218, which Hubert and Langton agreed should remain.[88] Henry III therefore made grants that were valid only until his majority. It was not until January 1227, as we shall see, that this restriction was lifted. Nonetheless, this was a milestone in Henry III's journey toward adult rule, for the seal remained with him from this point, allowing us to trace his movements with greater precision and providing a glimpse into his growing role in government. Moreover, Hubert had timed the enactment of the papal letters perfectly for his interests. The bishop of Winchester did not attest another royal letter until 1232, the year that the justiciar finally fell from office; at the same time the bishop's close relative Peter des Rivaux, who had served as treasurer of the king's wardrobe, was also dismissed.[89] The papal letters, which had been intended to unite the country by placing the king in more direct control of the royal authority, had rather the opposite effect: While Henry III moved out of the wings and onto the political stage, a number of other players were pushed off. Before the end of the month, Hubert and Langton pushed through the resumptions that the Holy See had long sought, starting with the earl of Chester and proceeding with Falkes de Bréauté, who had to give up most of his six shrievalties, and Peter des Roches, who relinquished three major castles. The loyalists at court did not appear to escape unscathed, either; Hubert gave up six castles, and the earl of Salisbury one.[90] They were still on the inside track at court, however, while the foreigners and their allies were out. Moreover, the chronicler Coggeshall observed that the loyalists' concessions were quickly regained. The justiciar's constable at Dover simply transferred oversight of the castle to a knight of Langton's, while Salisbury's withdrawal never took place.[91] Langton, ironically, was rewarded for his assistance by Hubert's approval of the return to England of his brother Simon, the subject of the conspiracy letter of 1220.[92] A thorough redistribution of properties followed into the winter of 1224, all to the advantage of the loyalists.

These sweeping changes provoked a major reaction within months, one that threatened a renewal of civil war and proved immensely costly to Henry III in the long run. The dispossessed foreigners demanded early in 1224, through an ambassador to the Holy See, to be restored on the grounds of their loyal service to King John during the civil war.[93] Essentially this was the same reasoning that had prevailed through the earlier minority; since Henry III could not make permanent alienations, those made under King John must still be valid on behalf of his minor heir, even though this entrenched the magnates and fragmented the power of the government. The appeal did not receive a favorable response, and in the late winter of 1224 the government went further, finally approving the marriage of the king's youngest sister to the earl of Pembroke and ordering Falkes de Bréauté on 29 February to surrender to Pembroke his hold on the lands and properties of the earldom of Devon, along with similar orders to other barons in the dissident camp.[94]

Although a number of dissidents including Chester were (formally, at least) reconciled to the new state of affairs in April and recovered some of their lost properties, this was not true for Falkes, who in the same month was threatened with outlawry, a sentence that would deprive him of everything.[95] In the following month, however, as it proceeded to turn up the heat on Falkes, the government received news that Louis VIII was at the head of an army preparing to invade Poitou, and by the beginning of June it was apparent that Hugh de Lusignan had defected, throwing his support behind the French king—in return for which Hugh received custody of Bordeaux from Louis VIII.[96] This made clear what Louis intended: a clean sweep of the Plantagenets from France. A perfect storm had thus converged over Hubert and Henry III, and in the circumstances the government placed a higher priority on ruining Falkes than on preventing ruin in Poitou.

In June, the king's justices convened at Dunstable to hear a range of petty assizes against Falkes in order "to hear and correct complaints of many people of rapine and plunder of their lands and goods."[97]

Whether legitimate or not, a number of complaints were brought forward.[98] While the most decisive action was not legal but military, it was these proceedings that pushed the crisis to breaking point. On 17 June, Henry of Braybrooke, one of the justices, was arrested and imprisoned by Falkes's brother, William.[99] The response was swift. By 20 June, the king and Hubert had besieged Bedford castle, and William put up a stiff resistance with Falkes's apparent support. The veiled threat that Falkes had voiced two years before to make war on the "native men of England" seemed to be coming true.[100]

Falkes found, however, that he was bereft of allies; much like the count of Aumâle in 1220–21, no other major foreign dissident rallied to his cause, and after an eight-week siege William was forced to capitulate on 15 August. Two days later, letters arrived from Honorius III condemning the government's actions against Falkes, primarily because the pope sensibly viewed Hubert's priorities as backward—he should have sent the army to Poitou rather than Bedford.[101] This was too late to save the garrison, however, nearly all of whom—over eighty knights as well as William de Bréauté—were hanged from the walls of the castle.[102] Falkes, forced to resign all his properties to the king, abjured the realm, dying in exile in 1226.

It was also too late to save Poitou. There, the collapse of the English position almost exactly coincided with the siege at Bedford: Louis VIII gathered his army at Tours on 24 June, and besieged La Rochelle on 15 July, exacting its surrender on 3 August and the fealty of the town fathers ten days later. Thus, by the time the situation at Bedford was resolved, Poitou was already in the hands of the French king, who had won in his own realm in 1224 what he could not in England in 1217. Obviously the timing and outcome of events was no coincidence. Henry III's government, having promised too little aid—500 marks— to Savari de Mauléon, recalled even that for the Bedford siege. Coggeshall explained that the burgesses of La Rochelle surrendered because "they despaired of help from King Henry."[103] The government's failure in Poitou, however, was a prime factor in reinvigorating the English defense of Gascony, much of which had been overrun by Hugh de Lusignan in his effort to take up his French prize. Henry III and Hubert followed the advice of the mayor of Bordeaux and sent money, as well as a force under the nominal leadership of Henry III's younger brother Richard of Cornwall, to the province's defense. The expedition, ordered in February 1225, was actually led by Longsword, the earl of Salisbury who remained a major player in the administration.[104]

Throughout 1225, the campaign made steady progress in driving the Lusignan forces back, and by November the defense of Gascony was complete, despite Salisbury's return to England due to illness in the summer. A major reason for the government's success in Gascony had to do with the successful tax raised in 1225 to support the expedition. A fifteenth on movable property was assessed, which garnered some £40,000 in revenue.[105] While still not at the level of the previous tax on movables, a thirteenth levied in 1207 that had raised £60,000 for John, it was by far the most successful levy of the minority and a testament to the success of Hubert's administration at rebuilding the financial foundation of the Crown.[106] This increase was reflected further in two areas. The exchequer was far more efficient in its audits and receipts in 1225, bringing in revenues of £18,000 in that year, than it had been in 1218, when the figure was a mere £4,000. Moreover, there were continued improvements in coin production: Between March 1225 and July 1226, the mints of London and Canterbury together struck £21,700.[107] Another crucial difference between the situations in Poitou and Gascony is revealed by an order Henry III placed in July 1225 for 200 casks of Gascon wine.[108] England essentially monopolized the market for Gascon wine, and the king's firm control of the province eventually paid substantial revenues that allowed Gascony's defense to pay for itself.[109] At the same time, there was concern for the defense of England. Louis VIII renewed in 1225 his threats to invade and conquer England for himself, and sought pledges of assistance from the ports of both realms. In the event, the threat evaporated; Louis VIII became distracted by events in Toulouse, where he had pledged to assist the Church's efforts against the Albigensian heresy, and died in 1226.

If the defense of Gascony had been made possible by the success of the tax of 1225, the success of the tax was in turn made possible by its *quid pro quo*: the final reissue of the Charters. Henry III declared in February 1225, simultaneously with orders to collect the tax, that the reissue should be made public; moreover, it was made by his own *spontanea et bona voluntate* rather than by the advice of his earls and barons.[110] This was a crucial distinction, for it deprived Henry III of any plausible deniability (to borrow a current political phrase) in the future regarding his obligation to his subjects. It was also, obviously, a further sign of the king's exercise of his own political will. The expectation, however, was clear that in exchange for the free granting of the Charters, the English populace would just as freely pay the taxation requested for the government's needs. Indeed, the Charter itself stated in its final clause that "In return for this grant and gift of these liberties and of the other liberties contained in our charter on the liberties of the forest . . . all of our realm have given us a fifteenth part of all their movables."[111] One is tempted to see in this bargain the English origins of the famous principle of *quod omnes tangit ab omnibus approbetur* ("what touches all should be approved by all") that was beginning to find its way into the political theories of the thirteenth century. The reissues of the Charters in 1225 thus became a permanent fixture of English political life; they were subsequently confirmed, notably in 1297 by Edward I, but never rewritten.

The death of Louis VIII in November 1226, however, provided the closing drama of the minority. The French king's death was sudden and wholly unexpected, and he left behind him a minor heir, Louis IX, who at the age of twelve faced a substantial period of minority rule himself, under the regency of his formidable mother Blanche of Castile.[112] It was to take advantage of this situation and attempt to regain his French claims that Henry III declared in January 1227 his intention to issue charters under his own seal—effectively removing the final restriction on his full exercise of regal power.[113] The minority of Henry III ended only with the beginning of the minority of Louis IX.

Historians have generally seen in the declaration of January 1227 the definitive conclusion to the minority of Henry III. That was not necessarily how contemporaries saw matters. The king would not turn twenty-one until October 1228, and there was no formal statement by the papacy that Henry ought now to be fully adult. Nor did the king himself declare this in so many words. Yet the declaration of January 1227 meant that for all practical purposes the king was fully in control of the politics and government of his realm. The immediate purpose of the declaration, moreover, emphasized the importance of property: castle custodies, wardships, farms, and offices. Thus, the tangible matters that had been such important sources of friction during the minority remained important thereafter—more immediately important to the magnates than more abstract constitutional theories such as the king's "two bodies," an idea applicable to royal minorities that did not find full expression in the thirteenth century. If, however, we seek the end of the minority in terms of changes in administrative personnel, then it did not end in 1227. Hubert de Burgh remained in office until 1232, benefiting handsomely from the king's freedom to make grants in perpetuity as he received rewards commensurate with his service. Henry III made Hubert earl of Kent, as well as granting him custody of a number of important castles. Hubert's fall in 1232, though, was more abrupt than his rise had been, and lost him all he had gained; and it was his nemesis Peter des Roches who was his undoing, replacing him at the king's side. The office of justiciar effectively departed with Hubert, as no successor was appointed. The return of Bishop Peter, and his relative Peter des Rivaux, did not last long either; both were gone by 1234. Thus a case can be made, as David Carpenter has done in an important article, that the "personal rule" of Henry III did not begin until well after he had reached adulthood.[114]

FRANCE: LOUIS IX

Henry III's minority was hardly an anomaly in the history of thirteenth-century Europe. In fact, royal minorities occurred in several European states during this century in a variety of contexts. In France, Louis IX, seven years younger than Henry III, was crowned king at the age of twelve on 29 November 1226, only three weeks after his father had died.[115] On the way to Rheims, where the ceremony was to take place, he had also been knighted, although in a strictly legalistic sense he was too young, since this act was usually performed between age 18 and 20.[116] Like King John, Louis VIII had designated his son as his successor on his deathbed. Although the Capetians were firmly established as the royal dynasty, a quick coronation was advisable as it had been for Henry III; as unpredictable risks lay in the future since the monarchy was at war with the Albigensian heretics while the young king had two uncles with aspirations to the throne.[117] In this situation it is even more surprising that Louis VIII did not name someone to lead the government in his little son's name. The king's mother, Blanche of Castile, finally took responsibility for the boy, and with him for the kingdom, quite unlike the experience of Isabella of Angouleme in England.[118]

Of course, Blanche did not rule by herself. She was supported at various times by coteries of powerful temporal and spiritual magnates: her husband's half-brother Philip Hurepel (who later, together with Pierre Mauclerc, Duke of Brittany, became leader of the opposition), Hugh of Burgundy, Robert and Henry from the house of Dreux—the latter had just become archbishop of Reims—the Sires of Coucy, Bar and Blois, Joan of Flanders and Blanche of Champagne,[119] as well as Walter Cornut, archbishop of Sens, bishop Guérin of Senlis, the keeper of the royal seal until 1227, count Ferrand of Flanders (after he had been set free),[120] and Thibault IV of Champagne.[121] There were also quite a few persons in the royal household who actively supported the queen and her government, namely Bartholomew of Roye and John of Nesle.[122] Blanche's rule seems to have been much less formally organized than say, William the Marshal's regency in England. However, remarkably similar to the English experience, the revolving door of magnates who cooperated with Blanche just as easily opposed her when they saw their political objectives endangered, as Blanche was soon to experience.

From the beginning she tried to gather the sympathies of the French magnates. She tried to please Philip Hurepel by granting him the castles of Montain and Lillebonne as well as the county of Saint-Pol. Additionally he received an annuity of 6.000 *livres tournois*. Count Ferrand of Flanders was set free after twelve years in prison and Blanche tried to tie several powerful families to the throne by arranging future marriages with Louis's brothers and sisters.[123] Despite her efforts in patronage, Blanche never really managed to establish trustworthy relations with the French aristocracy. The fact that she was a "foreigner" from Castile—as Joinville described her in his famous biography of Saint Louis[124]—complicated this situation, and only half a year after Louis's coronation the barons were up against her in open revolt. The resentment against her seems to have been strengthened by her foreign roots, as is not unusual in patron-client relations.[125] But the opposition's aim was not to depose Louis. Instead they wanted to overthrow *her* regime. The baronial plan was to kidnap the child and replace Blanche as the ruler behind the child by themselves. However, Blanche and Louis were saved by the intervention of the citizens of Paris, but shortly afterward Blanche had to face a propaganda campaign arguing that her allegedly licentious lifestyle made her unworthy of governing the kingdom—the classic method of trying to get rid of a ruling woman.[126] Nevertheless, Blanche still had enough support as well as financial and military resources to prevail. She managed to stabilize her rule and by 1230–31 the time of crisis ended. Around that time Louis IX slowly began to show his own political profile. In 1230, he led military campaigns in Brittany and Champagne, he intervened in the strike of the University of Paris, and in the conflict with the bishop of Beauvais[127] Louis was the main actor whereas Blanche appeared to be more on the sidelines of political action. She was asked by Pope Gregory IX to make her influence on Louis felt, but to no avail.[128]

Fortunately Blanche could rely on comparatively well-ordered finances, administration, and offices that had been created in the course of the twelfth century,[129] the center of which were the three "departments" of financial service, the chancery, and the judicature (later called the Parlement de Paris).[130] Since the 1190s, these institutions had become increasingly centralized in Paris, which developed more and more into a real capital.[131] The royal demesne had been administered by *prevôts* well into the second half of the twelfth century, when the *bailli* was introduced to strengthen royal authority against an office that had become hereditary. Since the reign of Philip II, both the *prevôts* and the *baillis* had to come together in Paris three times a year.[132] They were the backbone of the royal administration.[133] That did not mean that neither Blanche nor later Louis could rule without the participation or consent of the magnates; they still had an important say in government matters and could not be ignored, if politics were to be implemented in the provinces.[134]

Louis's marriage with Margaret of Provence in 1234 changed the balance of power within the central government in favor of a more independent rule of the king. The first phase of Louis's government, the "real" minority government, ended with this date. Blanche increasingly moved into the background of government and politics. But she was not completely removed from the sources of power. Some rumors had it that she, feeling the change coming, tried to postpone her son's wedding as long as possible.[135] The "shift from the rulership of the aging Blanche to that of her youthful son occurred almost imperceptibly,"[136] but her influence on the government—even after Louis's marriage and his twenty-first birthday—remained strong, so strong that Le Goff calls it a "co-rulership."[137] Only in 1244 was Louis capable of "his own personal emancipation" when he vowed to go on a crusade against Blanche's will.[138] This may be considered the beginning of the third phase of Louis's rule, but again there are no indicators that governmental practice changed in a major way. Still, Blanche remained an important player in the political game. Louis actually made her regent when he left for the Holy Land, a position she held until her death on 27 November 1252.[139] Only then did Louis's minority government really end. His mother's death caused the king to leave the Holy Land; but he was obviously not in a hurry, because it took him until April 1254 to return to France. In the meantime, his minor son seemed to have been nominal head of the regency government.[140] Being only eight years old, he needed a council to conduct the actual political business. This was a more institutionalized council, a real regency council, in which Louis's brother also seemed to have held important positions.[141]

GERMANY: HENRY VII

While in England and France royal minorities ensued because kings had died leaving underage heirs, Henry VII of Germany was crowned king of Sicily in 1212 and eight years later, king of Germany, to serve as a political proxy for his father, Holy Roman Emperor Frederick II. To complicate things further the papal curia was actively involved in these events. Not long after Henry's Sicilian coronation, when Henry was one year old, Frederick left the Mediterranean island. He was to become *Rex Romanorum* with the help of Pope Innocent III who needed support against Emperor Otto IV. Since Henry was an infant, the Sicilian government was managed by his mother, Constance of Aragon. Charters were signed *una cum carrissimo filio suo Henrico rege Sicilie.*[142]

However, the plans of Frederick II, who had been elected *Rex Romanorum* in Germany in the meantime and wanted to be crowned emperor by the pope, required Henry and his mother to join him north of the Alps. Slowly he maneuvered Henry into a position where he could be elected German king, while Frederick would be away in Italy, trying to deal with the problems German emperors usually had south of the Alps. In 1217, Henry was made Duke of Swabia[143] and in 1219 he became *Rector Burgundiae.*[144] Around this time, he stopped carrying the title of king of Sicily, which he had not used since 1218. The precise reason for this is uncertain, but it very likely indicated that from now on his field of action would strictly be limited to Germany.[145] Finally in 1220, Henry was elected German king. The proceedings around this election are very complex. Contrary to what Frederick told the pope, it was no accident: Only a few days after the election of Henry (VII) in Frankfurt, the ecclesiastical princes were granted a number of privileges in return for their votes.[146] This *quid pro quo* deal is undoubtedly a sign of Frederick's cunning as well as his personal political strength, but certainly not of a structural robustness of the monarchy.[147]

Frederick compensated for a lack of institutional structures by installing Archbishop Engelbert of Cologne, a powerful magnate who Frederick could trust, as regent.[148] It therefore seems quite logical that Engelbert, regent and *tutor regis,* was not a member of the household but rather of the court. His office of Imperial Chancellor for Italy was more an honorary than administrative one. The so-called council of the minority government, consisting of a group of ministerials, counts, and bishops, was a much more ill-defined body than say, French *parlements* or English great councils of the same time period. At the political center were the minor king and his regent Engelbert. At first the new government functioned smoothly, but Henry VII obviously lacked legitimacy; thus in addition to the election he was formally crowned king in 1222[149]—an interesting parallel to Henry III who also required a second coronation to enhance his legitimacy.

In 1225, however, relatives murdered Engelbert for reasons that are not quite clear but seemed to have something to do with his rigid territorial rule, while Duke Louis of Bavaria took over the responsibilities of a regent in 1226, although Henry could have been old enough to rule by himself.[150] Under Louis's regency, the government also worked without any apparent problems during the first years. Then in 1228, the now barely eighteen-year-old Henry fell out with Louis, who left the court suddenly around Christmas 1228. The reasons for the quarrels remain unclear, but a good guess would be Henry's increasing desire to rule by himself. In fact this is the point where Henry's personal rule started. As was the case with Henry III and Louis IX, Henry VII's achievement of his majority was not determined by any rules or legal considerations about ages of majority; rather, it was purely political. Whether Frederick liked his son's behavior, or whether it coincided with his own political ideas and plans for a stable government in Germany we will never know. In any case, he did not intervene.

It is interesting to observe that the king's court began to shrink from that day until almost only members of what could be called the household appear in Henry's entourage. The magnates and princes preferred to stay away from him. Instead they took care of their own business, which most likely meant their own territory, rather than spending energies on the affairs of the kingdom. Henry's court was stripped bare of princes and magnates,[151] which meant that certain ministerials gained relative importance, but their influence on Henry cannot be measured. It is quite clear, though, that with the lack of more powerful magnates Henry's influence on politics in the Holy Roman Empire waned and at the same time difficulties with the princes began to emerge. Henry's radius of action was more and more limited to the Hohenstaufen homelands.

By 1232, the number of problems between Henry and the magnates must have reached critical mass. His father ordered him to come to Italy to meet him—their first meeting in about twelve years. Henry had to swear an oath of loyalty and was sent back to Germany. If he broke the oath, the German princes would no longer owe him fidelity. It was not that easy, however, to settle quarrels between the two members of the Hohenstaufen house. Clearly Frederick II still had strong influence on politics in Germany, but could only make his influence felt indirectly. Thus Henry was tied up in a network of his father's supporters and confidants who did not hesitate to travel to Italy to talk to the Emperor himself. This happened even more frequently under Henry's personal rule. It is quite clear that this was a custom-made construction for the needs of Frederick II. It was supposed to make his influence felt over the long distance. He did not want his son to act independently as the events in 1234 and 1235 made clear: Two years after he had sworn not to act against his father's will, Henry wrote several letters to cities of the Lombard League, obviously with the intention of winning them as allies against his father.[152] In October 1234, he had already tried unsuccessfully to explain his behavior and his politics to Bishop Conrad of Hildesheim.[153] The final breach with his father seemed inevitable. In spring 1235, Frederick came back to Germany to crush Henry's "uprising," deposed him, threw him into prison, and had his brother elected king.[154] Having learned from Henry's case, he made sure that Conrad IV was only elected but not crowned.

The case of medieval Germany, in which the development of administrative institutions lagged behind that of England and France, illustrates the personal nature of feudal political relations, and the problems inherent in Hohenstaufen desires to build a more centralized state in Germany. In this case, a minority regime was used as a political proxy for an ambitious emperor, with less than desirable results. The princes and magnates of Germany never took Henry seriously, nor did Henry have the chance to create his own network of supporters because everybody kept turning to Emperor Frederick II: He was the ultimate patron, and even from a distance he ruled the court. Henry's household was too weak and staffed with the wrong persons for an effective government. While the minorities of Henry III and Louis IX placed no obstacles in the way of continuing trends toward greater political centralization and cohesion, Frederick's victory over his son was a clear defeat for the institutionalization of imperial power.

HUNGARY: LADISLAS III

Like that of Edward V of England, the minority of Ladislas III was the story of failure. Born in 1201 as the son of the Hungarian king Emery and his wife Constance of Aragon, the sister of Peter II and later wife of Frederick II and mother of yet another minor king, Henry (VII), neither his career nor his life lasted very long. That makes it impossible to say anything substantial about his politics, because he never even managed to come close to ruling the country. Ladislas's father, King Emery II, just prior to his death, had signed a peace treaty negotiated by Pope Innocent III with his brother Andrew.[155] For the past few years Emery and Andrew had been rivals over the succession to the Hungarian throne that their father, Bela III, had left to Emery. In 1203, the conflict with Andrew escalated, as Emery had him arrested and imprisoned in Esztergom (Gran) after he had Ladislas, not even three years of age, crowned king.[156] The king obviously wanted to demonstrate that he was still the most powerful man in the kingdom. He also made that perfectly clear by sending home Andrew's wife, Gertrud, daughter of Berthold of Andechs-Merania.[157]

Then Emery did something strange. For reasons we can only speculate about, he signed a peace treaty with Andrew[158] and had him brought back from exile to be the tutor of Ladislas and the regent of the kingdom.[159] Why he preferred his archrival as regent to Ladislas's mother or some trusted member of the clergy, like for example emperor Frederick II, we cannot say. Maybe he considered the chances for Ladislas to find support within the Hungarian nobility too slim. Maybe he was afraid of too much papal influence after Innocent III had already tried to interfere in the question of succession,[160] or he wanted to make sure that the crown stayed in the family even if this meant that Andrew would usurp the throne in the long run, which is, of course, what he did.[161] After Emery had died in November 1204,[162] Andrew did not waste much time. He called back his wife Gertrud and prepared to take over the rule not just as a regent but as a king: "*Heinrichus rex Ungarorum moritur, et Andreas frater eius de captivitate ad regnum sublimatur. Qui etiam uxorem suam in regno Teutonicorum requisitam, cum gloria magna revocavit.*"[163] It is quite clear that he used his position as regent to move into the center of power, the first rung on the ladder to kingship as the *Continuatio Claustroneoburgensis Secunda* points out correctly: "*Quo defuncto frater de catenis eripitur, et sub nomine tutoris filii fratris sui, quem pater infantulum coronaverat, super regnum Ungarie sublimatur.*"[164]

The next step was, of course, to get rid of the three-year-old child, which Andrew did not see as necessary for a legitimate rule. As the son of Bela III and the brother of Emery he obviously had more support among the Hungarian nobility than Constance who apart from being a woman was also a stranger—the same problem as Blanche of Castile had to face in France.[165] But, in contrast to her, Constance had no support whatsoever: Only Archbishop John of Esztergom sided with her.[166] No other Hungarian magnate felt the need to lend support to the foreign queen, not even as Innocent III sent letters addressed to all lay as well as ecclesiastical princes reminding them to defend the minor king's interests.[167] The suffragans of the archbishop of Kalocsa seemed to have been the most promising potential supporters of the king, because they received a separate letter reminding them to be steadfast in their faith to the child. From this letter it can also be concluded that the archbishop himself, who had crowned the child,[168] could have been a supporter of Ladislas.[169] If it is true that it was still a custom in Hungary that not necessarily the eldest son but the eldest brother of the dead king should succeed the monarch,[170] it might explain why the magnates did not assist Ladislas. Why should they? Andrew had a legitimate claim to the throne.

In any case, these papal measures to support and protect the minority government were to no avail. Not even the personal protection he granted to Ladislas and Constance[171] kept Andrew from infringing on their rights. Constance must have feared for her and her son's lives, because she fled to Vienna under the protection of duke Leopold VI, where Ladislas soon after their arrival died on 7 May: "*Andreas reginam uxorem fratris et filium euis heredem regni persequens, terminos Austrie usque Wiennam intrare coegit, ibique puer moritur, et regina marito natoque orbata auxilio ducis Austrie ad terram suam Arrogoniam proficiscitur.*"[172] Together with the boy's dead body that was buried in Székesfehévár, the royal crown found its way back to Hungary which enabled Andrew to celebrate his coronation on 29 May 1205.[173]

Because Ladislas's reign did not last more than a few months, he did not have enough time to find allies and supporters. The king himself was barely three years old, so his mother could have been the natural regent. But obviously she did not manage to muster enough support to save the crown for her son. In a hurry they had to leave the country and after Ladislas's death she saw no sense in fighting Andrew any longer. She gave back the royal insignia and left for Aragon. A minority government that started under such bad auspices and ended that quickly could not leave a larger impression on the country's long-term constitutional development.

ARAGON: JAMES I

While Ladislas's minority ended tragically, this chapter shall conclude with a description of a very successful one. Like Henry III's accession in England, a far from precipitous set of circumstances ultimately came together in a powerful way to keep young James on his throne. When James's father, Peter II of Aragon, died in 1213 following his defeat on the battlefield of Muret, the five-year-old king became the prisoner of the battle's victor, Simon de Montfort the elder. It took the intervention of the Holy See, which had been informed and alarmed by a group of Aragonese nobles, to free James from his prison in Narbonne. The links between Aragon and the papacy had become even closer since Peter II himself had been placed under the protection of Pope Celestine III when he had been a minor.[174] In 1204, Peter had been crowned by Innocent III and had sworn to be faithful and obedient to Rome in return. "Then Peter offered his kingdom to St Peter, the prince of the Apostles, and through a special document, which he gave to the pope upon the altar itself, the king made himself a tributary."[175] Therefore Innocent must have seen James's minority as a chance to widen his sphere of influence by doing what was his nominal right anyway. He dispatched the legate Cardinal Peter of Benevento not only to guide the boy back to Aragon in early 1214,[176] but also to arrange the minority government.[177] Once in Aragon, he was placed under the care and guidance of Guillem de Mont-rodon, the Master of the Templars.[178]

These first steps to secure James's succession to his father's throne had to be followed by more decisive measures, because there was at least one other pretender to the throne from the royal family: James's uncle Ferdinand, abbot of Montearagón.[179] Therefore, the legate called a *cort*.[180] In 1214, Aragonese and Catalan Magnates met in Lérida for what could be termed the first *general cort* of the Kingdom of Aragon.[181] This seemed to have started a series of *corts* that lasted until the middle of the thirteenth century. By 1228, "the 'general court' had attained a recognized place in the Aragonese constitution."[182] After 1250 and for the rest of James's reign, *corts* became less frequent and less important again.[183] In 1214 anyway, even under the direction of the papal legate, it was hard finding enough support for James's rule. In the end, Peter of Benevento managed to institute a peace and to make the magnates swear an oath of fidelity to the king. Trying to win support from every possible source, even towns and cities were given the chance to send representatives to the *cort*. It was the first time they were allowed to and their envoys indeed did do homage to the king.[184] Later in 1283, towns became an integral part of the annual assembly.[185] The legate Peter of Benevento finally arranged for count Sancho to be installed as regent. Together with three deputies for the different parts of Aragon and Catalonia he was supposed to take care of the government affairs,[186] while the king was sent back to Monzón. The peace of Lérida—which was the first in a series of general peace treaties under James I, at least for the Catalan part of the kingdom[187]—did not last very long, although Ferdinand,

James's rival to the throne, had been invited and actually appeared at the *cort*.[188]

Two years later, in 1216, the pope was forced to intervene again on behalf of James in order not to let Aragon drown in anarchy. To bolster Sancho's minority government Innocent tried to win support among the nobility by writing exhortatory letters. In the end he had to put together an administrative council that was to aid the regent in government affairs. Apart from the archbishop of Tarragona, Aspàreg de la Barca, Guillem IV de Cervera, Guillem de Cardona, and the Master of the Temple, Guillem de Mont-rodon became deputy councilors for Catalonia, and Garcia Frontin, bishop of Tarazona, as well as Pedro Ahones and Jimeno Cornel for Aragon.[189]

In any case, not even the administrative council managed to stabilize the situation. While James was still in the custody of the Templars, where he was to stay until June 1217, the political situation deteriorated. Count Sancho was more and more drawn into conflict against Simon de Montfort and was in danger of losing the new pope's favor. Honorius III even threatened to invade Catalonia. Count Sancho resigned his office in 1218.[190] It does not seem quite clear what happened to James and how the government was reorganized which it must have been because James was still not old enough to rule by himself.[191] According to Damian Smith, the pope simply installed a new regency council in 1219, which comprised almost the same members as the old: Archbishop Aspàreg, Jimeno Cornel, Guillem de Cervera, and Pedro Ahones.[192] But a closer look at the charter Smith quotes makes it more probable that James and the kingdom of Aragon were taken under papal protection. The advisors mentioned are in fact the old regency council minus Count Sancho (who had resigned), the bishop of Tarazona, and Guillem de Cardona, who simply died.[193] Guillem de Montcada, who seems to appear as *procurator domini regis* was rather a *procurator* restricted to financial matters and "certainly not a papal appointee."[194]

Around 1218–19, the second phase of James's reign began to take shape: the rule of the council.[195] Still not able to control the kingdom by himself, because of his young age as well as the constant opposition of rivaling factions of nobles—among them time and again Ferdinand—the eleven-year-old had meanwhile to rely on his advisers, who eventually advised James on whom to marry.[196] His marriage to Eleanor of Castile in 1221, however, did not bring any change as far as government practice is concerned: The council remained the center of politics; warring factions of nobles again and again took up arms against the king and his supporters. In 1223, James reached an understanding with his uncle

Ferdinand,[197] but his troubled situation did not change until the peace of Alcalá of 22 March 1227, which may count as the end of his minority.[198] After this peace treaty, James was able to stabilize his rule and with his first great military success—the conquest of Majorca—"the king had won independence of action as well as prestige."[199]

The whole picture of James's minority governments reveals quite a few things different from the minorities we have talked about so far. It comes as a surprise that neither the pope nor the nobles who supported James considered a coronation necessary. His father did not have a chance to think about it, because he died in battle with his son in the hands of his enemy. As with Henry III, the pope intervened in favor of the minor. But he did it in a much more active way: The legate seemed to have had a much more robust mandate and at one point Innocent even considered an invasion—an option that would have been unimaginable in the English case. Neither the procurator nor regent nor the administrative council needed the person of the king to be constantly around to exercise a legitimate rule, although there seem to have been "attempts to entice him from Monzon."[200]

In other words, possession of the *person* of the king was not nearly as important in Aragon as it was in other European, and later English minorities. In fact, James's personal presence was only needed in the beginning. After his release from de Montfort, he was presented to the public, consisting of the lay and ecclesiastical nobility as well as delegates from the towns. After that he disappeared for the next almost three years in Mozón. There, according to his own memory was left "in the care of a lieutenant."[201] Of course one can assume that in addition to being educated James also had something like a staff of servants. But this cannot be compared to anything like a real royal household with all its offices and officers. The administration of the kingdom was in the hands of regent and the council.[202] There was no household officer who could use his access to the king to gain influence on the government during James's time with the Templars.

The one important constitutional development of the minority was the institutionalization of the *cortes*: "The Cort(e)s of both realms may thus be said to date from the reign of James I. That was when the occasional summons of magnates to form plenary sessions of the king's court was transformed into an institution of the estates of Aragon and Catalonia."[203] The question whether this institutionalization took place due to James's minority can be answered with a tentative "yes." It is certainly no accident that the papal legate viewed the *cortes* as an appropriate means to stabilize the minority government. The estates on the other hand certainly embraced this chance of more participation in matters of the realm and it seems quite probable that they worked toward a certain regularity of these assemblies. This question certainly deserves more scholarly attention in the future. It also appears as if the administration of the kingdom became more "professional." More and better-trained officers began to take care of the ever-growing administrative tasks under James.[204] Finally, it should be mentioned that James seemed to have learned from his own experiences as a minor and integrated his son and designated successor early on into his government. This seemed to have worked so well that following generations adopted this practice.[205]

CONCLUSION: THIRTEENTH-CENTURY ROYAL MINORITIES IN ENGLAND AND EUROPE

The royal minorities that engulfed many of the kingdoms of Western Europe in the early thirteenth century shared a number of important characteristics, and resulted in important changes in politics and government. In many instances, the Papacy took advantage of the succession of a minor to further its aim of what Colin Morris has referred to as a "papal monarchy": The notion that the papal office was, in practice as well as in theory, supreme in the temporal as well as the spiritual sphere.[206] It is undeniable, however, that in most instances papal intervention was beneficial, stabilizing an otherwise unstable situation. In domestic politics, the minorities of this generation tended to expand both the personnel of the court and the importance of consent in the political process. Henry III's minority was not unique in highlighting the divisions and factions lurking just under the surface of politics, and in England and elsewhere the kings who survived their minorities found, sometimes uncomfortably, that they had to continue to take into account the wishes of a broader group of subjects. The struggles for access to a minor king are therefore very revealing in terms of the nature and personnel of the court, a concept that as recently as the late twelfth century had defied description by informed contemporaries.[207] In the case of Henry III in particular, however, we are left with several questions. What did the minority mean for Henry's adult reign? And, perhaps more importantly, how did the minority of Henry III affect those of later kings?

There can be no question that the minority laid the foundation for much that was wrong, and much that was right, in the adult reign of Henry III. By 1227, the deep division and mutual resentment between the "native English" and "foreigners" was fully developed, and the adult Henry III was easily manipulated first by des Roches and later by both his own Poitevin half-siblings and the Papacy, leading eventually to the supreme irony of the foreign earl of Leicester, Simon de Montfort, leading the effort to expel "foreigners" from political influence in the name of the "English."[208] But as the minority created long-standing problems, so it also suggested remedies. It is here that we find the origins of government not merely by *counsel*, but by a broadly-based *council* that could, and did, assist the king—whether he wanted it to or not—in shouldering the burdens of government. The magnates who had governed collectively in the king's name during the minority had set a precedent that would have a lasting impact on government, evolving over the rest of the thirteenth century into a parliament that would take account of the views of the "community of the realm" and would bring pressure to bear on Henry III in 1244, 1258, and beyond. The Charters were also perpetual; having been reissued in 1216 as a desperate expedient, they could not, in their final form, be undone without a renewal of civil war. They remain to this day the bedrock of the English constitution.

In the larger context of Europe, Henry III's minority stands with those of Louis IX of France and James I of Aragon, success stories that offer ample testimony toward a sliding scale of required prerequisites; the necessity of sophisticated administrative forms, the support of a powerful papal monarchy, and a critical mass of subjects determined to support an underage king, for a state to weather the storm of a royal minority. In England in particular, the continued development of the representative element, specifically great councils and parliaments, would prove crucial in making the option of a royal minority a viable possibility for the remainder of the English middle ages.

NOTES

1. D. Carpenter, *The Struggle for Mastery: Britain, 1066–1284* (New York, 2003), 300.
2. Matthew Paris, *Chronica Majora*, 7 vols. ed. H. R. Luard (Rolls Series, 1884–89), 3:3–5, cited in D. Carpenter, *The Minority of Henry III* (London, 1990), 12 n. 14. As the notes below indicate, this massive and thorough study has been invaluable to the preparation of this chapter.
3. *Foedera, conventiones, litterae, et cujuscunque generis acta publica*, ed. T. Rymer (London: Record Commission ed., 1816–69), 1:145, cited in Carpenter, *Minority*, 22.
4. *Regesta Honorii III*, 2 vols. ed. P. Pressutti, (Rome, 1888–95), no. 131, cited in J. Sayers, *Papal Government and England During the Pontificate of Honorius III, 1216–1227* (Cambridge, 1984), 167.

5. S. Painter, *The Reign of King John* (Baltimore, 1949), 297.

6. *History of William the Marshal,* in *English Historical Documents,* III, *1189–1327,* ed. H. Rothwell (London, 1975), 3:82 (hereafter cited as *EHD* III).

7. Sidney Painter observes that the theory of the king's "two bodies" and the undying nature of the king's "body politic" had not yet developed. Consequently the death of John on 27–28 October had effectively left the English throne vacant, making the coronation of his son imperative. Richard I and John had both been styled *dominus Anglie* in the interval between succession and coronation. See Painter, *William Marshal* (Baltimore, 1933), 192 n. 2.

8. It is unclear which of the two men actually placed the gold circlet that served as a crown on Henry's head; N. Vincent, *Peter des Roches* (Cambridge, 1996), 134, asserts that it was the bishop of Winchester, whereas D. Crouch, *William Marshal,* 2nd ed.(London, 2003), 125, claims that it was Guala.

9. Painter, *William Marshal,* 193; Crouch, *William Marshal,* 125; *History of William the Marshal,* in *EHD,* III, 3: 82–83.

10. *History of William the Marshal,* in *EHD,* III, 3: 83–84. All of the major players in the decision (Guala, Peter des Roches, the Marshal, and the earl of Chester) had been named by John as executors of his will. The list of executors may therefore be taken as a reasonably reliable guide to the personnel at the core of the royalist party. See the text of the will in W. L. Warren, *King John,* rev. ed. (New Haven, 1997), 255.

11. This occurs in several places, such as in letters patent of 2 November at Gloucester, in which the Marshal was styled *iusticiarius noster Anglie* (*Patent Rolls of the Reign of Henry III, 1216–1225,* p. 2). This was also the case in a document announcing the reissue of Magna Carta, probably early in November 1216. The document was phrased as though directly from the king, but it was clearly the idea of others, and it may have been the work of Guala. See *Select Charters,* ed. W. Stubbs, 9th ed. (Oxford, 1913), 333.

12. F. J. West, *The Justiciarship in England, 1066–1232* (Cambridge, 1966), 229.

13. For the office of justiciar generally, see West, *Justiciarship.* According to Matthew Paris, Hubert seems to have held a lasting resentment against the Marshal for serving Henry III in a manner which Hubert apparently assumed ought to be reserved to him.

14. Chester seems to have appealed to the legate in the spring of 1217 for approval to be recognized as *coadjutor* with the Marshal, on the grounds of the regent's age; but Honorius III advised Guala to reject Chester's plea. See *Royal and Other Historical Letters Illustrative of the Reign of Henry III,* ed. W. Shirley, 2 vols. (Rolls Series, 1862–66), 1:532, cited in Crouch, *William Marshal,* 126 n. 56.

15. Painter, *William Marshal,* 198.

16. *Select Charters,* ed. W. Stubbs, 9th ed. (Oxford, 1913), 336–39, wherein the Marshal is described as *rector nostri et regni nostri;* translation in *EHD,* III, 22:327–32.
17. Carpenter, *Minority,* 30–31; "between the end of May and the middle of August, there were over 150 submissions" (Carpenter 42).
18. *History of William the Marshal,* in *EHD,* III, 3:89–90; Carpenter, *Minority,* 39.
19. *History of William the Marshal,* in *EHD,* III, 3:93.
20. R. C. Stacey, *Politics, Policy, and Finance Under Henry III, 1216–1245* (Oxford, 1987), 4.
21. Carpenter, *Minority,* 56.
22. All references to manuscript sources on Henry III refer to documents held in the National Archives, Kew (TNA). TNA C 47/34/8 preserves nearly thirty of these charters, from men such as William de Arundel (no. 2), William de Kinellworth (no. 18), and a man named Ivo Pantolf (no. 20). A document of Ranulf of Chester was also included in the file as no. 24 in June 1928, apparently in error.
23. Carpenter, *Minority,* 65.
24. Carpenter, *Minority,* 65–66.
25. Carpenter, *Struggle for Mastery,* 303.
26. C. E. Blunt and J. D. Brand, "Mint Output of Henry III," *British Numismatic Journal* 39 (1970): 63.
27. The London mint figures, the only ones available from such an early period in the minority, are recorded in (oddly enough) the final pipe roll of John's reign. See *Pipe Roll 17 John,* ed. R. A. Brown (London, 1964), 20–22.
28. TNA E 368/1, m. 1d.
29. For this important point, see J. L. Watts, *Henry VI and the Politics of Kingship* (Cambridge, 1996), 115.
30. Ralph of Coggeshall, *Chronicon Anglicanum,* ed. J. Stevenson (Rolls Series, 1875), 187; Paris, *Chronica Majora,* 3: 43.
31. *Patent Rolls,* 177; *Rotuli Litterarum Clausarum in Turri Londinensi Asservati* afterward referred to as *RLC,* ed. T. D. Hardy, 2 vols. (London, 1833–44), II, 75b.
32. On this seal see G. G. Simpson, "Kingship in Miniature: A Seal of Minority of Alexander III, 1249–1257," in *Medieval Scotland: Crown, Lordship and Community,* ed. A. Grant and K. J. Stringer (Edinburgh, 1993), 131–39.
33. See Carpenter, *Minority,* 18, for an insightful discussion of this point.
34. Crouch, *William Marshal,* 136–37.
35. *Patent Rolls,* 173.
36. *History of William the Marshal,* in *EHD,* III, 3:96. The bishop of Winchester began attesting royal letters in place of the Marshal on 10 April, suggesting that the regent formally resigned the previous day: *RLC,* I, 390.

37. Humphrey duke of Gloucester, the uncle of Henry VI, mentioned the Marshal's office specifically in his appeal of that year to the lords of Henry V's council for a similar form of authority, which he felt Henry V had intended for him: C 49/53/12, published in S. B. Chrimes, "The Pretensions of the Duke of Gloucester in 1422," *English Historical Review* 45 (1930): 101–3.

38. *Calendar of Papal Registers Relating to Great Britain and Ireland, 1198–1304,* p. 65.

39. For this see Vincent, *Peter des Roches,* 177–80.

40. *Royal Letters,* I, no. 28, cited in Vincent, *Peter des Roches,* 178 n. 223.

41. Carpenter, *Minority,* 132, 135.

42. In this respect, the "triumvirate" bears resemblance not only to the original triumvirate in the last century of the Roman Republic, but also to the governing arrangement during the early minority of Henry VI, when the infant king's three uncles of Beaufort, Bedford, and Gloucester jointly—and very uneasily at times—controlled the royal administration.

43. C 60/11, m. 6, now available online in *Calendar of Fine Rolls, Henry III, 1218–1219,* no. 238 (http://www.finerollshenry3.org.uk). Carpenter (*Minority,* 130) suggests that "this was almost certainly a measure to prevent Pandulf drawing directly on the king's revenues for his own and papal purposes."

44. F. A. Cazel, "The Legates Guala and Pandulf," in *Thirteenth Century England II,* ed. P. R. Coss and S. D. Lloyd (Woodbridge, 1988), 19–21; see also F. M. Powicke, "The Chancery During the Minority of Henry III," *EHR* 23 (1908): 220–35, esp. 229, where Powicke asserts that Pandulf "captured" the administration for himself.

45. SC 1/6, no. 37; translation in Carpenter, *Minority,* 131.

46. Carpenter, *Minority,* 131; Vincent, *Peter des Roches,* 183 and n. 252, citing *RLC,* I, 391b-448.

47. *Pipe Roll 3 Henry III,* 14–15, cited in Stacey, *Politics,* 13. The manors were Chippenham, Devizes, and Rowde.

48. Stacey, *Politics,* 13.

49. K. Norgate, *The Minority of Henry III* (London, 1912), 121–23; and see also the detailed study of R. V. Turner, "William de Forz, Count of Aumale: An Early Thirteenth-Century English Baron," in *Proceedings of the American Philosophical Society* 115, no. 3 (1971): 221–49, esp. 236–38.

50. Stacey, *Politics,* 15; Norgate, *Minority,* 155–56.

51. Stacey, *Politics,* 14.

52. For much of what follows on the various crises of castle custodies I am indebted to the very useful study of R. Eales, "Castles and Politics in England, 1215–1224," in *Thirteenth Century England II,* 23–43.

53. *Patent Rolls,* 201; Stacey, *Politics,* 14–15.

54. *RLC,* I, 398b; Carpenter, *Minority,* 159–60.

55. Carpenter, *Minority,* 185–86.

56. See Carpenter, *Minority*, 182–83, for a very useful summary of this transition.

57. SC 7/50/3, dated 14 May 1220, is a damaged bull that nonetheless orders the earls and barons to restore to Henry III the various castles they detain and to assist Pandulf, presumably by fulfilling this instruction. A bull dated a fortnight later, TNA SC 7/18/8 (28 May 1220), contains the restriction on the number of castles mentioned above. See Eales, "Castles," 33.

58. Carpenter, *Minority*, 187.

59. *Annales Monastici,* ed. H. R. Luard, 5 vols. (Rolls Series, 1864–69), 3:57.

60. Turner, "William de Forz," 237.

61. Carpenter, *Minority*, 199. It is notable that she played no role in the minority government, not even being granted custody or guardianship of her son. Given the priority she placed on her interests in France, which at times placed her and her husband at odds with her son's government, this was probably a good thing.

62. *Patent Rolls,* 240.

63. Carpenter, *Minority*, 199.

64. Carpenter, *Minority*, 123.

65. Carpenter, *Minority*, 254.

66. This bad feeling was expressed in two letters to Hubert de Burgh, one from Salisbury and the other from Pembroke, detailing the war of words between the two men over John's custody of the wood at Norton in Northamptonshire. According to Salisbury, Falkes imprisoned John Marshal's bailiff at Norton and called "all native men of England" (*omnes naturales homines Angliae*) traitors, accusing them of desiring war against the foreign-born magnates. Clearly such an explosive outburst over a relatively small matter indicates genuine animosity, which was mutual, given that Salisbury in his letter also proudly claimed for himself the label of an English native. See *Royal Letters,* I, nos. 196 and 197.

67. Carpenter, *Minority*, 268.

68. Carpenter, *Minority*, 276, 292, 299.

69. Blunt and Brand, "Mint Output," Table I. For the broader economic picture, see P.D.A. Harvey, "The English Inflation of 1180–1220," *Past and Present* 61 (1973), 3–30, and J. L Bolton, "The English Economy in the Early Thirteenth Century," in *King John: New Interpretations,* ed. S. D. Church (Woodbridge, 1999), 27–40.70. Blunt and Brand, "Mint Output," Table II.

71. Carpenter, *Minority*, 263–65 (Langton), 277–79 (the forest).

72. Carpenter, *Minority*, 282–85.

73. *Chronica Majora,* 3:75–76.

74. *RLC,* I, 569.

75. *RLC,* I, 506–507.

76. See Carpenter, *Minority*, 301–6, for a thorough discussion of the papal letters and a convincing revelation of the people behind them. The

"bomb" metaphor is also Carpenter's (p. 289), but fits the circumstances perfectly.

77. The letters, copied into the Red Book of the Exchequer (E 164/2, fol.
171v.) are printed in various places; that to the earls and barons can be
found in *Foedera*, I, 190, while the letter to Neville is in *Royal Letters*, I,
no. 358. The quotation above is from Carpenter, *Minority*, 301.

78. SC 7/50/4.

79. Quotation in Carpenter, *Minority*, 301.

80. See the discussion of this point in F. M. Powicke, *King Henry III and
the Lord Edward*. 2 vols. (Oxford, 1947), 1:17, 171 n.1 and J. Beverley
Smith, "The Treaty of Lambeth, 1217," *EHR* 94 (1979): 570 n. 4. No
such clause appears in the text of the treaty, and Louis's pledge is
mentioned only by Wendover (*Chronica Majora*, 4:31).

81. Powicke, *King Henry III*, 1:171.

82. Henry's officials had enlisted papal aid the year before, when Honorius
III had issued letters demanding that Hugh return the dowry: SC
7/18/28, 25 June 1222.

83. *Patent Rolls*, 481–82.

84. *Annales Monastici*, 3:84.

85. *Patent Rolls*, 417; Powicke, *King Henry III*, 1:59.

86. C 54/30, m. 16, printed in *RLC*, I, 578. The writ of *liberate* the king
attested was probably intended to further block the plans of the justiciar's opponents, who were intending to gather at Northampton, by re-
leasing 100 marks in preparation for holding his own Christmas court
there.

87. Powicke, *King Henry III*, 1:59, where he states that the enactment of
the papal letters "brought the minority to an end."

88. Carpenter (*Minority*, 322 and n. 6) discusses this point, observing that
the restriction was probably put in place only in December 1223. The
letters patent of November 1218, however, make clear that the principle
was already established; it may be that Hubert and Langton actively decided to reinforce or renew the restriction at this time, when it would
have been appropriate to reconsider the situation.

89. Carpenter, *Minority*, 322; T. F. Tout, *Chapters in the Administrative
History of Mediaeval England*. 6 vols. (Manchester, 1920–33), 1:191.

90. Carpenter, *Minority*, 326–27; Powicke, *Henry III*, 1:59–60.

91. Coggeshall, 204; *Patent Rolls*, 425.

92. *RLC*, I, 630b.

93. Carpenter, *Minority*, 331, who goes on to point out the irony that, in-
voking John's memory, this would have perpetuated a political situation
"which John, in the circumstances of 1223, would not have tolerated
for a moment" (332).

94. *Patent Rolls*, 426–27.

95. *RLC*, II, 72–73.

96. Carpenter, *Minority*, 358, citing *RLC*, I, 603, where Hugh was described as "the king's enemy."

97. *Royal Letters,* I, no. 199, cited in Carpenter, *Minority,* 357.
98. See TNA KB 26/85, mm. 3-2d., described on the inside cover as "Martin de Pateshull's Roll" for the Michaelmas term of 8/9 Henry III, which records several complaints against Falkes. These are also printed in *Curia Regis Rolls,* XI, *7–9 Henry III,* 383–88.
99. Carpenter, *Minority,* 361.
100. See above, n. 91.
101. *Royal Letters,* I, pp. 543–545.
102. Norgate, *Minority,* 296–98, provides extracts of all the primary accounts of the execution of the Bedford garrison.
103. Coggeshall, 208.
104. See N. Denholm-Young, *Richard of Cornwall* (Oxford, 1947), 4.
105. Carpenter, *Struggle for Mastery,* 307.
106. Carpenter, *Minority,* 379.
107. N. Barratt, "Finance on a Shoestring: The Exchequer in the Thirteenth Century," in *English Government in the Thirteenth Century,* ed. A. Jobson (Woodbridge and London, 2004), 73; Blunt and Brand, "Mint Output," Table I. The mint situation continued to improve: By 1234–35, the two mints struck a combined total of £38,077, while by 1249 they produced £121,251.
108. *Patent Rolls,* 540.
109. By the last year of the reign of Edward I, the province paid £6,267 in customs revenues into the king's treasury: Carpenter, *Minority,* 378.
110. *Patent Rolls,* 560–67. The Latin text of the reissue of Magna Carta of 1225 is found in J. C. Holt, *Magna Carta,* 2nd ed. (Cambridge, 1992), 501–11.
111. Translation in *EHD,* III, 26: 346.
112. See below, and also the discussion in J. Richard, *Saint Louis* (Cambridge, 1992), 11.
113. *RLC,* II, 207.
114. D. Carpenter, "King, Magnates and Society: The Personal Rule of King Henry III, 1234–1258," *Speculum* 60 (1985), 39–70, reprinted in idem, *The Reign of Henry III* (London, 1996), 75–106.
115. Jacques Le Goff, *Ludwig der Heilige* (Stuttgart, 2000), 76.
116. Régine Pernoud, *La Reine Blanche* (Paris, 1972), 141.
117. Goff, *Ludwig der Heilige,* 64–65 and 80.
118. For the question whether Blanche was designated as a regent or not see Thomas Vogtherr, "Weh dir, Land, dessen König ein Kind ist. 'Minderjährige Könige um 1200 im europäischen Vergleich,'" *MST* 37 (2003), S. 291–314, p. 307.
119. Pernoud, *La Reine Blanche,* 145.
120. Goff, *Ludwig der Heilige,* 91.
121. Goff, *Ludwig der Heilige,* 84.
122. Goff, *Ludwig der Heilige,* 84 and 91 and Pernoud, *La Reine Blanche,* 145.
123. See Goff, *Ludwig der Heilige,* 81–82 and Pernoud, *La Reine Blanche,* 155–56.

60   Christian Hillen and Frank Wiswall

124. Jean de Joinville, *Das Leben des heiligen Ludwig*, 2.16, ed. Erich Kock, trans. Eugen Mayser (Düsseldorf, 1969), 84 explicitly states that Blanche coming from Spain did not have any relatives or friends in the kingdom. See also *Récrits d'un Ménsestrel de reims au Treiziéme Siècle*, 32.336, ed. Natalis de Wailly (Paris, 1876), 174 [. . .] et si enfant estoient petit, et elle esoit un seule famme d'estrange contrée.
125. Rolf, Pflücke, *Beiträge zur Theorie von Patronage und Klientel. Eine vergleichende Soziologie der Gefolgschaft* (Augsburg, 1972), S. 71: "Im Milieu ethnisch oder rassisch fremder Patronage kann das Ressentiment gegen die Patrone durch das Motiv ihrer Andersartigkeit verstärkt werden."
126. Goff, *Ludwig der Heilige*, 84–86; Pernoud, *La Reine Blanche*, 159. For references to Henry IV see I. S. Robinson, *Henry IV of Germany, 1056–1106* (Cambridge, 1999), 31.
127. Goff, *Ludwig der Heilige*, 92–100.
128. Goff, *Ludwig der Heilige*, 98–101, especially 100.
129. Hans Hattenhauer, *Geschichte des deutschen Beamtentums*, Handbuch des öffentlichen Dienstes 1 (Köln, 1993), 37. For Marion F. Facinger, "A Study in Medieval Queenship: Capetian France 987–1237," *Studies in Medieval and Renaissance History* 5 (1968), 1–48, 31 "the initial steps leading to a bureaucratization of the government" were taken under Philip I.
130. William Chester Jordan, *Louis IX and the Challenge of the Crusade. A Study in Rulership* (Princeton, 1979), 35 refers this statement only to the time of Louis's reign but their origin is under Philip II, in particular the financial service and the later so-called *Trésor de chartes*, see Joachim Ehlers, *Die Kapetinger* (Stuttgart, 2000), 131–32.
131. Ehlers, *Die Kapetinger*, 133. See also Annie Renoux, "Pfalzen und königliche Staatsbildung. 25 Jahre Pfalzenforschung in Frankreich," *Orte der Herrschaft. Mittelalterliche Königspfalzen*, ed. Caspar Ehlers (Göttingen, 2002), 55–83, 71–73.
132. See Hattenhauer, *Geschichte des deutschen Beamtentums*, 39 and Ehlers, *Die Kapetinger*, 133.
133. Hattenhauer, *Geschichte des deutschen Beamtentums*, 39–40.
134. Jordan, *Louis IX and the Challenge of the Crusade*, 46 and 47.
135. Goff, *Ludwig der Heilige*, 108.
136. Jordan, *Louis IX and the Challenge of the Crusade*, 7.
137. Goff, *Ludwig der Heilige*, 108.
138. Jordan, *Louis IX and the Challenge of the Crusade*, 7. According to Jordan, this decision created "the most public tension between the king and his mother and played the most symbolic role."
139. Goff, *Ludwig der Heilige*, 171. Blanche did not rule completely by herself, though. She was supported by a council and Louis himself still tried to deal with French matters, although not very effectively, from overseas.
140. Goff, *Ludwig der Heilige*, 171.

141. Andrew W. Lewis, "Royal Succession in Capetian France: Studies on Familial Order and the State," *Harvard Historical Studies* 100 (Cambridge, MA, 1981), 179.

142. See Regesta Imperii 5.2, No. 3836, 3844, and ibid. 5.4 Nachträge, No. 551-552A. See also Peter Thorau, *König Heinrich (VII), das Reich und die Territorien. Untersuchungen zur Phase der Minderjährigkeit und der "Regentschaften Erzbischofs Engelberts I. von Köln und Herzog Ludwigs I. von Bayern (1211) 1220–1228*, Jahrbücher des Deutschen Reichs unter Heinrich (VII), Teil 1 (Berlin, 1998), 26–31.

143. For the problem of the exact date, see Thorau, *König Heinrich (VII)*, 36–37, who considers February 1217 the probable date of Henry's enfeoffment with the Swabian duchy.

144. For this date also see Thorau, *König Heinrich (VII)*, 48.

145. Frederick II was to take over the rule in Sicily himself again; see Gerhard Baaken, *Ius Imperii Ad Regnum. Königreich Sizilien, Imperium Romanum und Römisches Papsttum vom Tode Kaiser Heinrichs VI. bis zu den Verzichtserklärungen Rudolfs von Habsburg*, Forschungen zur Kaiser- und Papstgeschichte des Mittelalters, Beihefte zu J. F. Böhmer, Regesta Imperii 11 (Cologne, Weimar, Vienna, 1993), 226–27.

146. Regesta Imperii 5.2, No 1114. This election had long been prepared by Frederick and therefore could not have been an accident; see Gerhard Baaken, "Die Erhebung Heinrichs, Herzog von Schwaben, zum Rex Romanorum (1220/1222)," *Aus Südwestdeutscher Geschichte. Festschrift für Hans-Martin Maurer. Dem Archivar und Historiker zum 65. Geburtstag*, ed. W. Schmierer, G. Cordes, R. Kieß, G. Taddey (Stuttgart, 1994), 105–20.

147. In 1196, Henry VI's so-called "Erbreichsplan"—a plan to make the monarchy hereditary—had failed and since then the princes had gained even more rights and privileges. In fact Frederick II himself as well as Henry (VII) granted extensive rights to the magnates: See Erich Klingelhöfer, *Die Reichsgesetze von 1220, 1231/32 und 1235: Ihr Werden und ihre Wirkung im deutschen Staat Friedrichs II* (Weimar, 1955). For the "Erbreichsplan" see Peter Csendes, *Heinrich VI* (Darmstadt, 1993), 171–78.

148. Christian Hillen, "Engelbert, Erzbischof von Köln, als Gubernator für Heinrich (VII.)," *Geschichte in Köln* 46 (1999), 35–49.

149. For the relevance of the coronation, see Heinrich Mitteis, *Die deutsche Königswahl. Ihre Rechtsgrundlagen bis zur Goldenen Bulle*, 2nd ed. (1944; repr. Darmstadt, 1987), 48, who states that "die ganze Herrschererhebung als ein einheitlicher, sich stufenweise verwirklichender Akt gesehen werden muß," in which "die Akte, die wir heute als Wahlakte charkterisieren können [. . .] teilweise zeitlich nach der Krönung liegen können" (p. 54). Brühl considers the coronation to be the "wichtigste staatssymbolische Vorgang beim Herrschaftsantritt eines neuen Königs" next to the unction; see Carlrichard Brühl, "Krönung," *Handwörterbuch der deutschen Rechtsgeschichte*, 2 (Berlin, 1978), 1235–36. The coronation

was in any case necessary for legitimate rule. For the coronation of the Roman King see Percy Ernst Schramm, "Die Krönung in Deutschland bis zum Beginn des salischen Hauses," *Zeitschrift der Savigny-Stiftung für Rechtsgeschichte—Kanonistische Abteilung* 55 (1935), 184–332. The importance of the coronation can be seen in Henry (VII)'s case as well, because he was only crowned when, during a quarrel about the investiture of bishop Konrad of Hildesheim, it became clear that peace and stability in Germany were in danger. The coronation apparently strengthened his authority; see Josef Lothmann, *Erzbischof Engelbert I von Köln (1216–1225): Graf von Berg, Erzbischof und Herzog, Reichsverweser* (Cologne, 1993), 304. For a more detailed description of the quarrels surrounding the bishop of Hildesheim see Irene Crusius, "Bischof Konrad II. von Hildesheim: Herkunft und Wahl," *Institutionen, Kultur und Gesellschaft im Mittelalter. Festschrift für Josef Fleckenstein zu seinem 65. Geburtstag*, ed. L. Fenske, W. Rösener, T. Zotz (Sigmaringen, 1964), 431–68.

150. Christian Hillen, " 'iustum est, ut eum sequar, quocunque ierit.' Der kölnische und der staufische Hof im 12. und 13. Jahrhundert," *Geschichte in Köln* 50 (2003), 37–54, 52.

151. See Christian Hillen, *Curia Regis. Untersuchungen zur Hofstruktur Heinrichs (VII.) 1220–1235 nach den Zeugen seiner Urkunden* (Frankfurt a. M., Berlin, Bern, New York, Paris, Vienna, 1999), 224–26.

152. Regesta Imperii 5.2, No. 4358-60.

153. Regesta Imperii 5.2, No. 4348.

154. The reason why Frederick II acted in such an unforgiving way and why Henry appeard so "stubborn" was conflict about their honor; see Theo Broekmann, *Rigor iustitiae. Herrschaft, Recht und Terror im normannisch-staufischen Süden (1050–1250)* (Darmstadt, 2005).

155. Z. J. Kosztolnyik, *Hungary in the Thirteenth Century*, East European Monographs (New York, 1996), 30. We know nothing about this illness.

156. *Continuatio Admuntensis*, MGH SS 9, p. 590.

157. *Continuatio Admuntensis*, MGH SS 9, p. 590.

158. Potthast, August, Regesta Pontificum Romanorum inde ab a. post christum natum MCXCVIII ab a. MCCCIV, vol. 1, Berlin 1874, No. 2016.

159. *Patrologia Latina sive bibliotheca universalis*, ed. Jacques Paul Migne (Paris: 1855), I, 215, p. 595, No. XXXVI: "*ex regis ipsius* [Emery] *dispositione, ob teneram filii ejus regis Ladislai aetatem, pueri curam et regimen regni susceperis.*" See also Pál Engel, *The Realm of St. Stephen. A History of Medieval Hungary, 895–1526*, trans. Tamás Pálosfalvi (London, New York, 2001), 89.

160. Kosztolnyik, *Hungary*, 29–30.

161. Kosztolnyik, *Hungary*, 31 offers as an explanation that Emery had doubts about the legality of Ladislas's coronation. Concluding from the other European cases of minority governments in those years it seems

highly unlikely that this was the case. In no other European country did doubts about the legality of the coronation of a minor arise.

162. The exact date of his death seems not to be clear. In the literature dates range from September (Pál Engel, *The Realm of St. Stephen. A History of Medieval Hungary, 895–1526*, trans. Tamás Pálosfalvi [London, New York, 2001], 89) to December (*Continuatio Admuntensis*, MGH SS 9, p. 590, n. 80). Th. v. Bogyay, Emmerich, *LexMA* 3, c. 1889–1890 has September as well as November. The most probable seems to be 30 November; see Gyula Kristó, *Die Arpaden-Dynastie. Die Geschichte Ungarns von 895 bis 1301* (Szekszárd, 1993), 174 who refers to the Hungarian sources which he seems to consider to be the most reliable.

163. *Continuatio Admuntensis*, MGH SS 9, p. 590.

164. *Continuatio Claustroneoburgensis Secunda*, MGH SS 9, p. 620.

165. If a queen, besides being a woman, was from a different country this seems to have provided a very good argument for the "native" magnates to dispose of her. It had already happened to Richeza, the polish queen, in about 200 years earlier, just to name one example; see Hedwig Röckelein, Heiraten—ein Instrument hochmittelalterlicher Politik', *Der Hoftag in Quedlinburg 973. Von den historischen Wurzeln zum Neuen Europa*, ed. Andreas Ranft (Berlin, 2006), 99–135, 106.

166. Kosztolnyik, *Hungary*, 32.

167. PL 215, c. 597.

168. Kosztolnyik, *Hungary*, 31.

169. PL 215, c. 598, no. XLII.

170. Kosztolnyik, *Hungary*, 29.

171. Z. J. Kosztolnyik, *Hungary*, 32.

172. *Continuatio Claustroneoburgensis Tertia*, MGH SS 9, p. 634. The *Continuatio Admuntensis*, MGH SS 9, p. 591 adds the detail that Constance took a large treasure with her: "*per vim occupatis portis et custodiis terminorum Ungarici regni, versus Wien ducens secum filium suum cum thesauris et diviciis magnis et comitatu copioso egrassa est, et a Luipoldo duce, de quo propter affinitatem plurimum presumebat, magnifice suscepta. Paucis igitur transactis diebus. Ladezlaus infans moritur.*" See also Engel, *The Realm of St. Stephen*, 89.

173. Gyula Kristó, *Die Arpaden-Dynastie. Die Geschichte Ungarns von 895 bis 1301* (Szekszárd, 1993), 174.

174. Damian J. Smith, *Innocent and the Crown of Aragon. The Limits of Papal Authority, Church, Faith and Culture in the Medieval West* (Burlington (VT), 2004), 21. Already in 1068, Sancho Ramírez had handed his kingdom over to the Holy See; see Michael Borgolte, *Europa entdeckt seine Vielfalt 1050–1250*. Handbuch der Geschichte Europas, vol. 3 (Stuttgart, 2002), 85.

175. Smith, *Innocent and the Crown of Aragon*, 43–44.

176. Thomas Vogtherr, "'Weh dir, Land, dessen König ein Kind ist.' Minderjährige Könige um 1200 im europäischen Vergleich," *FMST* 37 (2003): 291–314, 304.

177. Smith, *Innocent and the Crown of Aragon*, 146–47.
178. Although it is not quite clear when exactly this happened, it is a fact that James was indeed handed over to Guillem de Mont-rodon; see Smith, *Innocent and the Crown of Aragon*, 150 and 153. The king himself mentions it in his autobiography: "*E agren acort, can foren en Catalunya, qui ns nodriri. E acordaren-se tots que ns nodrí lo maestre del Temple en Montró. E son nom d'aquel maestre era En Guillem de Montredon, qui era natural d'Osona e maestre del Temple en Aragó e en Catalunya,*" Jordi Bruguera (ed.), *Llibre dels Fets del Rei en Jaume*, Els Nostres Clàssics. Texts en Llengus Catalane, dels Origens al 1800, B 11, vol. 2 (Barcelona, 1991), 14–15. Thomas Vogtherr, " 'Weh dir, Land, dessen König ein Kind ist.' Minderjährige Könige um 1200 im europäischen Vergleich," *FMST* 37 (2003), 291–314, 304 on the other hand states that James was under the protection of Cardinal Peter for the first few months after his return from Narbonne. According to Smith, *Innocent and the Crown of Aragon*, 150 and 153 and more importantly the king's autobiography it seems as if James was sent to Monzón right away, then taken to the cort at Lérida and then returned to the Templar's castle where he was to stay from August 1214 to June 1217; see *The Book of Deeds of James I of Aragon. A Translation of the Medieval Catalan Llibre dels Fets*, Crusade Texts in Translation 10, trans. Damian J. Smith and Helena Buffery (Burlington [VT], Aldershot, 2003), 27, fn. 57 as well as Bruguera, *Llibre dels Fets*, 14–15.
179. Thomas Vogtherr, " 'Weh dir, Land, dessen König ein Kind ist.' Minderjährige Könige um 1200 im europäischen Vergleich," *FMST* 37 (2003), 291–314, 305. James remembered also count Sancho to have nurtured hopes to become king (Bruguera, *Llibre dels Fets*, 15). Smith considers it not to be likely that Sancho aimed at the throne; see Smith and Buffery, *The Book of Deeds of James I of Aragon* 26, fn. 55.
180. For the Spanish *cortes*, which were a form of parliament, and the Aragonese in particular see Luis González Antón, Cortes III: Krone Aragón, *LexMA* 3 c. 289–91 and Joseph F. O'Callaghan, *A History of Medieval Spain* (Ithaca, London, 1975), 435–45.
181. Vogtherr, *FMST* 37 (2003), 291–314, 305.
182. Thomas N. Bisson, "A General Court of Aragon (Daroca, February 1228)," in *Medieval France and her Pyrenean Neighbours. Studies in Early Institutional History*, ed. Thomas N. Bisson, 31–48, 33 (London, Ronceverte, 1989).
183. Evelyn S. Procter, *Curia and Cortes in León and Castile 1071–1295* (Cambridge, New York, Melbourne, London, New Rochelle, Sydney, 1980), 256.
184. Procter, *Curia and Cortes*, 225.
185. Aragon was therefore the first of the three Iberian kingdoms to admit towns on a regular basis; see Procter, *Curia and Cortes*, 256.
186. Thomas Vogtherr, " 'Weh dir, Land, dessen König ein Kind ist.' Minderjährige Könige um 1200 im europäischen Vergleich," *FMST* 37

(2003): 291–314, 305. F. Darwin Swift, *The Life and Times of James the First, the Conqueror, King of Aragon, Valencia, and Majorca, Count of Barcelona and Urgel, Lord of Montpellier* (Oxford, 1894), 16 names Pedro Ahones and Pedro Fernandez de Azagra for Aragon. The name of the deputy responsible for the Catalan part of the kingdom seems to be unknown.

187. Erich Wohlhaupter, *Studien zur Rechtsgeschichte der Gottes- und Landfrieden in Spanien,* Deutschrechtliche Beiträge, vol. 14.2 (Heidelberg, 1933), 101–7 mentions four peace treaties which he calls Landfrieden. They were concluded during or shortly after James's minority, "damit scheinen wir in Katalonien über das Zeitalter der gro;szen Landfrieden hinaus zu sein," 107.

188. Although the king notes that neither Ferdinand nor count Sancho had attended the meeting, there seems to be evidence that both in fact did come to Lérida; see Smith and Buffery, *The Book of Deeds of James I of Aragon,* 26, fn. 53. Unfortunately there is only a very incomplete edition of James's charters, that in addition only starts in the year 1216, which makes it hard to check the attendance of the *cort* by going through the witness lists of the charters; see Ambrosio Huici Miranda, Maria Desamparados Cabanes Pecourt, eds., *Documentos de Jaime I de Aragon,* vol. 1: 1216–36 (Valencia, 1976). James seems to have been wrong in another point: Count Sancho very likely had no aspirations to the throne.

189. Smith, *Innocent and the Crown of Aragon,* 168. Thomas Vogtherr, " 'Weh dir, Land, dessen König ein Kind ist.' Minderjährige Könige um 1200 im europäischen Vergleich," *FMST* 37 (2003), 291–314, 305, only knows of the two clergy men and one worldly magnate, who he does not name. This gives the impression of James being a "rex clericorum" and even more under the control of the Holy See than he actually was. In fact the lay nobility constituted the majority of the administrative council.

190. Thomas N. Bisson, *The Medieval Crown of Aragon. A Short History* (Oxford, 1986), 60.

191. Swift, *The Life and Times of James the First,* 20: "Of the young king's fortunes during the next two years little is known, and his movements are difficult to trace. He had now shaken off the regent, and the government was carried on by a council." That is about all Swift has to report about the two years after Sancho's resignation.

192. Smith and Buffery, *The Book of Deeds of James I of Aragon* 29, n. 70.

193. According to Swift, *The Life and Times of James the First,* 20, James was just taken under papal protection with only a passing mention of the advisors of the king, which is in fact the wording of the document; see *La Documentetiòn pontifica de Honoria III (1216–1227),* ed. Demetrio Mansilla (Rome, 1965), 177–78, no. 234. For the list of the advisers see Salvador Sanpere Y Miquel, "Minoria de Jaime I. Vindicacion del Procurador Conde Sancho. Años 1214–1219," in *Congreso de Historia de la Corona de Arágon dedicado al Rey D. Jaime I y á su Época,* vol. 2,

(Barcelona, 1909), 580–694, 692, n. 1 (cont.): "*Spargum praterea Tar-raconensem Antistem, Simonem Cornelium, Guilielmum Cerveram, et Petrum Ahonensium Consilio Regis primarios administros, propter pueri aetatem, praeficit.*" See also ibid., 685–94.

194. Thomas N. Bisson, "The Finances of the young James I (1213–1228)," in *Medieval France and her Pyrenean Neighbours. Studies in Early Institutional History,* ed. Thomas N. Bisson (London, Ronceverte, 1989), 351–92, 361–62. The source for the procurator title seems a bit obscure: See ibid., n. 52.

195. Swift, *The Life and Times of James the First,* 32–33 suggests roughly the same phase.

196. Smith and Buffery, *The Book of Deeds of James I of Aragon,* 30, 32, 34; Bruguera, *Llibre dels Fets,* 18, 20, 22.

197. Swift, *The Life and Times of James the First,* 24.

198. Swift, *The Life and Times of James the First,* 32; see also Odilo Engels, Jakob I. "der Eroberer," *LexMA* 5, c. 281–82.

199. Bisson, *The Medieval Crown of Aragon,* 65.

200. Swift, *The Life and Times of James the First,* 18.

201. Smith and Buffery, *The Book of Deeds of James I of Aragon,* 27. Bruguera, *Llibre dels Fets,* 15.

202. For an overview of the royal administration, see Swift, *The Life and Times of James the First,*149–83. There were no court ordinances before the year 1276/77, but some of the offices date back to the time of James's rule. It is possible to identify a few like the majordomus and one can also sketch his responsibilities, but the overall picture remains rather blurry; see Karl Schwarz, *Aragonische Hofordnungen im 13. und 14. Jahrhundert. Studien zur Geschichte der Hofämter und Zentralbehörden des Königreichs Aragon* (Berlin, Leipzig, 1914), 4–19.

203. Bisson, *The Medieval Crown of Aragon,* 80.

204. Bisson, *The Medieval Crown of Aragon,* 81.

205. Swift, *The Life and Times of James the First,* 154.

206. See C. Morris, *The Papal Monarchy: The Western Church from 1050 to 1250* (Oxford, 1986).

207. Even Walter Map, one of the most experienced administrators at the court of Henry II, said of the *curia regis* that "what the court is God alone knows, I do not": Walter Map, *De Nugis Curialium,* ed. M. R. James (Oxford, 1914), 1:248, cited in W. L. Warren, *Henry II* (London, 1973), 301.

208. The most recent biography is J. R. Maddicott, *Simon de Montfort* (Cambridge, 1994).

CHAPTER 2

THE MORE THINGS CHANGE: ISABELLA AND MORTIMER, EDWARD III, AND THE PAINFUL DELAY OF A ROYAL MAJORITY (1327–1330)

J. S. Bothwell

Until quite recently, the historical image of Edward III's minority has been overwhelmingly negative. Perhaps part of this view lies in the perennial shock felt when examining the overthrow of a king in a country that has always seen monarchy as integral to its national fabric, part also in the idea of Isabella as an overly active queen, a mixture of misogyny and labeling that has yet to completely disappear. Another ingredient may be the sight of an overmighty noble helping to tear a royal marriage asunder, and part, of course, the more sensational stories of "screams in the night" heard from Berkeley Castle in the autumn of 1327—which, if nothing else, helps to stir the interest of even the most reticent of students in a late afternoon seminar. Most chroniclers at or near the time do look to one degree or another on the Minority as a problematic, if not downright disturbing, period. The *French Chronicle of London* mentions Edward II being "traitorously murdered" in Berkeley Castle and seems to question the propriety of executing the earl of Kent in 1330,[1] while the *Anonimalle Chronicle* has his son Edward III hearing on the eve of the Nottingham Coup the "many ways in which he had had foolish counsel and that he and his realm were on the point of being lost by treachery and his people destroyed."[2] Geoffrey le Baker venerates Edward II, paint-ing his last months as a sort of martyrdom, and so unsurprisingly has a very negative view of the regime that replaced him.[3] More recently, the emphasis of the discussion has shifted from condemning the Minority Regime as a whole to considering who was the controlling factor: whether it was Mortimer who held the power behind the throne,[4] or Queen Isabella—though, when the latter is argued to be the case, it is portrayed in an increasingly positive light.[5] This chapter's aim, how-ever, rather than continuing to try to figure out where the blame lay and/or who was ultimately in charge—which, though not just "an in-triguing, rather than important question,"[6] is too complex an issue to try to deal with here—is instead briefly to step back and take the broader view, especially in light of recent research, and understand the factors that came into play in the events of Edward III's minority, the nature of politics in the period, and whether or not the exercise of au-thority during Edward's minority was, as it is so often now implied, an interlude or break with what came before and/or after, or whether the shift seen was far more to do with the surface of power in its various guises, and less to do with the actuality of it. Finally, though the work-ing out of "blame" itself may be rather difficult, if not counterproduc-tive, perhaps we should step yet further back, and think more generally, again, if any "blame" should really be apportioned in the first place.

It would first, however, perhaps be useful to put forth a basic outline of the uncontested events of the period from which to work, as well as indicating some of the more important background fac-tors. For the two decades prior to 1327, England had, of course, been ruled by a king known more for his favorites than either his military or political skills. Up until the time of Edward II's over-throw by his wife, Queen Isabella and a band of 1000 or so Hain-aulters in the autumn of 1326, the country had been dominated to one degree or another by royal favorites, whether Piers Gaveston, the Court Party of 1316–19, or the Despensers—all ostensibly act-ing in the name of the king. Indeed, while monarchs before and af-ter had favorites, it is generally agreed that the problem with these men was that not only did Edward II allow them to dominate him to varying degrees, but also it was only the Despensers who made any real, arguably positive, difference to the governance of the king-dom.[7] The reign has, as a result, been considered a disaster for the monarchy and those who supported it, and few were sad to see the back of it. Upon the deposition of Edward II in January 1327, with the new king, Edward III, still a minor, there was initially set up a council constituted by parliament in order to run the kingdom, headed by Henry of Lancaster and a select group of churchmen and nobles. However, it was soon obvious to all that the real power in the kingdom increasingly lay with Queen Isabella and her lover, Roger Mortimer—though who was the "dominant" partner in the relationship, as we have already heard, is open to debate. Nonetheless, the pair's control not only became crucial at the peace negotiations with the Scots later in the coronation year,[8] but also with the redistribution of lands of various supporters of Edward II's regime, most notably those of Hugh Despenser the Elder and Younger, and the earl of Arundel, all of whom were executed on Isabella's assumption of effective control in late 1326. Indeed, with many of the properties going to either themselves or to buy the support of a few other tactically crucial men in the kingdom, including two of the ex-king's brothers and some well-placed henchmen, as well as the generally popular reversals of the judgments of 1322 and the death of Edward II later in the year, by the end of 1327 Isabella and Mortimer were as secure as anyone in such a position could have expected. The crowning aspect of this accumulation of power was the wedding of the young King Edward and the daughter of Isabella's invasion ally, John of Hainault, in January of the next year—that which had started with a political alliance ended with a matrimonial vow of the highest order.[9] However, this was in many ways the apex of the regime's successes, and thereafter more substantial problems manifested themselves. Whether it was the ill-judged promotion of Mortimer to the new earldom of March in the autumn of 1328, the Bedford Rebellion later in the year, or the execution of the earl of Kent in the spring of 1330 for trying to free the supposedly still living Edward II, the goodwill that the regime had started with in late 1326/early 1327 had now all but evaporated. The Nottingham Coup of October 1330 signaled the end of that decline, and the beginning of Edward III's majority, but even then it was not entirely clear which path the young king and his kingdom were going to follow thereafter.

However, it was not merely domestic political events most narrowly defined that helped decide the course of Isabella and Mortimer's regime, it was also a number of underlying issues which had, and would, play an important part in the policies of the monarchy or those who controlled it for decades to come. In particular, there were three long running "external" factors—two "foreign" and one "domestic"—that weighed heavily upon the royal government in this period, and would influence many of the decisions made during

Edward's minority. The first was the Scottish problem. Ever since the catastrophic defeat of English forces at Bannockburn in 1314 by Robert the Bruce, the Scots had effectively free run of the northern border, raiding at will, and causing no end of headaches for both landowners of the area and the English in general. There had been attempts to subdue the Scots, or at least contain their ambitions, most notably in 1319, and in 1322/3, but neither had come to anything except to encourage the supposedly treasonous negotiations of a number of members of the nobility,[10] including that which resulted in the fall of Andrew de Harcla, the earl of Carlisle and the victor of Boroughbridge.[11] With another phase of raiding on the English border, reaching a climax in the summer of 1327 after faint-hearted attempts at negotiations,[12] and ending with the disastrous Stanhope Park campaign on the part of the English forces later in the year, Isabella and Mortimer realized that military force was perhaps not the best approach at the time. Thus, in what has come to be known as the "Shameful Peace," the Treaty of Northampton (preceded by the Treaty of Edinburgh), Robert Bruce was recognized as king of the Scots, Edward III's sister was to marry David, son of Robert the Bruce, and England was to get a 20000 mark payment, all of which appear to have gone into the purses of Isabella and Mortimer.[13] However, this was by no means the end of the problem. The existence of "The Disinherited," a group of men dispossessed by the seizure of the kingdom by Robert the Bruce (many of whom were also English landowners now based in England), would keep the sore festering well into the next decade. With the death of Bruce in 1329, and the minority of his five-year-old heir David, many saw it as the perfect time to start planning revenge on the usurping dynasty, a revenge that would come to at least partial fruition with the Dupplin Moor (1332) and Halidon Hill (1333) campaigns, and the placing of the ineffectual Edward de Balliol on the Scottish throne.[14]

The second major "foreign" issue was that of France, both English lands on the Continent, and what was to become of the French throne itself. The relationship between the English and French kings over lands England held in France had been theoretically settled in 1259 with the Treaty of Paris—when Henry III surrendered the English crown's claim to lands in northern France lost in 1204 in exchange for acknowledgement of English rights over Aquitaine, subject to liege homage to the French king. Nonetheless, thereafter, the area had remained a flashpoint for Anglo-French relations: in 1294, with a dispute between English and French mariners ending in Philip the Fair confiscating Gascony; and in 1323–24, with the so-called

"War of Saint Sardos," in which Charles IV again took it upon himself to invade the Duchy.[15] The new Minority government, however, in the first two years at least, was saved from either confrontation, or the necessity to bow to the French king in person by Prince Edward's earlier homage in 1325—one of the few primarily positive acts for all concerned during Isabella's sojourn in France, though arguably further weakening any future claims the English might have in the region.[16] However, the end of the Capetian line—as luck would, or would not, have it, England, Scotland, and France would all change kings in the late 1320s—caused a change in the situation which Mortimer and Isabella had to face. Initially, Isabella arranged that, in addition to the £60000 relief promised to the French king as a result of the 1325 negotiations, she would pay 50000 marks as a war indemnity, with an offer of amnesty for most Gascon rebels.[17] However, with the establishment of the new French line in 1328, that of the Valois, and the threat of the young prince Edward's claim to the French throne through his mother, the situation became more tense—it was now not only the issues of vassal versus lord that divided the two kings, but the claim to the French throne itself. To start with, a protest by the English was made concerning the accession of Philip of Valois to the French throne, making clear that the young King Edward had a more valid claim.[18] That said, mainly due to the worsening domestic situation, it quickly became obvious that it was more sensible if the regime forwent the right for the present and instead sent the young king to pay simple homage for the Duchy of Gascony to Philip VI of France in 1329—though the nature of this homage has been open to many questions, then and since.[19] Though this was to settle the issue for the moment, the French homage, as the "Shameful Peace," did not sit well with the young Edward or many of his nobles, and lay seeds for future strife. Even at the time, chroniclers had little good to say about the Minority regime's handling of the situation: the *Scalacronica,* for instance, calling their counsel "malign, slothful and negligent."[20]

The final main background issue of the Minority period was not to do with foreign politics but with social evolution within England itself, an issue that nonetheless helped explain a number of contemporary events. Indeed, the position and treatment of the nobility and the impact it would have on the fortunes of the regents and the functioning of the country during the Minority was an aspect that had even deeper roots in the history of the period than either of the issues discussed above. The nobility, as is well known, had been gaining strength and power over the previous two centuries, both in its hold over its lands, and in its coherence as a social grouping.[21] From the nascent ideas of noble collective rights in the twelfth century, through the events of 1215, 1244, and 1265, this class had gradually honed its perception of itself as a social, political, and economic group, even if its conflicts with the king to this point had been generally unsuccessful. Even the monarchy had in essence admitted that not only hand-picked councilors should be called to advise on the running of the kingdom from time to time, but also the necessity of the involvement of a larger *quorum,* one which took in all the major landowning families and which would develop into the House of Lords, and more generally, parliament. By the end of period, according to Powell and Wallis, not only was there an increasingly defined and structured parliamentary peerage, but also one whose membership had stabilized considerably to the point where it would be seen as more and more hereditary by most historians.[22] By Edward II's reign, moreover, there was a fairly clear idea of noble rights, and the relationship between the king and nobility, as most recently put forth in the Ordinances (1311) and in the Treaty of Leake (1318), as well as, in theory at least, the *Modus Tenendi Parliamentum* and Walter of Milemete[23]—showing that there were also areas in which major problems could arise. The first serious indications of crisis in this relationship during Edward II's reign ended with the execution of Gaveston and the instabilities of the early 1320s, but even the role that the nobility played in the Usurpation of 1326/7, while not the dominant one, was still of enough importance to remind the magnates and lesser barons that they should have a key part to play in the Minority Government.[24] The fact, then, that the original minority council (in which the nobility had considerable voice—see below) was effectively sidelined even before it had really started its work, and that, at an individual level, though there was reseisin and, more noticeably redistribution of lands, the latter was nowhere near as wide as many nobles would have wanted, tended to help sour relations with the nobility from the beginning. Finally, there was more generally a recognition arising in the later 1320s, but looking back both to the *Modus* and even further back to Magna Carta, that if the nobility did get on the wrong side of the monarchy, there had to be certain set procedures, including the beginnings of trial by peers, in order to deal with the situation.[25] This not only helped to put the nobility in a stronger situation, if nothing else by widening the chance of justice, it was to help cause increasing tension—though the issue was not to be brought to the boil until the crisis of 1340–41.[26] Add all these issues together with the deposition of a king and the execution of a number of titled nobles, and the Minority regime had its work cut out for it when it began to govern in early 1327.

Facing the challenges that it did, then, how did the government of the realm function during Edward III's minority, and what part did the young king have to play? To begin with there was, as indicated, some attempt to rule the realm by common consensus, or at least advice and counsel, of the most important of the land—though the council which was then founded, as had been pointed out, had "no executive power,"[27] and indeed the only mention of the council's constitution in the Parliamentary Rolls for January 1327 took the form of an intent rather than a specific plan of action.[28] Nonetheless, a committee was set up of four bishops, four earls, and four (or six) barons, and including the archbishops of Canterbury and York, the bishops of Winchester and Hereford, the earls of Lancaster, Norfolk, Kent, and Warenne, and the barons Thomas Wake, Henry Percy, Oliver Ingham, and John Ros— though the composition of this council does vary slightly depending upon the source one reads.[29] All these, according to one much later account, "were s[w]ore treuliche for to conceile the king and they shulde ensuere every yeire in the parlement of that shulde be done in the tyme of that governayle."[30] Unsurprisingly Lancaster, who also initially had physical possession of the deposed Edward II in Kenilworth castle, was made the "chief guardian of the realm" and, with four members of the group (a bishop, an earl, and two barons), was to be permanently at the king's side.[31] According to Tout, the other Lancastrian supporters on the council included the Bishop of Winchester and Wake, Percy, and Ros,[32] though whether this group overlapped with the abovementioned inner group is not clear. Notably, the council did not include Mortimer (supposedly at his own wish), though it did include his supporter (Ingham) as well as two uncles of the king (Kent and Norfolk) who were also to receive large grants of land from the regime:[33] in other words, a group that included the spectrum of opinion, as well as some moderates, and deliberately excluded easily the most controversial noble of the period. Initially, considering the number of Lancastrians or neutrals on the council, as well as the general goodwill of the country toward Henry of Lancaster in light of the fate of his brother after Boroughbridge in 1322, the Lancastrians potentially held a considerable amount of sway over the governance of the realm as a whole.[34] Not only were the sentences and forfeitures of 1322 reversed in the first parliament of 1327, much to Henry and other Lancastrians' benefit, there was even talk of canonization of his brother (ultimately, however, felt inappropriate).[35] Thus, for whatever reason—whether Isabella and Mortimer did not yet think they were strong enough to take complete and unquestioned power, or as a way to help sell the change in government to the country as a whole—the initial version of the minority regime tried to bring in most shades of opinion, and act as a healer of the many past divisions.

And at first some very important duties, such as the choice of keepers of the peace, were decided by the minority council: according to Baldwin, "not only was there a stream of letters by warrant of the king and council, but at least one definite act is attributed to the earl of Lancaster and his fellow councillors."[36] The *Memoranda Rolls* of the exchequer for 1326–27 also list a number of important bits of business dealt with by the king and council at this time, including the unaccounted for issues of chamber lands for Edward II's reign, and concerning the setup of the escheatory.[37] Moreover, many of the members of the original minority council were also very active in royal charter witnessing, an indicator of a more general engagement with the business of government: all the titled members of the minority council, along with John Ros and Thomas Wake, witnessed at least a third of all royal charters in 1327.[38] Likewise, at a more mundane level, some of these minority council men were in control of many of the more practical aspects of the running of the kingdom. Obviously this was the case with the titled lay and ecclesiastical nobility, who had considerable sway both at court and their own spheres of influence, but even the lesser men on the council, such as again Ros and Wake, initially held important jobs such as Steward of the Royal Household, Constable of the Tower of London, and Justice of the Forest south of Trent.[39] Quite quickly thereafter, however, Isabella and/or Mortimer assumed control of the government as they had gradually the court, and the wishes of the minority council came to be ignored. The fact that the couple had arranged the overthrow of Edward II was obviously a key factor in their increasingly dominant position—whatever else they had shown, they had proved that they had the energy and determination to make at least one serious change. Also important was the arrangement in the November 1326 parliament (presumably under pressure from Isabella and Mortimer) to get the Londoners onside by regranting them lost liberties as well as giving them new ones[40]—a relationship that the Londoners were more than willing to reciprocate,[41] and a wise act considering their compromised position if the usurpation was later reversed. Similarly, support in the rest of the country, even if just through apathy, gave most a part in the revolution of 1326, and some local officials at the very least would therefore be held as complicit if the usurpation had later been reversed.

In part, though, the seeds of this dominance of Isabella and Mortimer were also planted by omission around the time of the Coronation and the setting up of the original minority council. In particular, the Ordinances of 1311, the main rallying cry of Thomas of Lancaster, were not revived:[42] this was a major omission, especially considering how long and hard Lancaster had fought for them since their composition, and how important the idea of noble council was to their makeup. Instead, thereafter, even more of the Lancastrian legacy was eroded, with old supporters of Thomas and Henry also steadily being removed from their offices under pressure from Mortimer.[43] Indeed, considering that the Lancastrians were the only other "organized" noble grouping in the kingdom at this time, it was unsurprising that Mortimer and Isabella worked to downgrade their influence—they clearly did not want the revival of the Contrariant party of earlier in the decade, dangerous as it had been both to the peace of the kingdom and the position of the monarch. And finally at a more personal level, aside from the queen's position as mother to the king, the friendship between Isabella and Richard Bury, Edward III's confident and former tutor, was useful for the queen and Mortimer as a way to keep control over the young Edward and know what he was thinking.[44] A similar attempt at personal influence also seems to have been used on John of Eltham, the king's brother, who was granted the earldom of Cornwall in 1328—for the sake of which he was later, after the end of the Minority, granted 2000 marks worth of land by Edward III.[45] According to the *DNB*, after Edward became king, John was often in his presence and was clearly active in the court more generally, being a frequent witness to royal charters starting in 1329—thus clearly an important person for Mortimer and Isabella to retain influence over.[46]

That said, when Mortimer and/or Isabella publicly and officially asserted their dominance over the royal administration is far from clear—the sham of conciliar government seems to have been kept going at the very least through most of 1327 and into 1328. In particular, while the Queen Mother clearly had to be an important part of any governance, the position of Mortimer in this period is less than obvious: he was noticeably an influence in the background, but when he was accepted as a key player is open to question. Indeed, though charter witnessing by Mortimer was high throughout the minority,[47] he remained firmly outside the council, and for the first year of the minority at least relatively quiet. Rather, the *French Chronicle of London* puts the clear dominance of the couple just after the wedding of David Bruce and Joanna of the Tower, the sister of the king, at

York in late July 1328, arranged by Mortimer and Isabella as part of the peace with the Scots, by which time Henry of Lancaster, referred to in this chronicle as "the chief guardian of the realm . . . by common consent of all the realm, could not approach him or counsel him."[48] Notably, Edward III was not present at the wedding,[49] and, in the next year, the *Lanercost Chronicle* referred to Mortimer in particular as "more than king in the kingdom, forasmuch as the queen mother and he ruled the whole realm."[50] However, whenever their public dominance began, Isabella and Mortimer started to grab and rearrange wealth and land as soon as possible after the usurpation, something that was done even before the official minority council had become effectively defunct. First, and most sensibly, they looked to the basis of their power. They quite quickly made arrangements for Philippa of Hainault, the bride of the young king and the daughter of their invasion ally, setting aside 1000 marks payment for the expenses of the chamber, though notably no dower lands were arranged until after 1330.[51] This was, of course, not only living up to the bargain made with the Count of Hainault in 1325–26, but was also crucial if Isabella wanted the use of troops from Hainault in the future—not inconceivable considering the continuing problems with the Scots, if no one else. Thereafter, however, the focus of patronage narrowed. In particular, Isabella's fast and lucrative arrangements for herself were not designed to make friends with the nobility as a whole. She assigned to herself £8722 4s 4d worth of lands spread throughout southern England and Wales, and had a dower worth 20000 marks,[52] thereby clearly limiting the amount of land available to the rest of the nobility. Moreover, in 1327, she also bought, for £10000, the Montalt inheritance—using, it would seem, money from a parliamentary subsidy.[53] Later, in 1328, the *Brut* accused her of taking into her hands the Lordship of Pontefract and almost all lands of value appertaining to the crown "so þat þe Kyng had nouȝt forto dispende, but of his Vsues and of his escheker,"[54] an act that would also upset Henry of Lancaster as its rightful owner. Indeed, the material wealth of Isabella during this time had caused much comment, and envy,[55] especially rich as she was the betrayer of an anointed king, however incompetent and hated. Finally, at least according to the *Brut*, it was Isabella, rather than the minority council, who decided which lands the young Edward himself was to be granted for his sustenance "þat þe Kyng hade noþing þerof but at her wille and her deliuerance, neiþer of hir landes."[56]

Unsurprisingly then, and despite his undefined position early on, Mortimer also quite quickly built up his estate as well, especially through royal grants in fulfillment of a promise of lands to £1000 per annum, through which he received, in September 1327, a number of Despenser and Arundel properties including the lordships of Denbigh (previously held by Thomas of Lancaster), Oswestry, Shrawardine, and Clun.[57] Moreover, he was made Justice of Wales (during pleasure and then for life)—as well as chief keeper of the peace in Herefordshire, Staffordshire, and Worcestershire and justiciar of the bishopric of Llandaff[58]—thus reinforcing his position in the west during the Minority. Mortimer also married his daughters off to the heirs of the earldoms of Warwick and Pembroke,[59] among others, thereby reinforcing his newly found position within the higher nobility yet further still. But perhaps what pushed some of the most powerful noble families *qua* noble families in the land to breaking point, aside from not being allowed any real say in the running of the realm, the relatively limited redistribution of lands (though still wider than that practised by Edward II),[60] and the embarrassment of the "Shameful Peace" with the Scots, was the creation of the "novel" yet very important earldom of March for Roger Mortimer in 1328,[61] arguably the most important nonroyal title in England and in effect overriding the existing noble power structure.[62] Indeed, this seems to have upset the established nobility even more than Edward III's forced homage to the French king a little later in the year. The earldom of March, because of the identity of its current holder, was now in effect even higher in the actual pecking order than the earldom of Lancaster: the fact that it was also a new title, and the first not to be based on any existing county, did not help matters either.[63] At a somewhat less serious level, in this year Mortimer was also to be the impetus behind the Round Table celebrations at Bedford,[64] and by the time of his promotion, it was said that he would not walk behind the king, but would only keep pace, or sometimes even walk ahead.[65] Though not the cause of the Bedford rebellion, such posturing by Mortimer in many ways seems to have been the straw that broke the camel's back for the increasingly resentful nobles, and especially the Lancastrians, forcing them into revolt in late 1328.[66]

Indeed, it must be remembered that initially Mortimer was not only just another member, though moderately powerful, of the English peerage, but that he previously had been aligned with the Contrariant cause under the leadership of Lancaster—though, notably, he was later accused by one chronicler at least of "deserting" Lancaster and the other barons in 1322 and instead putting himself "at the king's mercy, the prime misfortune amongst their troubles."[67] However, it was more importantly Mortimer's growing relationship with the queen while at the Parisian court, which, looking from the viewpoint of other nobles, not only allowed him to dominate the kingdom's politics, but also to be given a wholly new earldom. But whatever the ultimate cause, none of these factors would have endeared him to an established nobility already overly tired with the issue of curial favorites. Moreover, his hastily found fame and newly exalted position would also put Mortimer in the situation, and it does seem to have been Mortimer *himself* in this instance,[68] that he had to orchestrate the downfall of the earl of Kent, a key noble who, while initially favorable to the regime, by 1328 was in direct opposition to it, and willing to believe that a rethroned Edward II was far better that any present system of government.[69] Such an individual was, at the very least, a severe test of Mortimer's power, if not Isabella's, especially with Kent's additional status as the old king's brother and the new king's uncle. Finally, at a more prosaic level, it could be argued that by seizing lands from both sides on the Welsh borders,[70] much as the Despensers had before him, Mortimer was helping to make a new generation of enemies, both English and Welsh—a generation just waiting for him to slip up. Overall, then, such acts did nothing to make the nobility of the realm feel secure and, rather, in many ways could easily have been reminded of the instabilities of earlier in the decade. Though mainly political events, the creation of the earldom of March and the downfall of the earl of Kent in particular both exposed noble pride, and noble sensibilities, which had been developing for generations previous, while also creating a clear target, Mortimer, at which to aim.

Even so, in the early stages of their power at least, Isabella and Mortimer did not forget to establish something of a base of support, especially amongst the royal titled nobility, and made large grants in particular to Edward II's two half brothers, the aforementioned earls of Kent and Norfolk. Though most of this was arranged under the auspices of the king and parliament, it was clear to all where the impetus lay. For instance, in 1327, the earl of Norfolk was given 1000 marks of land and rent entailed—including manors in Oxfordshire, Berkshire, Buckinghamshire, Cheshire, Gloucestershire, Essex, and Lincolnshire—all forfeited by Despenser the Elder in 1326 and granted by the king and council in parliament.[71] Isabella and Mortimer realized how alienated the higher nobility had become during the last two decades, and made an attempt to rectify the matter. That said, aside from favor to some other lower level henchmen such as John Maltravers and Oliver Ingham[72] and, as we have seen, simply restoring many of those who had lost their lands in 1322 (which those involved

would have seen as their right anyway)—the breadth of new patronage was nowhere near what was needed to create a solid power base.
Rather, considering the later rebellion, or at least passive disloyalty, of
most of the people they gave out, or returned, lands and favor to (esp.
in 1328–29)[73] it is arguable that such resources were wasted, and
would have been better spent if not more widely, then at least
augmenting the incomes of the couple, or better yet the government.
Instead they opted for the worst of both worlds: not spreading available resources wide enough to make a substantial support base
amongst the nobility, but spreading them too widely to enrich themselves to the point where they were potentially unassailable simply due
to the extent of their wealth.

Moreover, it was not just the personal patronage of Isabella and
Mortimer (as well as, of course, their luxurious lifestyle)[74] that was to
cause problems, it was also the financial policy that they implemented
for the kingdom as a whole. As is well known, one of the few things
that Edward II and the Despensers did right for the monarchy, if not
for the kingdom, was not to spend much money on foreign wars, and
so be able to leave a very full treasury when their rule came to an end
in 1326. According to most estimates, the treasury had in November
1326 £78156 18s 2¾d, along with other valuables—nonetheless, primarily due to the spending of Isabella and Mortimer, by the spring of
1327 it was down to £12031 2s 8d.[75] As a result, from early on the
regime had to borrow considerable amounts of money, mainly for
campaigning in Scotland. For the fourteen months after August
1326, the Minority regime borrowed £19453, mainly from the Bardi:
unsurprisingly the Bardi were not altogether happy with the arrangement, complaining in particular about the "inadequacy of customs
and other revenues assigned to them in repayment."[76] Indeed, most
of the warfare, according to Kaeuper, was on credit during the
Minority: for instance, both for the initial invasion, for which £13500
was owed to John of Hainault alone, and a further £41304 for his
part in the Scottish campaign.[77] Such loans were continually needed
throughout the period, as it is generally accepted that Mortimer and
Isabella had already gone through the massive amount of wealth
stored up by Edward II and the Despensers by the time of Stanhope
Park campaign in the latter half of 1327.[78] In some ways, this is
understandable, considering the need not just to buy support and
troops, but also to be able show a certain degree of material affluence
from early on. However, the idea that such an amount of money had
been wasted, and that the monarchy was deeply in debt to foreign
bankers without any victories, and quite a few failures, to their credit,

was not something that was likely to impress either parliament, or when they heard of it, the public at large. Even the money given to England by the Scots as a result of the Treaty of Northampton in 1328 appears to have been siphoned into the hands of Isabella rather than going into the kingdom's treasury.[79]

Unsurprisingly, then, the young king himself, as we will see, developed serious reservations about the government as run by Mortimer and Isabella—though it should first be noted that it was not just Edward who had problems with it. At least a few upper nobles and prelates may have been concerned about the actions of the new regime from the beginning. Indeed, not all men of power were quick to link themselves with Isabella and Mortimer. For instance, the earl of Hereford, a nephew of Edward II, was seemingly very reluctant to associate with the Minority government and its doings—though Crawford thinks that, in Hereford's case, this may also have been to do with bad health,[80] not to make even a limited effort through curial emissaries at such a time is also a pretty clear indication of a certain degree of coolness. And it is interesting how the earl of Norfolk, according to Fryde, drew up a "statement of his rights as Earl Marshal which suggests that he had encountered difficulties or opposition" as early as the summer of 1327.[81] Likewise, it is notable how little Henry of Grosmont, Lancaster's son and a future loyalist of Edward III, showed up on the curial witness lists of the period, despite being heir to one of the most important estates of the kingdom—and though again this may have, in part, been to do with personal circumstances, in this case his youth (he was born in 1310),[82] it was still to be expected that such a scion of a great noble family was to have more presence in court affairs at this time than he actually ended up having. Somewhat more substantially, the other main institution of the land, the Church, was by no means united by this overturning of order at the highest level either. According to Heath, few churchmen gave overly enthusiastic support to the overthrow of Edward II;[83] though, at least according to Geoffrey le Baker, the Bishops of Lincoln and Winchester did back the minority regime's line, and threatened to disinherit Prince Edward for "one not of royal blood,"[84] perhaps a veiled reference to Mortimer.

That said, the initial divide came more over policies than personalities. While the first major spilt between the administration and its critics more generally can be seen to have come as a result of the peace with Scotland in May 1328,[85] with many magnates voicing their dismay at the peace treaty,[86] the clearest and most forceful voicing of this dissent came in the Bedford rebellion of late 1328/early 1329, the first violent break between the Minority regime and the nobility. The rebels' issues and demands were neatly put in a letter to the citizenry of London, namely that the monarch should be able to "live of his own," yet at the same time have enough money to deal with enemies; that he should have the council of the great men, lay, and ecclesiastical of the kingdom, as set out in the parliament of 1327, and that peace should be maintained in the kingdom as a whole.[87] But in many ways, because the actual rebellion was so much more clearly about baronial power and position than about law and order or the overall health of the realm, especially considering the social makeup of the rebels and its leadership by Lancaster, it is unsurprising that it encouraged mixed emotions amongst the high and mighty of the land. For a start, the Church was divided about the rebellion. Though initially in general supporting the usurpation, if in a rather lackluster manner, during the rebellion of 1328 the divisions hardened: according to Haines, "the bishops were in disarray, Burghersh and Charleton (Hereford) . . . acted unobtrusively in their official capacities, but Mepham, Stratford and Gravesend clung together in opposition to the ruling clique."[88] Moreover, and more importantly, it is unsurprising that Edward III chose, even considering his view on the Scottish situation, to stay distant from events, both physically and emotionally. Instead of backing or spearheading the rebellious nobility, the young king decided to spend Christmas with his mother, Mortimer, and Philippa "in one company" at Westminster.[89] He had seen what disaffected nobles had done to the monarchy when encouraged during his father's reign, and clearly did not want to see this happen again. Nonetheless, the supposed lack of involvement by Edward III himself, as the sides in this dispute overall, was not always clear to contemporaries.[90] For instance, according to the *Anonimalle* Chronicle:

In 1329 at the feast of St. Hillary (13 January), the king on one side, through the counsel of his mother and of Mortimer, and the said sir Henry, earl of Lancaster, on the other side, collected and assembled a great army and great forces each against the other in the regions of Leicester and Bedford, but through archbishop Simon and certain other bishops and a number of lords of the land a form of agreement was made. The king's side humbled themselves to the queen, agreeing to answer in parliament and to make amends for the offences committed between them, on account of this dispute begun and now ended, and in order to prevent the country being delivered into great danger, and so that the king would be held as lord. Because of this (dispute), some Londoners had come into the company of the said sir Henry Lancaster, as if to oppose the king, except that the cause of the earl was just, that is to say that he (the king) should live of his own to maintain his land if he was (not) at war in other lands.[91]

Most accounts, though, distance Edward III more clearly from the Bedford rebels. Indeed the evidence lies in the king's own words, in the letter of December 1328 to the Mayor, Aldermen, and Sheriffs of the City of London among others:

> Though the Earl and his party declared that they were acting in the King's interests, and that their movements were not directed against him, but against certain of his subjects, the King considered that their proceedings would result in grave disorder, and thus directly affected him. In any case, it was not their duty but his, to act as judge and do justice.[92]

Also, it is notable from these and other sources that one of the key issues seems to have been the intra-noble problem between Lancaster and Mortimer in particular—most likely over Lancaster's being effectively ousted as chief councilor to the king and denied access to Edward III. However, there were other problems between the two men. Aside from Lancaster not getting back Pontefract or Denbigh,[93] there was also the "novel" creation of the earldom of March probably being seen in competition, when it came to prestige, with the earldom of Lancaster—as well as Mortimer's general arrogant demeanour,[94] and Lancaster's condoning of the murder of Robert Holand (the betrayer of Thomas of Lancaster at Boroughbridge) against the Minority Regime's peace.[95] Put together one begins to think that, rather than just a political issue between the rebels and government as groups, that this situation may also, in part at least, have been more individually oriented.[96] Even the abovementioned letter from the King to the Londoners is a very personal document, and though the interests of Mortimer and Isabella were clearly noted, the voice of the young Edward seems also to be coming out, as when one of the passages addressed the criticism that the king "should live of his own":

> The above answer being considered by the King, it seemed to him as regards the first point, namely, that he ought to live of his own, that it was impossible for him to be any richer, since both he and his people were impoverished by the present disturbances, but if any man knew how to make him richer, it would give him and his advisers great satisfaction.[97]

Whether between the king and the Londoners, Lancaster and Mortimer, or even the king and the rebels more general, then, all this dialogue often had a very sharp edge to it. In the end, however, the threat of confiscation of all estates and goods of the rebels, as well as the late desertion of the earls of Kent and Norfolk, helped bring an end to the revolt. Most rebels were forced to acknowledge financial bonds for their future good behavior, something that had previously been well used by the Despensers.[98] Nonetheless, this, along with the fact that most of the 1328–29 rebels were not imprisoned, as well as the defections of Bishop Orleton, Stapleton, and Archbishop Stratford, and the exile of other members of the 1328–29 rebels including Henry Beaumont and Thomas Wake, all made the situation increasingly tense and unsettled, and increasingly unlikely that a long-term solution would be found.[99]

Finally, there was indeed the issue of the role of the young Edward himself in the growing turmoil of the minority government. Edward had, right from the beginning of his reign, been given control of the great and privy seals, both clear manifestations of royal power and a definite break with the past.[100] However though both had been profusely used, neither seal can be proved to have been used specifically at the instance of the young Edward, and indeed the privy seal, probably the more important seal as it was the one more directly indicative of the royal will at the time, was actually under the control of Henry Burghersh, bishop of Lincoln.[101] Nonetheless, the young king was not hesitant to show his feelings, especially concerning the mismanagement of the kingdom. Edward had already, in the first year of his reign, "shed tears of vexation" at the ineffectual outcome of the Stanhope Park campaign against the Scots.[102] He also appears to have been dealing with separate French magnates in 1328 to join with him against the king of France, despite Mortimer and Isabella's efforts to arrange his homage to the French king.[103] As for his role in the rebellion of 1328–29, while there is some disagreement amongst the contemporary sources as above, this could at best be said to be self-interested. Though probably not really supporting Mortimer and Isabella, the young king obviously saw that backing rebellion against the government, as had happened during his father's reign, could only hurt the country, and more importantly the monarchy. Likewise, though he was present at the sentencing of the earl of Kent a year or so later, Edward again did not seem to have been particularly in favor of this act, especially considering the fact that Kent was Edward II's half brother, and therefore of royal blood.[104]

Rather, Edward kept a deliberately low, or at least ambiguous, profile throughout most of the period—while at the same time gradually realizing that the actions of the Minority regime were perhaps beginning, especially with the execution of the earl of Kent, to endanger his own position. By the end of the decade, then, we do also start getting clearer ideas on the young king's view of the situation and the vehemence of his feelings. Perhaps the most famous and important bits of evidence we have of the desire of an independent policy comes with his famous *Pater Sancte* letter to the Pope, which it would be useful to quote in full here:

Most Holy Father, because it will behove us many times to send letters to Your Holiness, not only for Our own needs, but also for the advancement of the people of Our household and for others, and on this matter We are informed by My Lord William de Montague that You will be pleased to have from Us some private countersign [*prive entresigne*], by which You can tell which petitions we have tenderly at heart, and which not; We affectionately beseech Your Holiness that the petitions which We shall send You in future by Our letters in Latin or French, sealed under Our Privy Seal or under Our Signet, on which shall be written these words in Our hand "Pater Sancte"— that these You will please to have specially recommended and You will understand for a certainty that We have them at heart; for Our intention is not to Press You over these matters by this sign, but to use it at least where we can and as we ought to; and know, Most Holy Father, that this matter is not known to anyone except My Lord William aforesaid and to Master Richard de Bury Our secretary, of whom We are certain that they will keep it secret in every event. This document was written by the hand of the said Master Richard, for by reason of diverse occupations that We had at the time of despatch of these letters, We could not devote Ourselves to so much writing.[105]

Sent to John XXII at Avignon through the young king's closest friend and confident, William Montagu,[106] not only does it show the desire "to protect a vital area of the king's patronage and power, namely his household, from control or manipulation by the regents,"[107] it clearly exhibits the next step of throwing off the controls of the minority regime. And, if the *Anonimalle* and *Lanercost* chroniclers, among others, were right, and Mortimer *did* have designs on the throne,[108] and considering Edward's age, the young king was moving none too soon. Indeed, as he matured, Edward was said to have despised the "rule of the queen his mother, and hating the earl of March, for the queen did everything in accordance with him"[109]—and in turn, Mortimer was said to have set spies on Edward, while both Isabella and Mortimer seem to have been responsible for the delay of Philippa's coronation until February 1330, as well as of course keeping the royal household in financial straits.[110] In many ways, therefore, the events of that autumn night in 1330, when Edward III, William Montagu, and a few close associates slipped into Nottingham Castle, seized

Mortimer, and quickly sent him to the execution block, should have been of no surprise to anyone. Ever since 1328, it was pretty clear that Edward, if not getting ready to throw off the shackles of the Minority government, was becoming increasingly displeased with it.

However, whatever its initial successes or failures, and whatever the role of the young Edward III in the proceedings, perhaps the bigger question that should be asked when looking at the minority period is what can be said to be its overall impact? How much did it differ from what came before, or from what came after? In other words, though the personalities are memorable, and many of the events dramatic, does this necessarily mean that Edward III's minority itself witnessed overall any real, substantial, development or change in the exercise of power from what preceded or succeeded it? To understand this, it is probably best to view the scene in the broadest possible manner, and to break the analysis down into two main sections: the relationship between Edward II's reign and the minority period; and the minority period and Edward III's majority. First, it has to be admitted that there were some notable breaks with the recent past because of the "Revolution of 1326." As is well known, a handful of senior royal ministers, including the treasurer and chancellor, lost their jobs, along with, unsurprisingly, some castle constables and sheriffs; though of the latter only nine of twenty-four were replaced at the time of the revolution itself, including the sheriffs of Norfolk and Suffolk, Shropshire and Staffordshire, and Somerset and Dorset—all notably Despenser associates.[111] Likewise, the practice of governance more generally went through some major changes, superficially at least. Most importantly, the administrative "experiments" of the Despensers—the home staple, escheatery restructuring, and the designation of "chamber lands"—were brought to an end or modified: the home staple was abolished, the number of escheators brought back down from eight to two (north and south of Trent) and the chamber lands were suppressed.[112] Even the number of parliaments called before magnate critics came to blows with the Minority Regime in late 1328— six in total—showed an increase from immediate pre-usurpation policy, and an attempt to give at least the *appearance* of a more consensual system. Elsewhere in government, in terms of financial policy, there *was* a real shift from that of Edward II and the Despensers, who through aggressive economic tactics and a lack of military endeavors built up a large store of available funds in the treasury, to that of the Minority Regime of Mortimer and Isabella, which seemed determined to spend this inherited wealth as quickly as possible on ultimately useless campaigning as well as gifts and luxuries—[113] indeed, when Archbishop Melton regained control of the treasury after the Nottingham Coup of 1330, he found only £41 2s 11d remaining.[114] As a result, the Minority regime of Mortimer and Isabella were also to again start the substantial expansion of the use of credit which would continue into Edward III's majority and beyond, in particular in helping to fund the early phases of the Hundred Years War.[115]

That said, though there were clearly changes from Edward II's regime to the Minority period when it came to the exercise of power at both the high political and mundane administrative levels, most were not as substantial as may initially appear, and do not seem to have outweighed the continuities. First, as noted above, though the administration did change, not only was little blood spilt except at the highest levels, but the change itself was not nearly as thorough as might have been expected. The middling ranks of the royal administration— those who usually actually designed and implemented policy—were mostly retained: most famously, according to Tout, "a curiously small number of ministerial changes heralded the reign of Edward III, and a rule beginning with a revolution was conducted by almost the same officials as had administered the fallen tyranny."[116] This was true especially in the Chancery, Wardrobe, and Exchequer, the three departments that would, in many ways, decide the success or failure of a regime, or at least its ability to function efficiently. Even the above-mentioned change in two of the highest administrative posts in the land—chancellor and treasurer—was not actually that shocking: in total in the period 1300–1350, there would be twenty-four changes of chancellor (on average a change every two years or so), and thirty-five changes of treasurer.[117] More fundamentally, it must be remembered (though is often forgotten) that the much discussed administrative "system" of the Despensers had only been developed over the four years previous to Edward II's deposition: itself, then, a recent innovation, and, after their fall, royal governance returned to the system that had been developing for decades before. Likewise, at the parliamentary level, while the number of sessions was more frequent during the Minority period than those held during Edward II's tyranny, they nonetheless, again, look back to the regularity of parliaments earlier in Edward II's reign, and in Edward I's.[118] Even the treatment of the royal finances, one so important to both parliament and the kingdom as a whole, was not as surprising as it might first appear. Though Isabella and Mortimer did take a vastly different tack when it came to the finances of the kingdom, or at least the preserving of them, than their immediate predecessors, it was nonetheless to be expected from a regime that had just seized power and, through display and patron-age, needed to shore up its support—Henry I and Stephen had used similar tactics in the twelfth century, as would Henry IV and Edward IV in the fifteenth. But there were also more conscious, positive, links to past percep-tion and use of royal power, both recent and more distant. Most no-tably, the addition to the coronation oath made in 1308 was kept for 1327: whereas parliament (and in the background more than likely Mortimer and Isabella) could easily have rejected this as recent in-novation that had helped cause the troubles of the last reign, they instead preferred to accept it as previous tradition going back two de-cades and forced the young king to do the same. The new clause, namely

"Sire, do you grant to be held and observed the just laws and customs that the community of your realm shall determine, and will you, so far as in you lies, defend and strengthen them to the honour of God?" *To which was the response:* "I grant and promise them."[119]

was one that had caused a considerable amount of debate when it was first added, and was clearly still controversial almost twenty years later;[120] nonetheless, it was kept, if not always adhered to, and used thereafter throughout the later Middle Ages. Likewise, when it came to the running of the kingdom, it was accepted, as during Henry III's minority, that the nobles had to take part in one form or another, de-spite any possible consequences. Whether it be as parliamentary sup-port for actions taken, or even as key councilors of the king (as the initial minority council headed by Lancaster, or even with Mortimer acting more or less as sole councilor, along with of course Isabella), the idea was usually forefront that the nobility had to play a significant part in the governance of the realm.

And, looking at an even wider constitutional scenario, there was no real attempt by either Edward II's regime or the minority government to influence the development of parliamentary peerage, the main con-centration of landed families—and therefore nonroyal power—in the kingdom, or indeed the growing role of parliament itself—in the lat-ter case, probably because Mortimer and Isabella needed its backing for both legitimacy and support. Instead, the lists of individual parlia-mentary summons continued to stabilize, despite the ability of both regimes to influence them, and by the end of the 1320s, there was an increasingly set parliamentary peerage, a development that would have repercussions for centuries to come.[121] Ostensibly in defense of the monarchy against the designs of problematic members of such a progressively more powerful institution, though in point of fact obviously to build and sustain their own position, the Minority Regime under Mortimer and Isabella also followed the continued expansion of the definition of treason and other acts against royal authority started in the 1280s and 1290s, and including statutory laws against riding or going armed contrary to the peace of the realm.[122] And, in terms of justice toward the most powerful in the land more generally, punishment for such crimes likewise continued to evolve and harshen. For physical penalties, Isabella and Mortimer kept to the unforgiving treatment (including execution) of their worst enemies, previously used by Edward I, and even more so by Edward II—as Fitz Alan, the Despensers and the earl of Kent all found to their cost. All these continued developments were crucial considering the problems with the nobility in the earlier part of the decade, and so it is also unsurprising that connected material penalties were no less severe. When necessary, the Minority Regime retained the policy not only of heavy financial bonds for good behavior, but also of relatively merciless treatment of lands confiscated, especially the subsequent long-term regranting of properties involved to their supporters, foreshadowed in Edward I's reign though really brought to the fore in Edward II's treatment of some of the Contrariant estates.[123] Finally, using these and other resources, Isabella and Mortimer also followed both Edward I and Edward II in a narrow use of new patronage (as opposed to the reversals of the 1322 forfeitures in the first parliament of 1327), only granting to those who would directly back them or were immediately useful to them—such as the earls of Norfolk, Kent, and henchmen such as Maltravers and Beresford.[124]

Thus, there was much in terms of the exercise of power to link the two regimes—despite a royal deposition and the execution of a handful of top men—much more than should have been expected, especially considering the novelty, brutality, and the public nature of the criticisms at the end of Edward II's reign. And, if there were many continuities here, there were those also between the Minority period and that of Edward's early majority (i.e., after October 1330). To start, aside from the fall of Mortimer and a few close henchmen, again there was limited harsh reaction toward the majority of the previous administrators of various levels, and many of them again stayed in their posts. The most problematic individuals were of course removed, such as the Steward of the Royal Household (Hugh Turplington), killed during the coup itself; the Chancellor, Henry Burghersh replaced by John Stratford, and the Treasurer Robert Wodehouse was replaced by William Melton and then William Airymn, an old Edward II loyalist.[125] However, a number of other individuals, even at the higher levels, were kept on. For example, Thomas Garton, appointed Keeper of the Wardrobe in September 1329, remained in office until October 1331, when he was made a Baron of the Exchequer;[126] Peter Medbourne remained as Controller until November 1331,[127] John Houton appears to have been Cofferer until April 1331;[128] and Richard Bury, the king's old tutor, stayed as Keeper of the Privy Seal from 1329–34,[129] as did William de la Zouche as Clerk of the Great Wardrobe.[130] Others had a continuity based further back, such as John Fleet, who held office continuously as Keeper of the Privy Wardrobe from 1323 to 1344; Gilbert Talbot, whose appointment as King's Chamberlain ran from 1327 to 1334,[131] and Archbishop Melton, who had controlled the treasury on the eve of the usurpation, and was again appointed after the Nottingham Coup.[132] Moreover, though there were some political partisan appointments, the functioning of the lower reaches of the royal central and local administration was more or less unaffected, save for natural wastage and normal office turnover—castles and shrievalties did see a change of individuals, as had happened in 1327,[133] but most lesser offices appear to have gone on much as before. Indeed, as pointed out as long ago as the 1940s, the period between 1327 and 1336 had an administrative coherence, so much so that the three-volume case study, *English Government at Work*, was set during the period, and according to Morris, one of its editors, "October 1330 marked a change in political control rather than in method or machinery."[134]

But the two regimes had a more widely based coherence as well. Summons to parliament continued to stabilize during the early 1330s; and even when major additions were made, as they were throughout the rest of Edward's reign, there were still some longer term developmental continuities. Most notably, the landed endowment of new or revived titles which came to prominence with the earldoms of Carlisle (1322) and March (1328), however controversial at first, continued throughout this period, and was one of the keystones of Edward III's policy toward his nobility. Such policy, indeed, would become more or less standard for new promotions in the later Middle Ages. Moreover, while individually the "new men" of Edward's majority did much better out of royal patronage than the established nobility over his reign as a whole, a considerable number of grants (402 of 835) went to these individuals as well, including to many loyalist families of both

Edward II's and the Minority Regime—and notably ultimately to the descendents of the Despensers, Fitz Alans, and Mortimers.[135] And, when it came to parliament more generally, peers or commons, the adult Edward III, as the Minority Regime, not only made the effort to consult (if not always listen to) this institution when dealing with affairs of state, as concerning the Scottish and French situations,[136] but also made sure to get its official authorization when making major grants and other acts that impacted upon the common good.[137]

However, in terms of the adult Edward III's governmental policy, it was two other points of continuity that stand out. First, there was the continued widening of an increasingly controversial definition of treason and other "political crimes"—which, as we have seen, had been kept going through Edward III's minority regime and was a process that would only really be brought to a halt by the 1352 Treasons Statute.[138] This process was indeed part of a wider trend to attempt to bring problematic subjects to justice which would continue throughout the later Middle Ages. Similarly, when it came to the treatment of confiscated estates of such individuals, though the young Edward III might justifiably have felt nervous about such a precedent considering its past associations (especially the opposition that he might face from the landowning classes), nonetheless his government chose to follow and further develop a longer term disinheritance policy (in granting if not in duration) for an increasingly varied selection of crimes.[139] Thereafter he used the estates so forfeited (including Mortimer, Maltravers, Beresford, as well as some old Despenser lands) to establish a broader group of "new men" than the Minority's more "select" supporters—a policy not only meant to consolidate his control of the monarchy but also for the sake of fighting the Hundred Years War.[140] Secondly, there was the often noted importance of reform of law and order in the localities, revived by the minority regime and continued throughout Edward's early majority. There had been expressions of such intent at least as early as the end of 1326,[141] and, throughout the minority and early majority periods there was a genuine push for judicial reform, which Kaeuper calls a "concerted attempt" to reestablish law and order.[142] The Statute of Northampton of 1328 is probably the clearest exposition of this interest by the Minority regime, and certainly the most forceful.[143] As Cam noted as early as 1924, the policy connected with the statute "carried out, if not by the ill-famed Mortimer, at least under his auspices" was to bring back law and order to the kingdom, and had as its foundations: (1) appointment of guardians of the peace; (2) harsh laws against maintainers, highway robbers, and the like; (3) appointment of newly strengthened *Oyer and Terminer* commissions; and (4) renewal of the general eyre.[144] These, according to Verduyn, were a reaction to the political situation of the period, but notably the themes involved were also revisited before and after the Minority itself.[145] In other words, whatever the reasons for the interest in justice evidenced in the minority period—and it may well have been as much to do with regime stability as the more general regional lawlessness of the first part of the fourteenth century—the young Edward III, for the first few years at least, chose to continue to emphasize many of the minority regime's legal policies (and even, some have argued, Edward II's post 1322 policies) after his assumption of independent power in October 1330.[146]

So, if we bring the three periods of rule together, though we see some discontinuities, we also see many continuities between two and sometimes all three regimes. Indeed, though some high-level administrators changed, we see a more general stability in the personnel (as we in part already knew, if overshadowed by recent interest in the characters of Mortimer and Isabella), and more interestingly, the policy and practice, of both central and local governance—especially if we view the Despenser regime as something of an aberration in the annals of both political and administrative history. Even the fact that some trends stopped during Edward III's minority, and others began, itself gave a certain degree of coherence to the history of the period—if nothing else as but a transitional phase in which certain developments were allowed to disappear, and others start, without any particular blame being attached to the two monarchs involved. However, at base, the fact remains that though the personnel sometimes changed dramatically at the highest levels as a result of the turbulence of the 1320s and early 1330s, not only did the administration throughout this period remain intact and functioning despite the first deposition of a postconquest English king (as well as the first violent overthrow of a post conquest regency), but also, and more significantly, the more general ethos of controlling and running the realm which had been developing since at least Edward I's time. As for the impact of Mortimer and Isabella's governance, or even the minority council as initially set up by parliament, over the fourteenth century as a whole, evidence of any sort of substantive impact is even less conclusive.[147] Though a minority council was again looked to when Richard II came to the throne, it seems to have been far different in practice (aside from the fact that it had also more clearly not technically been set up as a minority) from that which was arranged in 1327. In this case (and unlike the council set up in 1327), at least until 1381, the "continuity council" had a fair degree of administrative power throughout its lifespan, despite the ever increasing importance of the royal household (as well as Gaunt and the earl of Buckingham) in the running of the realm at this time.[148] Moreover, when Richard II's officials *did* look back to the governance of the period 1327–30, few seemed to have remembered the original minority council as set up by parliament (as opposed to Mortimer and Isabella's regime) anyway, and so its impact on their thinking is very difficult to identify. Rather, over the longer term at least, as it can be said that it was the characters of Mortimer and Isabella that really dictated, and as their governance was built more on the dominance of personality than innovation in personnel or procedure, it is unsurprising that we see few changes. Indeed, Mortimer and Isabella, despite having taken control of the country, knew they were in a difficult situation, especially with Edward only a few years away from his majority, and therefore tended to take a cautious, restrained approach to power in many ways. Although they made sure that they and their friends were secure in their wealth and position, they also realized that to meddle with the governmental apparatus too much could spell disaster: therefore, they unsurprisingly tended to act conservatively when it came to the administration of the realm, and also, unless severely tested (as in the Bedford rebellion and the treason of the earl of Kent), the politics.

Rather, if we want to identify crucial factors for longer term impact when it came to the minority of Edward III's reign, we must look back again to the three major "background" factors mentioned at the beginning of this chapter. Indeed, it was these three long-term issues—Scotland, France, and the continued development of the power of the nobility—and the reaction of Isabella and Mortimer's minority regime to them that really helped define the longer-term impact of the minority period. In the Scots case, the acceptance of the "Shameful Peace" by Mortimer and Isabella would set a fire under Edward III, which would lead to continual campaigning, but also the gradual recognition that it was very hard to control the Scots, whatever the period. From the early victories at Dupplin Moor (1332), Halidon Hill (1333), and Neville's Cross (1346) and the capture of David Bruce, to the less clear-cut relationship between England and Scotland of the later Middle Ages, much of this can be traced back to both the Treaties of Edinburgh and Northampton and the precedents it set for Anglo-Scottish relations thereafter. Likewise, in terms of the French situation, again the initial backing down by Mortimer and Isabella, both in terms of payments made in 1325 and 1327, as well as the acceptance of the necessity of accepting feudal homage to the

French king in 1329, all caused Edward III no end of concern, and would influence both his reign and those beyond. Indeed, these acts in many ways weakened the English claim to both Aquitaine and the French throne, and despite many victories thereafter, the fact that an English king had acknowledged (even if under duress) the Valois and more generally French rights, would both rankle Edward III and weaken his claim. Whatever the case, English attempts to regain "honor" concerning these and connected issues would continue until the final defeat at Castillion in 1453. Finally, it was the nobility that in some ways both was most influenced by, and influenced, the historical position of Edward III's minority. Not only by clear restatements being made by the Lancastrians in 1328 of the relationship between king and nobility and the kingdom as a whole, but also allowing the hereditary parliamentary peerage to continue to develop despite the potential threat to Mortimer and Isabella's power,[149] and allowing even clearer statements of noble "issues" to be voiced (esp. the retention of the fourth clause of the coronation oath, and the continued development of idea of trial by peers as backed up by 1327 judgments), Isabella's and Mortimer's control of the minority government helped to solidify, and enhance, the power of the parliamentary peerage for the rest of the Middle Ages. The fact that not only a relatively minor one of their number, Mortimer, had influenced proceedings so drastically, but that the peerage itself was considered important enough to play a part in the deposition of a king, the setting up of the minority government, and even the downfall of Mortimer and Isabella themselves, all would have repercussions for centuries to come, including helping to lay the precedential basis for both the rise of impeachment and the development of appeal and even, if more tangentially, the rise of attainder later in the fifteenth century.[150] It was these three established yet ever developing issues that both were affected by the Minority, and affected its future reputation, for good and ill: and it was mainly a mix of the effect of these three issues which would ultimately lead to the downfall of the government in 1330. Mortimer and Isabella had an important impact, but it was an impact in reaction to far larger processes that had started long before Edward III's minority, and would continue long after its demise.

Determined campaigns of rehabilitation of individuals or regimes are, of course, usually as dangerous as they are suspect. Saying that, one does have the sneaking suspicion that, *if* we could separate our analysis of the government of Isabella and Mortimer from what came before, and what came after, though we would never give them a glowing review, we perhaps would not judge them that differently from the many of their predecessors and successors. They used excessive patronage to their friends and to buy support, but so did many others; they cut deals with the French and Scots, but so, again, did many others; they tried to restore law and order within the king, and rein in the nobility, but so did many others. Moreover, as we have seen in the comparison of the various periods of rule, there was in fact a considerable amount of continuity in two, and sometimes all three of the regimes, which in turn laid the foundation for at least some of Edward III's later successes. Rather it was larger processes that really made the difference to both the Minority and beyond—the histories of Scotland, France, and developments in the nobility itself. Indeed, what perhaps is more difficult to forgive is the fact that not only did Isabella and Mortimer push for the deposition of an, albeit incompetent, king, and that his adulterous wife was one of the main forced behind it, but, more importantly, there was no clear way out of the situation at the other end, save what actually happened. Though many historians would hate to admit it, they do like the "what ifs" of history: however, with the violent usurpation of a regime, the deposition and murder of a king, and the advanced youth of Edward III, though the "what ifs" survive, any life is bound to be ephemeral. What if the Regime had not given way to the Scots, and to the French, where would England be thereafter? Probably not in that different a situation: after all, both issues had long histories, and had as much impetus from the other sides as from the English, if not more. What if the development of the parliamentary peerage had been put more in check during the minority period, especially when it came to the stabilization of parliamentary summons and the overall confidence of the nobility? Again, going from the previous trend for the last few decades and the more general rise of parliament and stratification of society, such trends would have continued sooner or later. The machinery was set in motion by sets of circumstances arising previous to and in the main exogenous to the Minority itself, Isabella and Mortimer merely responded in a way usually most suiting to their own interests. The pair's actions were dramatic—but very rarely were they decisive in the larger scheme of things. Their charge, on the other hand, with none of the blame of the deposition, full right to the throne, and with his whole life in front of him, was another matter, and would prove himself a far more determined, and often proactive, agent in the decades to come.

NOTES

1. *The French Chronicle of London,* ed. H. T. Riley (London, 1863), 268.
2. *The Anonimalle Chronicle 1307 to 1334,* ed. W. R. Childs and J. Taylor (York, 1991), 143.
3. *Chronicon Galfridi le Baker de Swynebroke* (Oxford, 1889), 28–34; R. M. Haines, *King Edward II: Edward of Caernarfon, His Life, His Reign, and Its Aftermath, 1284–1330* (Montreal, 2003), 188.
4. W. M. Ormrod, *The Reign of Edward III* (New Haven and London, 1990), 3; Mortimer's overarching role has reached the mainstream in the new OUP history. M. Prestwich, *Plantagenet England 1225–1360* (Oxford, 2005), 220. An idea championed in the burst of popular history for the period by Ian Mortimer, *The Greatest Traitor: The Life of Sir Roger Mortimer* (London, 2003), chapter 13.
5. K. Allocco, *Intercessor, Rebel, Regent: The Political Life of Isabella of France (1292/6–1358)* (University of Texas at Austin PhD, 2004), chapter 6; S. Menache, "Isabella of France, Queen of England—a Reconsideration," *JMH* 10 (1984): 107–24. The popular champion for this side is Alison Weir, *Queen Isabella* (London, 2005), 265ff—though not quite as fervent.
6. N. Fryde, *Tyranny and Fall of Edward II* (Cambridge, 1979), 207.
7. On the role of the Despensers in the government of the realm, see M. C. Buck, "The Reform of the Exchequer, 1316–1326," *EHR* 98 (1983): 241–60; N. Saul, "The Despensers and the Downfall of Edward II," *EHR* 99 (1984): 1–33. Fryde, *Tyranny,* esp. chapters 7 and 8 sees the Despenser changes more encouraged by avarice than desire to innovate, let alone reform.
8. See below.
9. Notably, due to consanguinity to the third degree, the couple had to get dispensation from the Pope. The National Archives (afterward TNA) (SC7/24/5).
10. *Calendar of Close Roll* (afterward *CCR*) *1318–1323,* 525, 526.
11. *The Chronicle of Lanercost,* H. M. Maxwell (Glasgow, 1913), 245; H. Summerson, "Harclay, Andrew, Earl of Carlisle (*c.* 1270–1323)," *Oxford Dictionary of National Biography* (afterward *DNB*) (Oxford, 2004).
12. I. M. Davis, "The Weardale Campaign, 1327," *History Today* 21 (1971): 856.
13. For the treaty, see T. Rymer, *Foedera* (London, 1816–69), ii, 740–42.
14. For Edward III's relations with the Scots in the first years of this reign, see R. Nicholson, *Edward III and the Scots: The Formative Years of a Military Career 1327–1335* (Oxford, 1965); for chronicle excerpts connected with the campaigning, see C. Rogers, ed., *The Wars of Edward III: Sources and Interpretations* (Woodbridge, 1999), 4–41.
15. Most recently on Anglo-French relations in the later thirteenth and early fourteenth centuries, see M.G.A. Vale, "The Anglo-French Wars, 1294–1340: Allies and Alliances," in *Guerre et Société en France, en*

Angleterre et en Bourgogne, XIVe-XVe Siècle, ed. P. Contamine, C. Giry-Deloison, and M. H. Keen (Lille, 1991), 15–35.

16. *The War of Saint-Sardos (1323–1325),* ed. P. Chaplais (London, 1954), 241–45.

17. M. McKisack, *The Fourteenth Century* (Oxford, 1959), 111; also see C47/30/1/2-3.

18. Prestwich, *Plantagenet England,* 221.

19. Haines, *Edward II,* 330–31.

20. Thomas Gray, *Scalacronica,* ed. and trans. A. King (Woodbridge, 2005), 101.

21. See K. B. McFarlane, *The Nobility of Later Medieval England* (Oxford, 1973), updated by C. Given-Wilson, *The English Nobility in the Late Middle Ages* (London, 1987); also see D. Crouch, *The Image of Aristocracy 1000–1300* (London, 1992).

22. J. E. Powell and K. Wallis, *The House of Lords in the Middle Ages* (London, 1968), 303–15.

23. N. Pronay and J. Taylor, eds., *Parliamentary Texts of the Later Middle Ages* (Oxford, 1980), 13ff; C. J. Nederman, ed. and trans. *Political Thought in Early Fourteenth Century England: Treatises by Walter of Milemete, William of Pagula, and William of Ockham* (Temple, Arizona, 2002), 32–34.

24. For the most recent detailed discussion of the events of Edward II's fall, see C. Valente, "The Deposition and Abdication of Edward II," *EHR* 113 (1998): 852–81.

25. Magna Carta, clause 39; Pronay and Taylor, eds., *Parliamentary Texts,* 87–88.

26. For calls for trial by peers during the Minority, see SC8/196/9788 (with aid of PROCAT); SC8/50/2500; more generally on the issue of trial by peers, see L. W. Vernon Harcourt, *His Grace the Steward and Trial of Peers* (London, 1907).

27. Ormrod, *Edward III,* 3.

28. *Rotuli Parliamentorum* (afterward *RP*), ii, 10.

29. E.g., the *Brut* says four barons were to be called, while Knighton says six. R. M. Haines, "The Episcopate during the Reign of Edward II and the Regency of Mortimer and Isabella," *Journal of Ecclesiastical History* 56 (2005): 692 n. 163; also Haines, *Edward II,* 195–96.

30. From the "Chronicle of England" cited in J. F. Baldwin, "The King's Council," in *The English Government at Work, 1327–1336,* ed. J. F. Willard and W. A. Morris (Cambridge, 1940), 1:132.

31. Haines, *Edward II,* 195.

32. T. F. Tout, *Chapters in the Administrative History of Medieval England* (6 vols.) (Manchester, 1928), iii, 10–11.

33. *Calendar of Charter Rolls* (afterward *CCharR*), 1327–1341, 2–5.

34. Tout, *Chapters,* iii, 10–11.

35. *RP* ii, 7; on Lancaster's Cult, see J. Edwards, "The Cult of 'St' Thomas of Lancaster and its Iconography," *Yorkshire Archaeological Journal* 64

(1992): 103–22; J. Edwards "The Cult of 'St' Thomas of Lancaster and its Iconography: A Supplementary Note," *Yorkshire Archaeological Journal* 67 (1995): 187–91.

36. Baldwin, "King's Council," in *English Government*, ed. Willard and Morris, 1:133.

37. *Calendar of Memoranda Rolls* (afterward CMemR), 1326–*1327*, 124, 230–31.

38. C. Given-Wilson, "Royal Charter Witness Lists 1327–1399," *Medieval Prosopography* 12 (1991): 61–62.

39. Tout, *Chapters*, iii, 10–11; vi, 42. Ros is also noted by Tout as "Steward of the Household of Queen Isabella" in roughly the same period (Tout, *Chapters*, iii, 18n).

40. SC8/120/5982; *French Chronicle*, 268.

41. *Calendar of Plea and Memoranda Rolls of the City of London 1323–1364*, trans. and ed. A. H. Thomas (Cambridge, 1926), 11–12.

42. *RP* ii, 7, 11.

43. M. Prestwich, *The Three Edwards: War and State in England, 1272–1377* (London, 1980), 111.

44. For Bury's time as keeper of the king's wardrobe in the late 1320s, see E361/2/30, 31; E361/9/25; E101/383/12, 17; E101/384/8,12; Bury as a filter through which the king heard petitions, see SC8/114/5658; SC8/157/7824. For Bury's seemingly close relationship with the Minority Regime, see W. M. Ormrod, "The King's Secrets: Richard de Bury and the Monarchy of Edward III," in *War, Government, and Aristocracy in the British Isles, c. 1150–1500*, C. Given-Wilson, A. Kettle, and L. Scales, ed. (Woodbridge, forthcoming 2008).

45. *CCharR 1327–1341*, 198.

46. Other important grants in this period include the manor of Milham (E40/5570), later granted to Eltham's retainer, Thomas de Weston, for life. SC8/156/7788 (with aid of PROCAT); also see *CCharR 1327–1341*, 53; for Eltham see S. L. Waugh, "John, Earl of Cornwall (1316–1336)," *DNB* (Oxford, 2004).

47. Given-Wilson, "Royal Charter Witness Lists," 61.

48. *French Chronicle*, 269; also see *Anonimalle Chronicle*, 141.

49. H. M. Maxwell, *The Chronicle of Lanercost* (Glasgow, 1913), 260.

50. *Lanercost Chronicle*, 265.

51. SC1/41/48; the actual document says 10000 marks, but, as Crawford notes, this is most probably a scribal error, A. Crawford, ed., *Letters of the Queens of England 1100–1547* (Stroud, 1994), 89–90.

52. *Calendar of Patent Rolls* (afterward CPR), 1327–*1330*, 66–9; G. L. Harriss, *King Parliament and Public Finance in Medieval England to 1369* (Oxford, 1975), 149; also confirmed in her control of the county of Cornwall, originally granted her by Edward II. E40/222.

53. *CCR 1327–1330*, 267; B. P. Wolffe, *The Royal Demesne in English History: The Crown Estate in the Governance of the Realm from the Conquest to 1509* (Athens, Ohio, 1971), 55.

54. F. W. D. Brie, ed., *The Brut or the Chronicles of England* (Oxford, 1906), i:257, also 254–55. For a list of Isabella's acquisitions, see Wolffe, *Royal Demesne,* 232–35.
55. For Isabella's material wealth, see H. Johnstone, "Isabella, The She-Wolf of France," *History* n.s. 21 (1936–7): 214–18.
56. Brie, *Brut,* 1:248.
57. *CCharR 1327–1341,* 55. However, as Holmes points out, in total these lands must have been worth nearly twice this. G. A. Holmes, *The Estates of the Higher Nobility in Fourteenth-Century England* (Cambridge, 1957), 13.
58. *CP* viii, 438–39.
59. Haines, *Edward II,* 200.
60. See J. S. Bothwell, *Falling From Grace: Reversal of Fortune and the English Nobility* (Forthcoming, Manchester, 2008), chapter 3.
61. Powell and Wallis, *House of Lords,* 301–2; there is no definite date for this creation, but the *Complete Peerage* narrows it down to the period between October 25 and October 31, 1328. *CP* viii, 439 note h.
62. For a list of lands of the Earl of March at the time of his forfeiture, see E142 Exchequer: Ancient Extents.
63. And one of the first after Harcla's earldom of Carlisle to be deliberately endowed with lands. For Harcla, see Powell and Wallis, *House of Lords,* 296.
64. J. R. Lumby, ed., *Chronicon Henrici Knighton* (London, 1889), i, 449; Fryde, *Tyranny,* 207.
65. Prestwich, *Three Edwards,* 112; also see *Brut,* 1:261–62.
66. For the rebellion, see G. A. Holmes, "The Rebellion of the Earl of Lancaster, 1328–1329," *BIHR* 28 (1955): 84–89.
67. Gray, *Scalacronica,* 93.
68. Mortimer, *Greatest Traitor,* 229–31; *CP* viii, 440.
69. S. L. Waugh, "Edmund, First Earl of Kent (1301–1330)," *DNB* (Oxford, 2004).
70. Holmes, *Estates,* 13–14.
71. *CCharR 1327–1341,* 3–4; for grants to Kent, see E42/487; *CCharR 1327–1341,* 2–5.
72. E.g., grants to Maltravers *CPR 1327–1330,* 59, 101, 346, 517; *CFR 1327–1337,* 53, 65, 73, 96, 107, 113, 128, 144, 149; grants to Ingham, *CPR 1327–1330,* 364, 512; *CFR 1327–1337,* 174, 190.
73. Including the Londoners who had previously been favored by the Minority Regime, but by now were clearly on Lancaster's side. See above and Prestwich, *Plantagenet England,* 222.
74. See E. A. Bond, ed., *Chronica Monastario de Melsa* 3 vols. (London, 1866–88), ii, 358–61.
75. Frdye, *Tyranny,* 208–9, 270.
76. R. W. Kaeuper, *War, Justice, and Public Order: England and France in the Later Middle Ages* (Oxford, 1988), 50–51; for evidence of loans and repayment arrangements, see E43/694(i); E43/144; E43/701(ii); and E101/127/26.

77. Kaeuper, *War, Justice, and Public Order,* 50. For details of some of the expenses of John of Hainault in this period, also see E101/17/14 and E101/18/4.

78. A. Tuck, *Crown and Nobility: England 1272–1461* (Oxford, 1998), 80.

79. Ormrod, *Edward III,* 5.

80. Crawford, ed., *Letters of the Queens,* 90–91.

81. Fryde, *Tyranny,* 217. And, for whatever reason, in early July 1327, the Earl Marshal hesitated to come to the king when bidden, supposedly because the Scots were at nearby Appleby (see *Calendar of Documents Relating to Scotland,* iii, 920); in the same year, there was also a case of problems between the Earl Marshal and the king's officers at Bordeaux, which might again indicate tensions. See SC8/281/14000.

82. Given-Wilson, "Royal Charter Witness Lists," 62.

83. P. Heath, *Church and Realm 1272–1461* (London, 1988), 103; for more details on the Church's somewhat divided stance in this period, see Haines, "Episcopate," 688 ff.

84. Baker, *Chronicle,* Thompson ed., 27; N. Fryde, "John Stratford, Bishop of Winchester and the Crown, 1323–1330," *BIHR* 44 (1971): 158. According to Fryde (p. 159), the minority government later extracted bonds from Stratford for good behavior.

85. Tuck, *Crown and Nobility,* 81.

86. Fryde, *Tyranny,* 217.

87. *Plea and Memoranda Rolls 1323–1364,* 68–69; R. M. Haines, "An Innocent Abroad: The Career of Simon Mepham, Archbishop of Canterbury, 1328–33," *EHR* 112 (1997): 562; many inhabitants of London had taken, or were to take, part in this rebellion. E163/4/27-8.

88. Haines, "Episcopate," 694; Mepham had only been consecrated as Archbishop of Canterbury a few months before. SC7/56/19; *Calendar of Papal Letters* ii, 272.

89. W. Stubbs, ed., *Annales Paulini* (London, 1882), i, 343.

90. See Fryde, *Tyranny,* 219ff for a discussion of the various versions. For a detailed overview of the events of the rising, see Haines, *Edward II,* 201–10.

91. *Anonimalle Chronicle,* 141–43.

92. *Plea and Memoranda Rolls 1323–1364,* 77.

93. R. Somerville, *History of the Duchy of Lancaster 1265–1603* (London, 1953), 1:34–35; P. Vinogradoff and F. Morgan, eds. *Survey of the Honour of Denbigh 1334* (München, 1981), x–xiii.

94. See above.

95. Fryde, *Tyranny,* 218, more generally 217–19; Lancaster also was having a hard time getting back, mainly through petition to the royal government, the manor of Chelveston from the Earl of Kent, which had been given by Thomas of Lancaster to Holand in the previous reign. SC8/342/16127 (with aid of PROCAT).

96. *Plea and Memoranda Rolls 1323–1364,* 77–83.

97. *Plea and Memoranda Rolls 1323–1364,* 81–82.

98. *CPR 1330–1334*, 35; *CCR 1327–1330*, 528–32; Prestwich, *Plantagenet England*, 222.

99. *Lanercost Chronicle*, 265–67.

100. F. W. Wiswall, "Politics, Procedure and the 'Non-Minority' of Edward III: Some Comparisons," in *The Age of Richard II*, ed. J. L. Gillespie (Stroud, 1997), 10–11.

101. And, though petitions were addressed to the King, among others, from the beginning of his reign, it was fairly clear that the decision-making lay elsewhere. See SC8 passim; also see W. M. Ormrod, "Coming to Kingship: Boy Kings and the Passage to Power in Fourteenth-Century England," in *Rites of Passage: Cultures of Transition in the Fourteenth Century*, ed. N. F. McDonald and W. M. Ormrod (York, 2004), 41.

102. *Lanercost Chronicle*, 258.

103. C47/28/1/19.

104. For Kent's trial, see *Brut*, 1:263–67; for Edward's lack of enthusiasm toward harsh treatment of Kent more generally, see Mortimer, *Greatest Traitor*, 298; churchmen also seem to have been involved with Kent: after the Coup of 1330, there were pardons and restitutions to the Archbishop of York, the Bishop of London, the Abbot of Langedon, and William de la Zouche, for their parts in the earl's activities. See SC8/173/8613; *RP*, ii 32b.

105. PRO 22/3. Translation from W. A. Paintin, *The English Church in the Fourteenth Century* (Toronto, 1980), 77–78. This letter probably also had the more immediate goal of furthering Bury's career. Ormrod, "King's Secrets," forthcoming.

106. Tout, *Chapters*, iii, 27; C. G. Crump, "The Arrest of Roger Mortimer and Queen Isabel," *EHR* 26 (1911): 331.

107. Heath, *Church and Realm*, 104.

108. *Lanercost Chronicle*, 266; According to the *Anonimalle* "the said sir Geoffrey (Mortimer) through madness even called himself king." *Anonimalle Chronicle*, 145.

109. Gray, *Scalacronica*, 105.

110. Ormrod, *Edward III*, 6.

111. Saul suspects the others were of similar backgrounds. Saul, "Downfall of Edward II," 21–22.

112. Tout, *Chapters*, iii, 11–12.

113. See above.

114. Fryde, *Tyranny*, 224.

115. For borrowing in this period, see Fryde, *Tyranny*, 214–15; E. B. Fryde, "Loans to the English Crown 1328–31," *EHR* 70 (1955): 198–211.

116. Tout, *Chapters*, iii, 5.

117. E. B. Fryde et al., eds., *Handbook of British Chronology*, 3rd edn. (Cambridge, 1996), 85–86, 104–5. Even some of Edward II's personal royal servants were kept on and patronized—such as Richard Potesgrave, the royal chaplain—while a number of Despenser loyalists were also pardoned. Fryde, *Tyranny*, 208–9.

118. *RP* passim.
119. *Statutes of the Realm* (afterward SR), 1:168.
120. R. S. Hoyt, "The Coronation Oath of 1308," *EHR* 71 (1956): 353–83.
121. Powell and Wallis, *House of Lords,* esp. 303–15.
122. SR 1:258.
123. Bothwell, *Falling from Grace,* chapter 3.
124. See above.
125. *Handbook of British Chronology,* 76, 86, 105.
126. *Handbook of British Chronology,* 80.
127. Tout, *Chapters,* vi, 29.
128. Tout, *Chapters,* vi, 31.
129. *Handbook of British Chronology,* 94.
130. Tout, *Chapters,* vi, 35.
131. Tout, *Chapters,* vi, 46.
132. Though at a more practical level, as has been recently noted, there were some important changes in royal mint personnel in both 1327 and 1330. F. Wiswall, "Royal Mints and Royal Minors in England, 1216–1389," *E-Sylum* 9:1 (2006).
133. Tout, *Chapters,* iii, 35–6. Many sheriffs seemed to have been deliberately changed in early December 1330 *(RP* ii, 60); but it should be noted, both by regulation and practice, the turnover of sheriffs and other officials was quite rapid in this period anyway, even without political events intervening. Indeed, looking back, change of regime and change of sheriff seem to be clearly connected, no matter how long they had previously held office: most sheriffs seem to have been changed both soon after Edward I returned from the Holy Land in 1274, and between the death of Edward I and the coronation of Edward II. See *Lists and Indexes IX: List of Sheriffs for England and Wales* (New York, 1963).
134. Willard and Morris, eds., *English Government,* 1:v.
135. J. S. Bothwell, *Edward III and the English Peerage* (Woodbridge, 2004), 145–53 & Appendices 3–6.
136. *RP* Edward III, passim.
137. The most famous example being the six earldom creations later in the 1330s. J. S. Bothwell, "Edward III, the English Peerage, and the 1337 Earls: Estate Redistribution in the Later Middle Ages," in *The Age of Edward III,* ed. J. S. Bothwell (York, 2001), 35–52; also see H. G. Richardson and G. O. Sayles, *The English Parliament in the Middle Ages* (London, 1981), XXI 2.
138. See J. G. Bellamy, *The Law of Treason in England in the Later Middle Ages* (Cambridge, 1970), chapter 4.
139. Bothwell, *Falling from Grace,* Forthcoming, chapter 3.
140. A. Ayton, "Edward III and the English Aristocracy at the Beginning of the Hundred Years War," in *Armies, Chivalry and Warfare in Medieval Britain and France,* ed. M. Strickland (Stamford, 1998), 173–206; Bothwell, "Edward III, the English Peerage, and the 1337 Earls," 35–52.

141. E.g., *Plea and Memoranda Rolls 1323–1364*, 15 and ff.
142. Kaeuper, *War, Justice, and Public Order*, 127; see also Haines, *Edward II*, 217.
143. *SR* 1:257–61.
144. H. Cam, "The General Eyres of 1329–30," *EHR* 39 (1924): 243ff. Though after 1331, the eyre "was of symbolic rather than real significance, and was used simply—and cynically—to the crown's advantage." A. Musson and W. M. Ormrod, *The Evolution of English Justice: Law, Politics and Society in the Fourteenth Century* (Basingstoke, 1998), 45.
145. A. Verduyn, "The Politics of Law and Order during the Early Years of Edward III," *EHR* 108 (1993): 842–67; A. Verduyn, "The Commons and Early Justices of the Peace under Edward III," in *Regionalism and Revision: The Crown and Its Provinces in England 1200–1650*, ed. P. Fleming, A. Gross, and J. R. Lander (London and Rio Grande, 1998), 87–106; also see *SR* 1:261–65.
146. Musson and Ormrod, *Evolution of English Justice*, 105–6. There was also a fair degree of continuity in higher level legal personnel (and also Barons of the Exchequer and Master of the Rolls) between two, and sometimes all three periods. See J. Sainty, *The Judges of England 1272–1990* (London, 1993), 6–7, 23, 45, 62, 91, 110–11; J. Sainty, *A List of English Law Officers* (London, 1987), 5; PRO 22/30.
147. Indeed, as Ormrod notes for the period as a whole, "there was no formal prescription in medieval England either as to what arrangements ought to be made for the governance of the realm when the king was obviously too young to rule or, indeed, as to when such a king might be thought to be ready to assume the reins of power." Ormrod, "Coming to Kingship," 32.
148. A. Tuck, "Richard II, 1367–1400," *DNB* (Oxford, 2004).
149. According to Powell and Wallis, "the list for the parliament of January 1327 was used, with relatively minor changes, for every parliament summoned in the next five years." Powell and Wallis, *House of Lords*, 312.
150. Of course, also all connected with Mortimer and Isabella's continued acceptance of both harsher bodily and property penalties for treason and similar crimes. See above.

CHAPTER 3

RICHARD II AND THE FICTION OF MAJORITY RULE[1]

Gwilym Dodd

INTRODUCTION: THE PROBLEM OF THE KING'S YOUTH

For Thomas Walsingham, one of the first occasions when Richard II revealed the true nature of his rule came in the Summer of 1383 when, accompanied by his new queen, he went on a "shrine-crawl" of the eastern counties, imposing himself and his household on the hospitality of the region's abbeys, apparently showing little consideration for the expense and inconvenience that his visits caused. It was not simply that the king had received "an abundance of gifts from both religious and seculars," but that these gifts had been "bestowed in great abundance upon the foreign countrymen of the queen, her Bohemians."[2] Moreover, when he had stayed at the abbey of Bury (St Edmunds) Richard had peremptorily confirmed Abbot John Timworth in office even though the latter had not yet received papal confirmation.[3] "After such action," Walsingham commented, "the king's unreliability, and that of his council, became known far and wide." All in all, if Walsingham's account represented broader opinion, Richard's progress through the shires had been a public relations disaster. It had exposed some deep-seated flaws in the exercise of his kingship—the unnecessary extravagance of his household, the misappropriation of money and the injudicious exercise of the royal prerogative. Over the next few years these faults would form the kernel of criticism leveled against the king until, in 1386, royal authority was overthrown completely and the king himself was forced into a quasi form of political exile. Perhaps the most telling aspect of this account lies in the explanation Walsingham offers for Richard's apparent excessiveness. It was in light of the king's visit to the shrines of Norfolk and Suffolk that the chronicler uttered those words, now so inextricably associated with minority rule, that a kingdom could expect nothing but misfortune if its king was a minor: "Woe to thee, O land, when thy king is a child."[4] The real sting in the tail lay in the fact that by 1383 Richard II was seventeen and a half years old and was, by any measure—contemporary or modern—of sufficient years to be considered an adult. The reference was therefore less an objective statement of fact than a subjective observation on the young king's disposition and abilities: the king, in spite of his age, was not yet mature enough to govern with the wisdom and good judgment expected of an adult.

That Richard "hadn't grown up" formed a common thread in the discourse employed by the opposition to his rule—and for good reason, for it provided a formidable rhetorical strategy to justify interference in decisions and actions that a fully fledged adult king would have expected, and would in normal circumstances have been allowed, to take unhindered.[5] The king's immaturity is the clear implication behind the threat issued by the Appellants in the Tower of London in 1387, that if Richard did not "correct his mistakes and henceforward submit himself to the control of the lords . . . he must understand that his heir was unquestionably of full age."[6] Some weeks later, in articles of accusation leveled against Richard II's courtiers and advisors in the Merciless Parliament of 1388, charges were laid before the assembly on the grounds that, "seeing the tenderness of the age of our lord the king and the innocence of his royal person, [the king's allies had] caused him to apprehend as truth so many false things . . . against loyalty and good faith."[7] In this instance, the Appellants were casting themselves in the mould of protectors of the royal dignity and were asserting their political agenda in terms of a legitimate programme of reform to allow for the apparent deficiencies in Richard's rule caused by his youth. It is significant that even as a twenty-one year old the king's inability to discern good counsel from bad was ascribed above all in terms of his age. The king's lack of maturity also constituted a cornerstone of the Lancastrian spin placed on Richard's downfall in 1399. In the critical moments following Henry Bolingbroke's enthronement in the parliament of that year, Archbishop Arundel delivered a sermon to the assembled Lords and Commons in which he justified the transfer of power on the premise that "in the place of a boy willfully running riot, a man will now rule over the people."[8] The significance of the fact that Richard and Henry were both the same age, that is to say 32 years old, has not been lost on historians,[9] and most certainly it would have been understood by contemporaries: this was what gave the sermon so much force. For Adam Usk, writing with the benefit of hindsight and also with an intimate knowledge of how the Lancastrian regime conceived the reign of Richard II, it was the latter's youthful tendencies which above all explained his downfall: "during the time of this Richard's youth, both because of it and because of what resulted from it, numerous misfortunes continued to plague the English kingdom . . . leading to great confusion in this realm, and, in the end, to the destruction of King Richard himself and of those who clung to him too fondly."[10] The underlying subtext was that youth was fundamentally incompatible with successful government. It was an attitude predicated on an assumption that effective rule was dependent on the ability of a king to exercise his will independently so as to be able to balance political factions, to exercise sound judgment, and to rule without pandering to the influence of others.[11] The assumption was that children were inherently incapable of possessing these qualities.

If the subject of the king's youth could be used to justify the course of history in accordance with a political programme espoused by Richard's opponents, it is important to note how the king himself came to use his age as a way of accounting for the problems he had faced in the course of his reign. Both Richard and his opponents considered the king's "tender years" to have been a weakness, but whereas his critics projected this as a cause of misgovernance and unsound policy, Richard considered it to have presented opportunities to his unscrupulous opponents to promote their own self-interested ambitions. In a letter written in the winter months of 1397–98 to the count of Holland, in which he rejoiced in his recent coup against the former Appellants, Richard mused that "posterity may learn what it is to offend the royal majesty, established at howsoever tender years; for he is a child of death who offends the king."[12] This reference to the circumstances of his accession, some twenty years after the event, is significant, for it suggests that for Richard his youth was an important factor in shaping his perception of the course of events since 1377, only for him this perception was formulated in terms of victimhood and oppression.

The Wilton Diptych provides a further clue in this regard, for its unmistakable depiction of Richard as a boy is surely intended to represent his coronation in 1377 in which his kingdom was "handed over" by the Christ child, Mary, and the heavenly body of angels.[13] In the mid-late1390s, when the Diptych is most likely to have been painted, such a scene would have reinforced the sense not only that Richard's authority lay beyond the encroachment of earthly forces, but also how the king had a divinely appointed mission to restore to himself the untrammeled power and authority that had been invested in his office at the point at which he had been made king in 1377. The Wilton Diptych was thus a visual depiction of Richard's kingship in its pure and unblemished state—a position that neatly mirrored the king's own circumstances at the point of accession when he was "so innocent and tender in age."[14] If the Diptych was painted toward the end of the decade, between 1397 and 1399, after Richard had crushed the former Appellants and had taken steps to build a new nobility whose loyalty to the crown was unquestioned, this would make the youthful depiction of the king in the altarpiece an even more powerful message about the king's entitlement to restore the prerogative powers that he had once enjoyed, but that had subsequently been taken away from him. Just as importantly, the boy-like appearance of Richard would have reinforced a sense in which the period of his later adolescence and early adulthood, when he had suffered these indignities, ought to be entirely erased from political memory. The Diptych thus had something important to say about the first twenty years of Richard's reign, but it also looked forward as a symbol of a new beginning in the reign, as a reminder of the unimpeachable authority Richard could now assert over his subjects by virtue of the heavenly mandate given to him at his coronation.

Richard's youth thus informed and in many ways determined the shape of the political controversies of the late fourteenth century. That the king had come to power as a boy was not simply a fact, but a matter of serious and prolonged debate as it came to be seen as a means of legitimizing, or discrediting, political action. For Richard's opponents, the root cause of the political tensions of these years was the king's failure to develop the critical facilities necessary for a fully functioning adult king; for Richard, it was that his youth had presented opportunities to his adversaries to make good their selfish political ends and in so doing to encroach on his royal prerogative. In essence, one side posited that Richard II had never grown up; the other, that Richard had never been *allowed* to grow up.

Richard II's reign is almost unique in the attention that was given by contemporaries to the king's age and in particular to the consequences of his youth on politics. It was a debate, which perhaps more than any other reign in which a king ascended the throne as a minor, was to have a lasting effect on his rule and on his subsequent reputation. The circumstances of Richard's succession to the crown as a ten-year-old boy, and the ensuing problems he experienced attracting broad political support, has certainly had a profound impact on the nature and shape of historical writing, as modern historians have come to depict the king as a willful teenager trying to come to terms with an unhappy and troubled upbringing.[15] These ambitious, if ultimately futile, attempts to psycho-analyze Richard's personality provide an interesting parallel with contemporary views that held Richard's youth to be the source of all his—and his kingdom's—problems.[16] The overbearing concentration on Richard's age and his apparently youthful tendencies are to be explained by the fact that there was only a short period of his reign in which he was seemingly at liberty to exercise authority in his own right without the constraints and limitations imposed on him by parliament or his magnates. Whether Richard was a capable ruler or not, the fact that it was not until the 1390s that he was finally in a position to assert his authority has no doubt reinforced the *impression* that for much of his reign he was deficient in a number of key areas. Had Richard ruled beyond 1399 the circumstances of his accession and the troubles of the 1380s might well have receded into memory, but the usurpation ensured that his youth, and the problems which were thought to have stemmed from it, remained at the top of the political agenda. In essence, Richard never really had the time or opportunity to shake off the stigma that he was immature and therefore unsuited to exercising authority without the "help" of advisors.

But all this stemmed from an even more fundamental problem attached to the circumstances of his rule. When he came to power in 1377, a decision was taken to maintain the fiction that Richard ruled as though he were an adult. This meant, in essence, that really important decisions were taken by other people, but were recorded in his name. The paradox of the situation was emphasized by the appointment of the councilors who were charged with the responsibility of day-to-day government soon after Richard became king. The day after his coronation Richard witnessed the swearing in of these advisors. On paper (or parchment) at least, this was the king's council, sworn in at his behest and answerable to the king for its actions, but in reality it was the king who was "ruled" by the council and it was he who required guidance and direction. The arrangements put into place in this year asserted the indivisibility of the king and crown and the basic principle that the crown must be perpetually adult. There were good reasons for these arrangements (as discussed below), but they created a set of circumstances that made it hard for the political community to accept when Richard really was ready to take over the reins of government, and even harder for Richard to assert this himself. Because there was no "official" minority there could be no "official" end to the supervision which the political community felt was rightfully theirs to give to Richard during his "tender years." The debate about when to end this supervision therefore hinged not on a formal and prearranged date which accorded to a particular age of the king, but rather on his kingly qualities or "capabilities," which became a matter of judgment and interpretation. It was undoubtedly the ambiguity surrounding Richard's status that above all created the conditions for political conflict and turmoil in the 1380s.[17] Even Richard himself seems tacitly to have acknowledged the ambiguity surrounding his abilities in the first twelve years of his reign when, in May 1389, he announced to his council that "his attainment of fully completed age put him in the position of an heir claiming his inheritance on reaching his twenty-first year."[18] It is interesting to speculate, though impossible to prove, that in finally articulating his right to exercise unimpeded political authority, Richard had been influenced by events across the channel, where six months previously the young Charles VI had staged a similar coup against his own overbearing uncles, asserting his right as a king of almost twenty years old to take control of affairs himself.[19] In the direct speech attributed to Richard II, he purportedly announced that, "I think it is fitting that I should . . . assume the conduct of affairs, since I have reached the age of maturity." If this accurately records what was said,[20] it is striking that Richard himself should have couched his reassertion of authority not in the straightforward language of offended royal dignity but in terms of reaching an age at which he might now rightfully assert his prerogative. The clear implication was that Richard himself acknowledged that he had not been sufficiently "mature" to conduct the affairs of state before his twenty-first birthday.

So a discussion on the minority of Richard II is in one sense an historical anomaly since one of the underlying problems of Richard's reign was that there was no minority as such. The word "minority" was never used in official documentation. It is significant in this respect that the councils set up in the first years of Richard's reign to supervise his government were not called minority but "continual" councils, though this fact has not stopped historians from using the term to describe the period when they were in operation.[21] The word "minority" assumes a set of formal circumstances which were not in existence in these years and which most contemporaries would have struggled to recognize or accept. It also suggests a "neatness" to the arrangements put into place to meet the challenge of Richard's youth when it was precisely the lack of definition and the absence of overall direction which characterized the young king's gradual assimilation of political power. It is, then, these very early years of Richard's reign that require careful re-examination, for these were the years in which the underlying tone of politics for at least the first half of Richard's reign, up until 1389, were to be defined. The period was once famously dismissed by Anthony Steel as "dreary in the extreme."[22] On the contrary, these years hold a particular fascination for the way in which the political community chose to respond to the particular challenges presented by the rule of a boy-king. The early years of Richard II's reign have been considered more favorably in more recent work, not least in the excellent narratives by Tuck and Saul, but whereas the emphasis of this work has tended to focus more generally on the basic question "how successful was the minority government of Richard II?" there are a number of subsidiary issues that would repay more detailed scrutiny. Where exactly did power and authority reside in the early years of Richard's reign? To what extent, if at all, did Richard partake in government from the very beginning of his rule? If limitations were placed on Richard's authority, were they imposed on him or did they reflect genuine deficiencies in the king's ability to discharge his kingly duties or indeed, like Henry VI,[23] a reluctance by the king to take on the full gamut of responsibilities that went with his office? Exactly what role did that key political personality of the period, John of Gaunt, play in these years? These questions provide the bedrock for the following discussion, but they also draw us into deeper concerns about the nature of late medieval kingship and its capacity to cope with minority rule. Above all, they invite a more general consideration as to whether we characterize the period in terms of "crisis management" or whether we should credit the system of monarchical government with the capacity to cope quite satisfactorily with the advent of a boy king.

"MINORITY" GOVERNMENT: 1377–1380
The Continual Councils

In retrospect it would be easy to say that what should have happened in 1377 was for John of Gaunt, in his position as the most senior royal prince and Steward of England, to have headed a regency or protectorate government that would not only have provided clear political leadership, but also a critical line of demarcation separating the period of Richard's royal "apprenticeship," when he was learning the ropes of what being king entailed, and the start of his rule proper when a formal and public declaration of his majority rule might have closed down the potential for political dissent on the grounds that the king still needed supervision.[24] But in the absence of any formal prescription as to what should happen in the event of a boy king acceding to the throne, the arrangements put into place in 1377 were determined above all by the politics of the moment and in this sense the appointment of continual councils between 1377 and 1380 made every sense. As is widely acknowledged, a general mistrust of Gaunt's motives made a regency government an impractical and potentially dangerous proposition. Gaunt was a highly controversial figure: he was widely associated with the discredited regime that had been attacked in the Good Parliament of 1376, and his heavy-handed and vindictive treatment of the Londoners in the Autumn of that year, and the first months of 1377, hardly instilled confidence in his ability to exercise authority in an even-handed and judicious manner.[25] His apparent championing of the religious dissenter John Wyclif in the summer of 1377 had also generated a strong residue of ill-feeling toward him from within the Church.[26] What the kingdom needed above all in 1377 was the restoration of a semblance of political equilibrium and the most practical means of achieving this was to institute some form of representative government in which all possible political interests were served—that is to say a government, so to speak, of "national unity." The expedient of collective government had already been attempted in the Good Parliament when a continual council had been installed at the request of the Commons.[27] Although short-lived, it provided an obvious model to tackle and to some extent neutralize the challenges faced by a fractured and unsettled political community at the outset of Richard II's rule.[28]

For understandable reasons, the continual councils have attracted considerable interest in scholarship and have consequently come to be regarded, in a sense, as the defining characteristic of royal government in Richard's early years. Particular attention has been given by historians to the political profile of the members of the council in order to demonstrate the lengths to which the political community went to ensure that they were inclusive and truly representative.[29] We certainly cannot ignore the divisions and tensions that existed within the political community, and the concomitant need to produce a politically balanced body of men, but to regard the continual councils only in these terms risks oversimplifying the political dynamics of the day by reducing the factors that governed the interaction of the council's members—and their patrons—to the rather inflexible straightjacket of faction and partisanship. There is a danger in assuming that the council members were wholly preoccupied with what had happened in the past, during the turbulent last years of Edward III's reign, when in fact it was the problems and challenges presented by the succession of a boy king at a very difficult juncture in the war against France which must have featured uppermost in their minds. Similarly, when scrutinizing the membership of these councils, we should countenance the possibility that the experience and competence of the individuals chosen, and their willingness to undertake an intensive period of service on behalf of the crown, were factors that were just as important in influencing decisions on appointment as whether they were "Gaunt's man," a former adherent of the Black Prince or a champion of the constitutional reforms advocated by the Commons in the Good Parliament. There were some exceptionally well-qualified administrators on these councils. Take, for example, William Latimer. The controversy surrounding Latimer's disgrace in the Good Parliament and his later rehabilitation by John of Gaunt should not obscure the fact that this man had been positioned at the very heart of royal government for almost a decade: he had been steward of the household between 1368 and 1370, and acted as chamberlain between October 1371 and 1376. He had also been appointed constable of Dover castle and was warden of the Cinque ports from 1372, and had been utilized on several critical diplomatic missions in the early 1370s.[30] Similarly, Sir John Knyvet could claim to be one of the leading statesmen of his time: he had been a chief justice of the king's bench since 1365 and had been chancellor for no fewer than four and a half years between 1372 and 1377.[31] William Wykeham, bishop of Winchester brought a similar level of expertise and experience to the third continual council of 1378: from 1361 he had acted a royal secretary; from 1363 he was a royal councilor and from this year until 1367 he had been keeper of the privy seal; from 1367 until 1371 he had served as chancellor and throughout the early 1370s had continued acting as a key member of the king's council.[32] Even the comparatively obscure figure of John Harewell, bishop of Bath and Wells had served as constable of Bordeaux and later chancellor of Gascony for much of the 1360s.

The appointments to the continual councils need not just be seen in terms of the administrative aptitude of the personnel; they contained

The membership of the continual councils, drawing on N. B. Lewis, "The 'Continual Council' in the Early Years of Richard II, 1377–80," *English Historical Review* 41 (1926): 246–51 (an asterix indicates appointment on more than one occasion)

July–Oct 1377	Oct 1377–Oct 1378	Oct 1378–Jan 1380
Courtenay, bishop of London*	Courtenay, bishop of London*	Wykeham, bishop of Winchester
Erghum, bishop of Salisbury*	Erghum, bishop of Salisbury*	Harewell, bishop of Bath and Wells
Earl of March*	Appleby, bishop of Carlisle	Earl of Arundel*
Earl of Arundel*	Earl of March*	Earl of Suffolk
William Lord Latimer	Earl of Stafford	Sir Robert Hales
John Lord Cobham	Sir Richard Stafford*	Sir Roger Beauchamp*
Sir Roger Beauchamp*	Sir Henry Scrope	Sir Aubrey de Vere
Sir Richard Stafford*	Sir John Devereux*	Sir Robert Rous
Sir John Knyvet	Sir Hugh Segrave*	
Sir Ralph Ferrers		
Sir John Devereux*		
Sir Hugh Segrave*		

an equally rich seam of military service and experience. Again, such considerations have tended to be obscured by the concentration on factional politics so that, for example, the appointment of men closely allied to the Black Prince has generally only been seen in terms of the counterbalance they represented to Gaunt and his followers. In fact, the selection of men who had formerly served the Black Prince meant, almost by default, that the councils could draw on an extensive and invaluable body of military know-how. This may have featured as strongly as political and administrative credentials in determining the choice of appointment. It should be remembered that the Anglo-French truce expired only three days after Edward III died on 21 June 1377, and this was followed very soon afterward by French attacks on the south coast of England, Calais and Aquitaine.[33] This, together with a rapidly deteriorating situation on the Scottish borders, placed a special premium on the ability of the councils to respond to the military threats that England now faced. In fact, a close scrutiny of the personnel appointed to the continual councils suggests that they were intended to be as much "war" councils as "administrative" councils: John Lord Cobham, for example, served in France in 1359–60, 1366–67 and 1369, and had been on the embassy which had negotiated the Anglo-French truce of 1375;[34] Sir Richard Stafford had been in the vanguard of the Crécy campaign in 1346, he was present at the siege of Calais in the same year and had been rewarded for his "good service" in the Poitiers campaign of 1356;[35] Sir John Devereux had taken part in the Black Prince's Nájera campaign of 1367, he was appointed seneschal of La Rochelle and the Limousin in 1370, and of Saintonge in 1372 and had served as captain of Brest in the same year;[36] Sir Ralph Ferrers was at the siege of Calais, he was present at Poitiers in 1356, in 1358 he had been appointed as captain of Calais and Guines and in 1370 had been admiral of the fleet which had taken Sir Robert Knolle's army to France;[37] and Sir John Segrave was noted by Froissart as participating in the ill-fated expedition of 1373 which had aimed to re-conquer those parts of Gascony that had been overrun by the French.[38] Both Henry Scrope and William Latimer, as well as Sir Robert Hales, had begun their careers as soldiers.[39] Even the appointment of Thomas Appleby, bishop of Carlisle, to the continual council of October 1377 would appear to have been underscored by military considerations: Appleby had been actively involved in border affairs for over a decade as one of the wardens of the west march (he had first been appointed in 1367).[40] His experience and knowledge of the Anglo-Scottish conflict would have proved particularly valuable in the autumn of 1377 a few months after a major cross-border offensive launched by George Dunbar, earl of March, heralded a new period of increased Anglo-Scottish hostility.[41]

In political terms, the councils undoubtedly achieved an admirable degree of inclusiveness and consequently they projected a very strong sense of political cohesion and administrative order. But this, in a sense, was one of their main purposes. The minority councils were the "public face" of government during the period. Their membership was announced in parliament, their terms of reference were defined in parliament, and their lifespan was determined by parliamentary sessions. They exuded an air of regularity, stability, and transparency: above all, a sense of well-being and reassurance that government was in capable and reliable hands. The councils did not, however, constitute the sum total of government in these years and we should certainly not regard them as a real substitute for the royal prerogative. At least from the point of view of the Commons, the members of the council appointed in October 1377 were "to be continually at hand to advise on matters concerning the king and kingdom with the king's officers," and to oversee the expenditure of the "money granted them for the wars."[42] The close working association of the council's members with the "king's officers" is particularly noticeable and suggests a close affiliation to what, in circumstances when the king was an adult, we might describe as the king's "administrative" council.[43] This is an important distinction, for in identifying the locus of power and authority in Richard's early years it is necessary to understand that this was an age of bureaucratic monarchy in which a large volume of business transacted in the king's name would routinely have been delegated to his principal ministers.[44] Many of the matters discharged by the continual councils of Richard's early years would therefore have been no different in kind or importance to the matters considered independently by royal councils at other times. Indeed, evidence of warranty notes issued by the council or by the king and council on letters patent in the first years of Richard II's reign suggests that the *volume* of business that the continual councils discharged in the course of their existence (i.e., 1377–80) was not noticeably higher than in later periods when the king's council was operating under less formal or prescribed conditions (figure 3.1 and figure 3.2). The period of continual council "rule" may not therefore have represented such a radical departure from the norms of royal government and administration in other periods. It might then be that the primary motivation of the Commons in having the councils convened with a fixed "aristocratic" membership was to ensure an adequate level of supervision over the actions and decisions of the king's principal officers—the chancellor, treasurer, and keeper of the privy seal.[45] Membership of the council would undoubtedly have been a mark of status, but the responsibilities were onerous and the condition attached to appointment, that reappointment should not occur within two years, though this was ignored in many cases, probably derived as much from a concern to "protect" councilors from further imposition as to ensure that government was not monopolized by a limited group of men.[46]

In assessing the record of the continual council we must therefore recognize that its remit was fairly limited. For sure, it fulfilled a vital role in discharging large volumes of administration, but in terms of *policy* making we must look elsewhere to identify the political initiative. Thus, when Saul sums up the record of "minority" government under Richard II as "lacking either clarity of vision or efficiency of policy-making," this judgment cannot be made simply on the basis of the workings and nature of the continual councils: it has to be seen in light of government in general during the early years of Richard's reign.[47] Crucially, if we are looking for the locus of power and authority in these early years, for the forum where the really important decisions were taken, we must countenance a system of government that was far less structured or prescribed than the appointment and operation of the continual councils alone suggests. We ought also to envisage a method of decision-making that was far less open to public

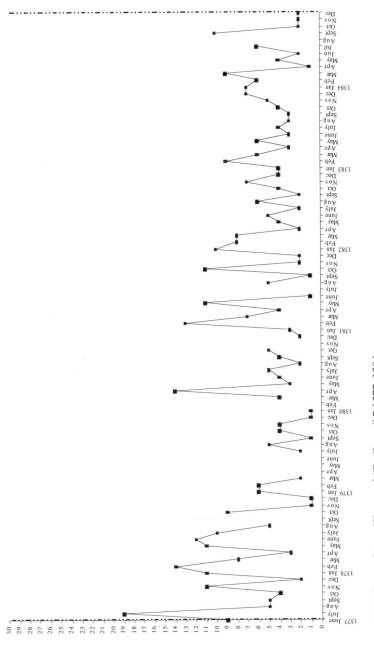

Figure 3.1 Letters Patent Warranted "By Council," 1377–1384.

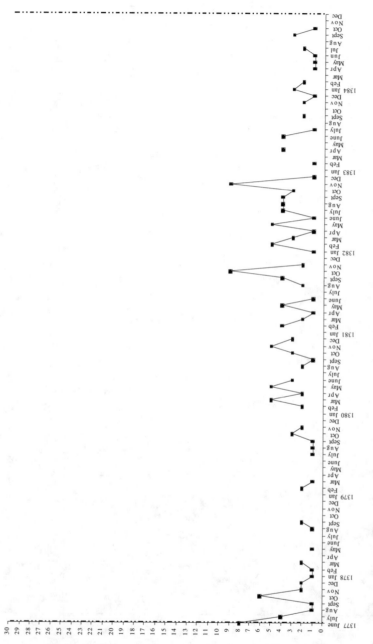

Figure 3.2 Letters Patent Warranted "By King and Council," 1377–1384.

scrutiny than the very public swearing in of the continual council in parliament intimated. This is the conclusion we are drawn to when considering the reluctance of the Lords in October 1377 to agree to the second of the Commons' requests to divulge the identity of "those who will accompany the person of our same lord the king."[48] The request was turned down on the grounds that "it seemed to them [i.e. the Lords] too burdensome and difficult to place anyone about their lord the king who did not wholly please him":[49] there was a keen sense in which the arrangements surrounding the "governance" of the king himself were to be decided behind closed doors. The response also highlighted the paradoxical position of the king himself: that is to say, that on the one hand, the way in which government was to function during Richard's early years was the subject of political debate within parliament, in recognition of his youth and inexperience, but on the other hand, a line was drawn on the extent to which the domestic circumstances of the king was to be considered "public" property, on the basis that the king himself possessed the ability and discernment to choose his own counselors and advisors.

If we regard the continual councils in rather less exalted terms than their prominence in the records would suggest we must clearly look elsewhere to obtain a complete picture of where power and authority lay in these years. This is not a straightforward exercise. It was in the very nature of the decision to maintain the notion that Richard was himself the source of political authority at this time that the official records of government usually hid the true origins of a decision or instruction by noting that it had been initiated by the king. Officially, the *king* ruled England in these years: his counselors and advisors merely facilitated his will. On the surface at least the English polity was very successful in maintaining the fiction that Edward III had been succeeded by a fully mature adult king. But if we investigate more closely it becomes apparent that the continual councils were but a single string in a many-stringed bow, and that the functions that its members performed were by no means the decisive factor in shaping the nature and dynamics of politics in these years.

The Great Council

First then, the Great Council, so-called because of its size and the high political standing of its members.[50] The period 1377–80 witnessed one of the most intensive periods of activity by this type of enlarged and reinforced royal council in the later Middle Ages. The meetings of the Great Councils were not routinely recorded; their

Figure 3.3 Letters Patent Warranted "By Great Council," 1377–1384.

existence, at least in this period, is indicated by the survival of formal summonses, by occasional references in chronicles or official records, and by the existence of warranty notes recording that an instrument of government had been authorized "by the Great Council." The warranty notes deserve special mention because it is in this period that an unprecedented number of letters issued on authority of the "Great Council" can be found in the chancery rolls. As figure 3.3 demonstrates, a spectacular surge occurred in the middle months of 1378 when a total of 424 and 80 such warranty notes were recorded in the patent rolls of March and May respectively.[51] This was a level of administrative activity that surpassed all normal levels and suggests that a Great Council, or several meetings of this body, had been convened to clear a large backlog of business that had built up since the beginning of the reign. In fact, a closer investigation of the sort of matters that were discharged by the Great Council in these months shows that the vast majority were letters of "inspeximus and confirmation" which in essence validated annuities or offices that had been granted in the reign of Edward III. Inevitably, the greater proportion of such grants was issued to men who held office in government or who discharged some function within the royal household.[52] Typical of the recipients of such letters were: master John Bray, physician of the late king; Gilbert del Spitel, groom of the ewry of the household; John Fastolf, a king's esquire; Robert Appelby, serjeant-at-arms; and John Gosebourn, one of the auditors of the Exchequer.[53] It is not known what part, if any, these individuals were expected to play in securing their annuities, but it is possible, given the sheer volume, that the process was undertaken more for auditing purposes than to consider in detail the particular merits of individual cases. Long lists of confirmations were drawn up in the course of the Great Council meeting. On 9 March 1378, for example, at least thirty confirmations were recorded;[54] on 11 March the number exceeded forty;[55] and on 23 March there were at least fifty cases.[56] The fact that these confirmations were attributed to a body described as a "Great Council" is important, because whether or not large numbers of bishops and nobles turned up to witness these ratifications—unfortunately no evidence exists to shed light on this point—it is clear that great value was placed on the broad consensus which usage of the term "Great Council" could bring to important decisions on crown expenditure. The other effect of having such a large number of confirmations recorded in the chancery rolls and broadcast as letters patent throughout the kingdom was no doubt to emphasize the continuity that existed between the old and new reigns. It may well be that the

accession of Richard II saw a resurgence in the fortunes of men associated with the Black Prince,[57] but in terms of sheer numbers of personnel who served and surrounded the king, Richard's regime—that
is to say his "establishment"—would have borne great similarity to
his grandfather's.

The warranty notes are an important source for conciliar activity,
but they have limitations and cannot be relied upon as a definitive
guide showing when Great Councils had convened. We know that a
Great Council met in February 1379, for example, shortly before the
parliament of April in that year, and yet no warranty notes recording
the activity of the Great Council were noted in the chancery rolls between December 1378 and May 1379. The Westminster Chronicle
also noted that "on the 5 August [1378] the king held at Reading a
council to which all the leading men of the country were summoned,"[58] and Walsingham recorded a meeting of an enlarged council at Windsor between 13 and 16 September (though he does not use
the term "Great Council" to describe it).[59] Again, there is very little
"administrative" imprint from these meetings in the records of government. Instead, they appear to have been convened to address key
matters of policy. It was a meeting of the Great Council in July 1377,
for example, which decided on the arrangements for Richard's early
years, including the key decision that a continual council would be installed instead of a regency.[60] The meeting of February 1379 is especially worth noting in this regard, for it had been convened to
consider the perilous military situation which the kingdom now
faced, partly it seems because the parliament of 1378 had failed to implement appropriate measures in this regard, and partly because the
members of the continual council felt themselves to be insufficiently
qualified to address these matters themselves.[61] The Great Council
put into place measures to ensure the defense of the realm[62] and, as a
stop gap measure, it secured loans from a broad cross-section of the
political community to pay for the military expenditure.[63] It did not
have the power to raise taxation, however, and so it was at this meeting that the decision was taken to call the parliament which met a few
months later in April. The Great Council meeting of September 1378
is also likely to have played an important role in determining the parliamentary agenda. It met amidst the controversy surrounding the infamous murder of Robert Hawley in Westminster Abbey and it was
almost certainly here that the crown's strategy was devised in meeting
the outrage of the bishops and Londoners over the incident.

We do not know who attended the meetings designated as "Great
Councils" between 1377 and 1380.[64] There was no clear contempo-

rary definition on what was needed to make a "normal" meeting of the council into a "Great Council," and it was probably the case that the latter was defined in rather opaque terms as a meeting that attracted an unusually larger gathering of the kingdom's political elite. The enlarged council meeting of 1379 was reported by Richard le Scrope to have been attended by "almost all the prelates, abbots as well as others, dukes, earls, barons, bannerets and other wise men of the kingdom," but no further details are known.[65] Scrope did, however, say that "all the lords there present voluntarily lent our lord the king various great sums of money." If the subsequent lists of lenders are any guide, the meeting of the Great Council was attended by the bishops of Chichester, Exeter, Bath and Wells, Winchester, Rochester, and Salisbury; the earls of Northumberland, Warwick, Suffolk, Angos, Arundel, and the duke of Lancaster; and a further twenty-one abbots and thirteen priors.[66] Of the less formal meetings, the endorsements of two petitions presented in February 1381, in which the lords of the council were named, may offer important clues about the first years of the reign: John of Gaunt; William Wykeham, bishop of Winchester; Edmund Langley, earl of Cambridge; Richard, earl of Arundel; William, earl of Suffolk; Hugh, earl of Stafford; and Henry Percy, earl of Northumberland were named in both documents; Simon Sudbury, archbishop of Canterbury; William Courtenay, bishop of London and Thomas Brantingham, bishop of Exeter were additionally named in one.[67] It is particularly interesting to see the presence of Gaunt, Langley, Percy, and Sudbury in these councils—individuals who were not appointed as permanent members of any of the three continual councils of 1377–80. It is a reasonable assumption to make that these individuals would also have attended council meetings in the first three years of the reign, and the presence of one or more of them at such gatherings may have been sufficient for the recording clerk to designate the meeting as a "Great Council."

Parliament

In the hierarchy of council meetings, the Great Council obviously took precedence over the continual council, but the Great Council was no substitute for a meeting of parliament which was attended, in theory at least, by every member of the noble and ecclesiastical elites, as well as representatives drawn from urban and gentry communities throughout the kingdom. Although parliament was in session for only a relatively short amount of time in the period 1377–80, its influence on the politics and the government of the realm was all pervasive. This was because the shape and direction of policy was to a great extent dependent on the ready supply of public money, which in turn could only be accessed with the approval of the Commons in parliament. The hold which the Commons had on the nation's purse strings was sufficient in itself to ensure that the representatives would have a key role to play in Richard's early years, especially as war against France was in full swing and the crown was in desperate need of taxation. But by 1377 the Commons had additionally developed over the course of fifty years into a political force of impressive maturity, with a deep understanding of the problems and workings of central government and an innate conviction in their right to question policy and to point out areas that needed attention.[68] Only a year before Richard's coronation, in the Good Parliament of 1376, the Commons had demonstrated a remarkable capacity to mount a sustained and concerted political assault on a group of unpopular courtiers, as a result of which the government had been forced to capitulate almost totally to their demands for reform.[69] The reforms may have been quickly quashed, but there can be no doubting the profound impact that the Good Parliament had in consolidating the Commons as a political force to be reckoned with. In general, the MPs of the late fourteenth century were respectful of their political superiors and they were acutely aware of their position as bystanders in the business of actually running the government. But this did not make them subservient or obsequious. This much is indicated in the caution exercised by the Lords in 1378 when MPs had requested that five or six of their number might join the Commons to discuss the "charge" given to them by the chancellor. The Lords rejected the request and suggested instead that a smaller delegation from each house meet separately to "consult with one another in an informal manner, without trouble, clamour or disturbance."[70] The exchange provides a rare insight into the dynamics of parliamentary debating in the late fourteenth century and confirms the impression that MPs were outspoken, opinionated, and very probably bad tempered in their discussions with each other and with members of the Upper House.

It should come as no surprise, then, to find that the Commons took a very close interest in the arrangements for Richard's "minority" government. Almost the very first points of business recorded in the opening parliament of the reign were the following three demands relating to these arrangements: first, that the names of the eight continual councilors should be openly declared in parliament; second, that those men surrounding the king should be identified, and assurances given that they would be "the most virtuous, honest, and worthy of the kingdom" and, additionally, that the royal household would be "governed with decent moderation"; and third, that the laws of the land should be upheld, with a particular demand that no law should be repealed without parliament.[71] The second of the requests is particularly significant, for it shows a real sense of proprietorship over the person of the king: the Commons were assuming for themselves the responsibility of ensuring that Richard's early years in power were correctly and appropriately administered. It was no doubt because Richard had not officially been declared a minor that the Commons felt compelled to justify their interference in such matters by pointing out what was obvious to everybody: that he was "at present so innocent and tender in age."[72] By asserting themselves as custodians of the king's welfare the Commons were giving practical expression to a fundamental principle underpinning medieval kingship: namely, that the king was seen to personify the realm and that his person was consequently regarded as *persona publica*.[73] In other words, because the private life of a king had such a profound effect on the public life of the kingdom, it was perfectly legitimate for the political community to voice its concerns over the arrangements put into place to help the king during his impressionable youth, because from the welfare of the king sprang the welfare of the kingdom.

If we see the crown, and the person of the king, in this way—in essence as "public property"[74]—this makes better sense of the rather presumptive attitude displayed by the Commons in their scrutiny of the king's private living arrangements. We should see their disclaimer at the end of their list of demands, that these ought not to be considered derogatory to the "regality and dignity of our aforesaid lord the king,"[75] to be further indication of the ambiguity attached to Richard's position and the fact that their enquiries sat very uneasily with the king's "official" status as a fully functioning adult king. But practicalities ruled the day, and no doubt because Richard was considered incapable of effectively expressing the royal will the Commons felt able to raise these concerns. To this, of course, we must add the more practical and enduring factor that questions relating to the conduct and disposition of the government, including the royal household, often turned on questions about finance and expenditure, areas in which the Commons felt fully entitled to expect cooperation given the strict conditions attached to the grants of taxation they provided for the crown's use.[76] These considerations thus provide context for the Commons' demands for assurances about royal expenditure and about the people surrounding the king. It explains, for example, why the Commons insisted on the appointment of war treasurers in October

1377 to make proper accounts of government spending;[77] and why, in 1379, a highly intrusive inquiry was made into the king's estate and his revenues, which included the inspection of fees paid to royal officials and of the annuities granted by the king and his grandfather, as well as a wholesale examination of household expenditure.[78] In a period when the king was considered incapable of bringing the discretion and wisdom imbued in his office to the implementation of royal government the Commons' aim was to make parliament substitute for the king in guaranteeing the good and proper conduct of his officials: in effect, they were not to be accountable to the king, but to parliament, and in particular to the Commons. Perhaps the clearest expression of this agenda was the MPs' demand in 1377 that "until [Richard] reaches the age to distinguish good from evil," all the chief councilors and officers of government "might be appointed and provided by parliament" and that any appointment of a chief minister between parliaments ought to be done only by the Great Council and in any case it should be a provisional appointment until ratification in the next assembly.[79] Although the demands were met only partially,[80] they demonstrate most emphatically how the Commons were claiming for themselves the right to participate in decisions that would fundamentally shape the course and direction of government in these years.

The circumstances of Richard's nonage, like the dotage of his grandfather, had the effect of significantly increasing the political profile of MPs. It is no accident that in these very years private petitioners began to address their complaints to the members of the Lower House in the hope that their intervention with the king and Lords might secure a favorable response.[81] This was a measure of the influence they were now considered to hold within the English polity. But we should be cautious in overstating the power that the Commons could wield. They might attach conditions to the grants they made in parliament or insist on careful and prudent royal spending, but the Commons did not have the ability to ensure that their demands were met. Some of their requests were not even agreed to. We have just seen how their request for the "public" appointment of the key officers of state in parliament was fudged, and it is also worth remembering the short shrift given to their demand to have the identity of those surrounding the king revealed.[82] The attempt of the Commons in October 1377 to revive the agenda of the Good Parliament, by having its ordinances confirmed by statute, was also dismissed peremptorily, in spite of the fact that the wool subsidy from that assembly—which the crown was still collecting—had been granted explicitly on this understanding.[83] Even the continual council was rather less the creature of the Commons than we might expect: the councilors were chosen only by the Lords, and at least in 1377, they were sworn to office in front of the Lords only. In 1379, parliament had ended before all the continual councilors had been chosen. The fact is that the Commons were first and foremost political lobbyists and while they could undoubtedly bring great pressure to bear on the crown by the hold they enjoyed over the supply of taxation, their powers—even at this high point of their political influence—remained limited.

To address the subject in this way, however, runs the risk of characterizing the political dynamics of parliament solely in terms of a trial of strength between MPs and peers. Undoubtedly there were disagreements, seemingly stemming in large part from the Commons' inaccurate appraisal of the crown's financial situation,[84] but the prevailing mood at this time was determined above all by the imperative to maintain political consensus and stability. In 1377, a ten-year-old boy had succeeded to the throne at a point when the fortunes of war had decisively turned against England and when, in the domestic political scene, serious fissures existed just beneath the surface. For many, the kingdom must have appeared very close to the brink of utter destruction.[85] In these circumstances differences of opinion or clashes over policy will always have been tempered by the need to retain a common sense of unity and purpose. Even over an issue as close to the Commons' heart as crown income and expenditure, we cannot assume that the political community was neatly divided along parliamentary lines into those (the Commons) who wanted the crown to account for its spending and those (the Lords) who cared little for such matters. It is interesting, in this regard, to note how the Commons couched their request in October 1377, where they asked for the repeal of all gifts "granted in deceit of our lord the king [Edward III]," in terms of saving the "estate of our most honored lords the sons of our lord [king] . . . who are of poor standing . . . [so that they may be] suitably relieved by some of the said gifts."[86] Petitions for financial recompense presented by Thomas Woodstock and other peers of the realm in the early years of Richard II's reign are a useful reminder that an insolvent crown frittering away public money was in nobody's interests (except, possibly, the small clique who benefited from the king's largesse).[87] Indeed, the point can be made more forcefully in light of the great state loan of March 1379 when a wide range of the king's subjects pledged sums of money to finance the kingdom's defense ahead of an anticipated parliamentary subsidy.[88]

The amounts loaned to the crown ranged from £100 (mainly earls and some bishops) to 5 marks; London, which was listed separately, raised a staggering £5,000.[89] The loan would certainly have intensified a common desire to ensure prudent government expenditure, but it is interesting to speculate that it would also have generated a significant lobby group within the Commons *in favor* of parliamentary taxation, so that the loans would be adequately paid off. The dubious methods by which the loan had apparently been solicited by members of the royal household might additionally explain why the Commons and Lords were prepared to countenance such an invasive inquiry into household costs later that year.[90]

For the officials, nobles, and ecclesiastics who either represented or acted for the crown during Richard's early years, the need to maintain political consensus in parliament was borne not simply out of the need to retain the Commons' favor so that they would grant taxation; it went to the very heart of what furnished their actions with legitimacy and authority. Royal power was predicated on the notion that the king's right to rule over his subjects derived from the representative qualities inherent in his office.[91] Without a king ruling effectively, parliament provided the most obvious mechanism to generate an alternative source of representational legitimacy by imbuing the actions of the king's agents with the assent and endorsement of the Commons. The government of Richard's early years was thus not "forced" into acting through parliament but rather saw the institution as a way of engendering a sense of collective responsibility and therefore support for its actions. It listened to, and frequently acted on, the demands of the Commons because not to have done so would have made a mockery of the claim central to its existence that it stood and acted for the common interest. It was this basic principle which explains the rather undignified way in which Gaunt made an issue out of the rumors that had been circulating in 1377 about his intentions toward the throne.[92] This was not just about wounded pride or offended ego; it was absolutely critical, if Gaunt was to command any authority in the coming months and years, that he not only asserted himself to be acting in the common interest, but that he had the explicit acceptance of the Commons that this was indeed the case. It also explains, at least partly, why it fell to the Commons to bring to an end the system of continual councils in 1380 because without the support of MPs, the councilors had no consensus on which to base their authority.[93]

John of Gaunt

Gaunt's role in the infamous Hawley/Shakell affair highlights the central position that he occupied in government at the time. The outlines of this episode are well known.[94] Shortly after Richard's accession, Robert Hawley and John Shakell had defied the wishes of the council by refusing to reduce the ransom of the count of Denia, who had been captured at the battle of Nájera in 1367. For their contumacy they had been imprisoned in the Tower of London in October 1377, but in August 1378 they escaped and claimed sanctuary in Westminster Abbey.[95] Sir Alan Buxhill, acting on the instructions of the council, then attempted to have the pair arrested and in the ensuing scuffle within the abbey Hawley and a sacristan were cut down and killed. It was almost certainly as a result of the outrage caused by this violation of sanctuary that the decision was taken to hold parliament at Gloucester rather than Westminster. Gaunt was actually overseas—or "on the high seas"—at the time of the murders, but this did not stop contemporary chroniclers holding the duke responsible for the outrage. To some extent, these sentiments are understandable because Gaunt would almost certainly have been at the very forefront of the defense mounted by the crown against the abbot of Westminster's accusations in the Gloucester parliament. Walsingham's account of Gaunt's return from his expedition, when he attended a council meeting at Windsor, is highly instructive on the matter. When the duke heard that William Courtenay, bishop of London had pronounced sentence of excommunication on all those who had been involved in the affair, in spite of royal letters ordering him to desist from such action, Gaunt was reported to be "very angry; and he said that he was particularly outraged at the impudence of the [bishop] who . . . had scorned the royal requests and persisted in [his] obstinacy."[96] Gaunt was apparently even more furious at the fact that when the bishop "had been invited by the king to attend the council, he had arrogantly scorned the invitation."[97] If the account is accurate, it shows how Gaunt had assumed the role of spokesman for the king and, by implication, how royal policy was being determined or directed by the duke. His angry reaction to the contempt shown by the bishop paralleled very closely the vigorous and aggressive assertion of royal dignity that was later to be displayed in parliament.

This leads to a series of more general points about Gaunt's role and position in the first years of Richard's rule. In the first place, we should, once and for all, scotch any notion that Gaunt was either snubbed in 1377 when the arrangements for Richard's "minority" were fixed or that his political ambitions and his authority were in some way curtailed in the early years of the reign by the combined forces of an unreasonably suspicious political community.[98] Walsingham's famous remark, that Gaunt elected to "retire from the court" following the coronation, can too easily be regarded as an act of pique by a nobleman who failed to achieve what he most desired: the position of regent.[99] The word "retire" suggests defeat, resignation, and failure—which well suited Walsingham's jaundiced view of the duke and his actions.[100] But Gaunt's standing in the realm was in practice not much different early in Richard II's reign than at the end of Edward III's reign. It is true that he was not made regent, but there is no evidence to show that this is what he desired. Indeed, we cannot be sure that the possibility of a regency was seriously considered in 1377: it is entirely possible that the sentiments articulated fifty years later in 1427, that a regency represented an accroachment of royal power, already formed the common currency of political thought in the last quarter of the fourteenth century.[101] In this respect, we must remember that Gaunt was nothing if not a staunch upholder of the royal prerogative. Besides, Gaunt was astute enough politically to appreciate that a more flexible system of government, in which he could direct royal policy by speaking "through" the king, was much more likely to bring him control and acceptance than a regency government in which the lines of authority were more clearly delineated—in other words, where the blame for failed policies could be laid more squarely on his shoulders and where there was consequently much greater scope for dissent.[102] Ironically, the more straightforward direction of a regency government would probably have better served the interests of a distrustful political community than the ambiguous system of government installed in 1377 which enabled Gaunt to influence his young nephew for the most part without any element of accountability.[103]

Aside from political considerations, a regency style government may not have suited the "hands-on" approach of Gaunt to the external threats facing the realm at this point: the energy with which he engaged in campaigning against the French and Scots in the late 1370s suggests that his primary interest lay in military pursuits rather than the day-to-day running of government. He, incidentally, would not have been alone in holding this view: it should be remembered that the Great Council of February 1379 had originally been intended to meet the previous month, but the plans had changed because "the prelates and lords excused themselves from attending; some of them saying that because of important and urgent matters which they had to attend to elsewhere, namely both the business of the kingdom as well as their own affairs, they were not able to come to nor stay at the said council, and especially so soon after the long labor they had undertaken at the said parliament of Gloucester."[104] Gaunt's modern biographer has portrayed him as remote and politically isolated, a man who found it hard—or was disinclined—to forge close political alliances or friendships and who devoted his interests and energies to fulfilling his own goals rather than those of the realm.[105] We should not dismiss the possibility that it was Gaunt's lack of appetite for regency, rather than the obstacles put in his way by a distrustful political community, which best accounts for the decision to creative an alternative form of government in 1377.

It has been argued that the "denial" to Gaunt of the regency highlighted the limitations of his power,[106] but it is equally possible to regard the less prescribed position he occupied in government in the late 1370s as an *affirmation* of his political ascendancy: he did not need to be made a regent, or to hold any other official "minority" title, in order to be recognized and treated as the premier nobleman of the kingdom whose opinion carried more weight than anyone else's.[107] His position as the senior royal prince, as the largest landholder in the kingdom besides the king, as Steward of England *and* as a king of a foreign land (i.e. Castile) assured him undisputed political preeminence at this time. The fact that only he appears to have been personally summoned to attend council meetings provides a measure of the importance attached to his opinion and suggests that important decisions on policy could not be reached without his involvement.[108] Within council meetings themselves it was Gaunt who appears to have assumed leadership. Again, we rely on Walsingham for elucidation on this point. According to the chronicler, during the meeting of the Great Council early in the Autumn of 1378 Gaunt had taken control of the subsidy which had been granted in the parliament of October 1377 insisting that he would determine how it was to be spent to ensure the proper and effective defense of the realm. If Walsingham is to be believed, Gaunt did not enjoy the wholehearted support of his fellow lords yet none felt confident enough to challenge his authority: "[t]he nobles, although unwillingly, agreed to this importunate request with, it is said, some bitterness of heart. They already knew that fortune was against them and that the duke held such power in the kingdom that it was extremely inadvisable for them to go against his wishes."[109] Though no doubt induced by the particular circumstances of Gaunt's declaration of loyalty to the king, the Commons' affirmation of the duke in October 1377 as their

"their chief aid, comforter, and counsellor in this parliament"—that is to say, the most important of the lords who they had nominated to be part of an intercommuning committee—most certainly reflected the reality that Gaunt, as the chief political figure within parliament, was best placed to convey the crown's needs to the assembled MPs.[110] The point is worth emphasizing, for it underlines an important difference between popularity and respect. Gaunt was not popular; but he commanded respect and authority within the polity by virtue of his power and proximity to the crown. In light of the actions of the Bad Parliament of January 1377, which rolled back the reforms implemented by MPs in the Good Parliament six months earlier, we may even question how far he was the politically isolated figure commonly depicted in contemporary and modern writing. Walsingham was at such a loss to explain the drastic *voltre face* of January 1377 that he assumed—quite erroneously as it turned out—that Gaunt had packed the assembly with his own supporters.[111] The chronicler was quite unable to contemplate the possibility that not everyone shared his harsh views of the duke, and that within the broader political community outside London there may have been a sizeable body of opinion that actually identified its interests with the nobleman.[112]

To a point, Gaunt's dominion within the polity is affirmed by the role ascribed to him, and his younger brothers, in the opening parliament of the reign: they were not expected to attend council meetings on a regular basis, but it was stressed that if "any dispute by maintenance in the country or elsewhere" occurred between council members, the latter should suffer grievous penalty "the cognizance and jurisdiction over which matters shall belong to the king himself, and his uncles of Spain, Cambridge, and Buckingham."[113] This was explicit confirmation of the political pecking order: Gaunt, with his brothers as deputies, was positioned at the very top of the scale, albeit below the king himself. More importantly, they were being accorded exclusive rights to exercise the sort of power of arbitration and judgment normally reserved for the king alone.[114] This was an explicit affirmation of their position of proximity to the king and, by implication, their removal or detachment from the rest of the political community. No doubt it was in recognition of the particular and extensive powers that Gaunt possessed as the most senior statesman of the realm that petitioners often chose to address their supplications to him, rather than to the king or council, in the first years of the reign: there was no question in their minds as to where ultimate authority lay.[115] So, it should be clear that the issue of whether or not a regency government should be installed related more to the structure of government than to questions about the location of power and authority within it. Gaunt's seniority meant that he did not have to be physically present at Westminster to ensure his central position in the running of the kingdom's affairs: a combination of his political stature and the placing of his friends and allies in key positions of responsibility (in particular, Richard le Scrope as chancellor[116] and Guichard d'Angle, earl of Huntingdon, as tutor to the king between 1377 and 1380[117]) meant that he retained a very tight and comprehensive grip on government. It was arguably the control of these key positions, rather than who was appointed to the continual council, which determined the real locus of power at this point. Technically Gaunt was not regent, but in reality this was what he was. It was this reality that probably explains why a number of contemporary writers were in no doubt as to where real power lay in these early years (indeed one chronicler, albeit a French writer, thought that a regency had indeed been installed).[118]

The King: Grace and Favor

We come then to the final piece in the jigsaw: the king himself, and the extent of his involvement in government from the very beginning of his rule. It is a question which has never received detailed scrutiny, quite possibly because it is so hard to decipher from the records how far decisions recorded in the name of the king actually reflected the king's active participation.[119] In the absence of explicit consideration the tendency is perhaps to assume that Richard had very little hand in the running of government for the first years of the reign.[120] No doubt the stories of Richard having to take a nap midway through the proceedings of his coronation, and his being carried through the crowds on the shoulders of Simon Burley, have contributed to the impression that Richard would have been far too young to have any real impact on government at this time.[121] And yet, we cannot dismiss Richard as a political nonentity. The fiction of Richard's majority rule remained a fiction insofar as he did not discharge the full gamut of responsibilities and duties that might be expected of an adult king. This is rather different to saying that he took no active part in government at all. For contemporaries, these early years of the reign were probably conceived in terms of an apprenticeship in which it was felt desirable to expose Richard as much as possible to the demands of kingship while reserving for institutions like the continual council, Great Council, and parliament the main administrative burden and important decisions on policy and expenditure. The Commons' demands in

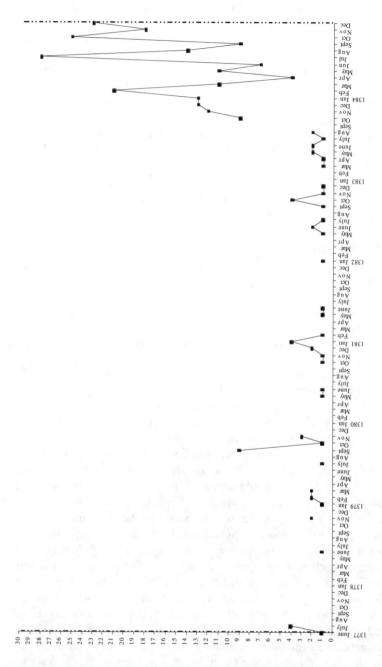

Figure 3.4 Letters Patent Warranted "By Signet," 1377–1384.

1377 to be given assurances about the arrangements for Richard's governance suggests that he was regarded as capable of exercising a sufficient level of discretion as to be a cause for concern. The Lords sought to reassure MPs by stating that "the knights, squires, and all about the king, should be restrained on pain of grievous penalties . . . from seeking anything from the king on their own behalf, or on behalf of others, which could in any way be charged to the king or kingdom."[122] The assumption was that Richard had the power to grant favor to those courtiers who surrounded him, but that he did not have the experience or wisdom to be able to refuse such requests if they made demands on royal revenues or on income derived from taxation.

In the notes of warranty attached to chancery instruments there are clear signs of the king's involvement in a variety of different decisions, though it must be stressed that the number of such occasions where his participation can be established beyond doubt, are relatively few.[123] In the very first months of the reign, before a continual council had been formally constituted and apparently while a privy seal was being made,[124] it can be seen in figure 3.4 that there was a very brief period in which the signet seal—the surest indication of the personal involvement of the king in a decision—was used to authorize letters issued under the Great Seal. In June 1377, for example, a signet letter was sent from the royal manor of Kennington to chancery ordering the appointment of Richard Story as keeper and surveyor of lordships in parts of Wales;[125] in July, a signet letter authorized the appointment of John May to buy stone and timber for repairs to the manor of Langley in Hertfordshire;[126] and another, in the same month, charged Walter Hanlee, a king's serjeant-at-arms, and John Clerc to organize ships and mariners to serve the king for six weeks.[127] In the following months and years, the appearance among the chancery records of the warranty note "by king and council" or "by king and Great Council"[128] shows that Richard attended council meetings on a fairly regular basis and was presumably consulted directly on those matters that had been authorized in his and the council's name. In early 1378, a large number of chancery instruments authorized in this way related to the confirmation of grants or annuities that individuals had received in the reign of Richard's grandfather.[129]

While other warranty notes such as "by council," "by Great Council," or "by petition of parliament" indicated very straightforwardly that the king had not been involved in decisions taken within government, the same cannot be said of the warranty note "by privy seal" which, as figure 3.5 demonstrates, was easily the most ubiquitous of chancery authorizations used in this period. Although the privy seal

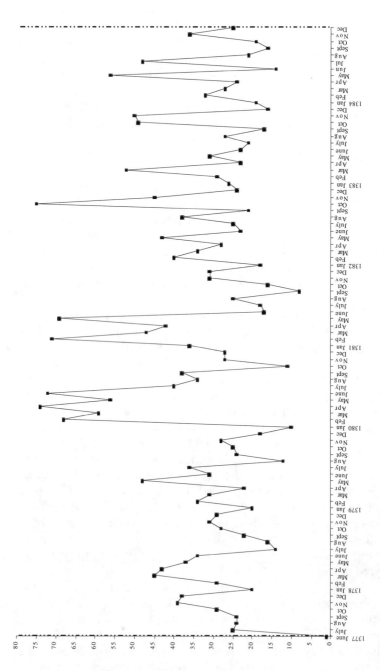

Figure 3.5 Letters Patent Warranted "By Privy Seal," 1377–1384.

could be mobilized by either the council or the king, detailed investigation into its use in the reign of Henry IV has shown that more often than not it was used by the king in preference to sending letters direct to the chancellor using his signet seal.[130] This was a more formal or solemn method of validating a royal mandate and might well have been most suitable for the circumstances of Richard's early years in power when he was spending much of his time traveling between royal manors and palaces in the Thames valley.[131] The great difficulty is that privy seal instruments disguise their true origins, so while it is perfectly possible that large numbers of writs were sent to the chancellor by the keeper of the privy seal at the behest of the council, it is equally possible that a good proportion emanated by royal order, more likely than not as a result of a signed bill or signet letter that the king had sent to the keeper for action.[132] The point is demonstrated by the fact that the keeper of the privy seal, John Fordham, appears to have divided his time in the first six months of the reign between Westminster and the itinerant royal court, for there are a large number of chancery instruments which were noted as having being authorized by privy seal letters issued at one of the king's Home Counties' manors.[133] The clear implication is that on these occasions the privy seal had been mobilized directly within the context of the royal court. At other times when the privy seal was removed from the presence of the king, we have only the letters of the signet seal to indicate what lay behind a privy seal letter. Unfortunately, the destruction of the greater part of the privy seal archive in the seventeenth century, which housed these written instructions, means that we will never be able to recover an accurate picture of the what lay behind the warranty note "by privy seal," but we should at least countenance the possibility that Richard was involved in a considerable proportion of privy seal letters issued in these early years of his reign.

Some extant petitions dating to the period 1377–80 would appear to confirm that Richard was actively involved in decisions affecting the welfare and circumstances of his subjects. Some examples, it is true, we must take at face value if we are to sustain such a conclusion, though it is doubtful in this context that decisions recorded in the king's name would have been rendered such without the king having been consulted in any way at all. To the petition presented in 1377 by the merchants of York, for instance, which made complaint against a group of Scottish merchants who had robbed the petitioners and suggested two ways of bringing the miscreants to justice, the endorsement read "the king wills the second option."[134] Another petition presented from York in 1377—this time from Richard de Ravenser, master of St Leonard's Hospital, who asked for the confirmation of his hospital's charters—was answered: "The king wishes this well as it is of royal foundation;"[135] and the response to a petition from Adam Ramsey, who asked for office and wages, was "This bill was granted by the king."[136] In other cases, we are on surer ground in concluding that Richard had personally considered the contents of a supplication. It is surely of some significance that the petition presented by William Windsor and Alice Perrers, against the judgments brought against Perrers in the parliament of October 1377, was initially brought before the king.[137] True, we learn from the endorsement that Richard subsequently sent the bill to his council, presumably because it related to such a sensitive political issue, but the fact that he had received it first shows that at least some contemporaries regarded it as worthwhile to send their requests directly to the boy king. This point is borne out by the fact that from the very start of the reign many supplications were addressed to the king alone.[138] An even more emphatic indication of Richard's capacity to deal with questions of patronage—or royal grace—in his own right is the endorsement to the petition of John de Cobham, who requested confirmation of the agreement he had reached with Edward III whereby the crown would inherit Cobham's estates upon his death.[139] In the endorsement, a clerk had specified that the petition was "For the king," and the full response noted that the "king wills that the said bishop of Lincoln and Guy de Bryan . . . be diligently examined" on the matter. The explicit reservation of the petition for the attention of the king is highly significant, for it clearly shows the importance that was attached to having the king's involvement in questions relating to the royal patrimony. An equally persuasive indication of Richard's active role in these early years is provided by the endorsement to a petition presented in the parliament of 1378 by John Blaunchard who asked to be repossessed of a bailiwick in the forest of Grovely (Wilts.) which had been unjustly seized into the king's hands.[140] It was ordained that Blaunchard was "to have a letter of the privy seal of *procedendo,* provided that they do not proceed to give judgment *without consulting the king.*" The case was to be decided in chancery, but only after the king had been directly consulted on the matter.

In all these cases, it should be stressed that the mention of the king in the endorsements to these petitions does not indicate that the king was handling the cases in isolation. What they do suggest, however, is that the arrangements put into place for government in the first years of Richard II's reign were multi-layered, and that alongside the more obvious "institutional" contexts, such as the council or parliament, in which the business of government was discharged, there also existed a more informal and much less clearly defined or prescribed context— the royal household would perhaps be the least contentious term to describe it—in which matters were referred to the king who reached decisions in consultation with the men and women who immediately surrounded him—the *familiars* of his chamber and household. That policy could emanate independently from this environment, even in these early years, is amply demonstrated by the controversy surrounding the Leybourne inheritance in which the king and his advisors chose to ignore the advice of parliament, and presumably also the wishes of John of Gaunt, by willfully obstructing the fulfillment of all the terms attached to Edward III's will (Gaunt was one of its executors).[141] In the parliament held at Gloucester in 1378, the executors of Edward III's will made complaint that the receiver appointed to administer the Leybourne lands had been prevented from making payment out of the issues "by certain of the council of our lord the present king," who had ordained that payments could not be made "without special mandate from the king." Crucially, the king had not provided this mandate.[142] The carefully worded grievance is interesting for its oblique reference to the king's "councilors"—or counselors. Almost certainly this did *not* mean the councilors appointed to attend the continual council, but rather the less easily identifiable individuals who surrounded the king and inhabited his court. The episode provides a striking illustration of the weight of authority that the court could already bring to bear over legal and governmental processes when policy was directly advocated by the king or in his name. It also highlights, in rather ironic terms, how much more freedom of action Richard enjoyed during his years of "minority" in comparison to the period between 1386 and 1388 when power was all but taken away from him by parliament and the Appellants.

The identity of the king's counselors is hard to pin down, but for the early years of Richard's rule they almost certainly would have included some of the men who had served with the Black Prince and who now filled important positions in the royal household. Sir Simon Burley, as the king's vice-chamberlain, is an obvious individual to cite; but there were others, such as William Packington, keeper of the wardrobe; Alan Stokes, keeper of the great wardrobe; Richard le Scrope, steward of the household (until March 1378), and his successor, Sir Hugh Segrave; Robert Braybrooke, king's secretary; and John Fordham, keeper of the signet seal.[143] Aubrey de Vere would also have held a key position in Richard's household as the royal chamberlain; and the appointment of the royal knight Sir Robert Rous (along with de Vere) to the third continual council to represent "court" interests suggests that he too was prominent.[144] In his role as the king's tutor, Guichard d'Angle, earl of Huntingdon, would presumably also have had an important influence on the young king, as would Sir Richard Abberbury, a chamber knight, who also served briefly in this capacity. Over a dozen more chamber knights were serving the king in his early years and these were for the most part either former members of the Black Prince's retinue or former servants of Edward III.[145] Nor should we forget the very considerable influence that Richard's mother, Princess Joan of Kent, probably exerted in these early years. It was, after all, Princess Joan who had engineered the reconciliation between John of Gaunt and the Londoners in February 1377, and it was she, with Simon Burley, who was absolutely central in the early negotiations for Richard's marriage.[146] Princess Joan had been present with the king in London during the Peasants' Revolt of 1381 and, according to the *Anonimalle* chronicle she had actually accompanied her son to the meeting with the rebels at Mile End.[147] At least one petitioner, the prior of Coventry, felt she possessed sufficient authority to warrant inclusion with the council in the opening address of a petition presented at some point early in the reign against the men of the same city.[148]

RICHARD'S ASSUMPTION OF POWER

If, as I have argued in the previous section, the incidence of privy seal writs in the years 1377–80 provides some measure of the volume of activity which Richard II engaged in from the very beginning of his reign, this helps put into perspective the decision by the Commons to insist on the abandonment of the continual councils in 1380, since it is clear that the activity of these councilors accounted for only a proportion of the business of government discharged at this time. It underscores the points that the councilors were not absolutely vital to the proper running of government; that the Commons were probably justified in seeing their role in "helping" Richard govern as increasingly unnecessary and irrelevant; and that the decision was driven as much by economic reasons (i.e., by the high wages paid to the councilors) as by an underlying unease at the incompatibility of an "artificially" constituted council with the free exercise of the royal will.[149] It also highlights the point that the abandonment of the councils did not mark any significant change in the underlying form of government, between a period in which the king did little and a period when the king suddenly found himself at the center of things. The ending of the continual councils indicated a reconfiguration of the framework of government, not a fundamental change in the extent of the authority which Richard was exercising.[150] As one recent commentator has pointed out, the very fact that the continual councils were abandoned must surely indicate that Richard had *already*, by 1380, proved his abilities and his willingness to "undertake at least some of the functions of an adult ruler."[151] Without a formally declared majority, however, the process by which Richard came to be seen, and came to see himself, as a fully functioning adult king could never be clear cut. In later years, as we have seen, this became a useful political weapon for the king's opponents to justify their impositions on Richard's authority, but in the comparatively benign years of the early 1380s this uncertainty fuelled a desire in contemporaries to place great store by events or episodes which *appeared* to show that Richard had at last matured sufficiently to be able to rule the kingdom effectively in his own right. For example, Richard's role in the Peasants' Revolt of 1381, in which he apparently met the rebels face-to-face, subdued them and then single-handedly led them away from London, became a major *cause célèbre* among the chroniclers of the day, Walsingham in particular seeking to contrast the decisive leadership of the king with the incompetence and cowardice of his useless courtiers.[152] This was the first time in the reign that contemporary writers had given Richard a real personality, with an important and positive influence on the events of the day. Richard's fourteenth birthday in January 1381, which marked a transition from *pueritia* to *adolescentia*—the point at which, according to canon law, a child entered adulthood—was a happy co-incidence which no doubt encouraged contemporary writers to emphasize Richard's part in dealing with the rebellion later in the Summer.[153] Richard's marriage to Anne of Bohemia in January 1382 was another clear "rite of passage" for the young king and was given great significance by the political community, though the failure of the union to produce offspring obviously greatly diminished its value for Richard as a way of shoring up political support.[154] Recent discussion has also argued that Richard himself sought to assert his adulthood in both symbolic and practical terms by consistently pressing parliament between 1381 and 1386 to fund royal expeditions to the continent.[155] The proposal was continually frustrated by the lack of adequate funding until, in 1385, Richard was able to lead an army in person to Scotland.

There are other signs that Richard was taking control of his destiny. In the past, great store was placed on the notable increase in the recorded use of the king's signet seal at the end of 1383 to authorize the dispatch of letters under the privy or Great Seals (see figure 3.4). The sudden prominence of the signet seal appeared to indicate that it was only now that Richard began taking on the responsibilities of government, and it also neatly fitted the idea that Richard was somehow predisposed to exercise his authority in a willful and "unconstitutional" way, because instructions sent to the chancellor on the authority of the signet seal avoided the safeguards provided by the privy seal office as intermediary between the king and chancery.[156] In its fundamentals, this interpretation can be dismissed, for the use of the signet seal almost certainly marked a change in bureaucratic procedure rather than a significant change in the level of Richard's participation in government. But as Saul has argued, for the change to have occurred in the first place, suggests a greater application of Richard to the government of his realm.[157] This was, in other words, the first sign that Richard was shaping government to suit his needs: it did not mark the invidious erosion of accountability in government, simply a more efficient and streamlined mechanism of conveying instructions from the king to his chancellor. It may also be significant that about this point petitions bearing the name of the king's chamberlains begin to appear in the archives. These were the supplications that had been presented to the king in his chamber and which, at least if later examples are any guide, were normally sent to the privy seal office to have a writ sent into chancery. The existence of these "chamberlain's bills" in files that had once pertained to chancery suggests that these endorsed bills, like the signet letters, were now being sent direct to the chancellor for action instead of via the privy seal. Again, we should not necessarily read anything sinister into this new procedure. They are, however, an excellent guide to show how much influence men such Simon Burley and Robert de Vere were having on the young king.[158]

Of all the incidents in these years that demonstrated Richard's desire to assert his independence from the supervision and close monitoring that had characterized his early years, it was the dismissal of his chancellor Richard le Scrope in July 1382 which is arguably the most illuminating. Scrope had made a stand over the king's apparently irresponsible distribution of the manors and lordships which pertained to the inheritance of the earldom of March.[159] According to Walsingham, who was writing some time after the event, Scrope "openly refused [these] requests, asserting that the king was weighed down by much debt from various quarters."[160] Scrope was said to have been motivated out of a concern to protect the royal patrimony from the youthful exuberance of the boy king: "he [Scrope] had no intention of issuing any confirmatory charters . . . made by the king, who had not yet passed his years of boyhood, lest, perhaps, he might himself suffer the king's ingratitude later on." Walsingham, never one to hold back on voicing his direct opinion, wholeheartedly agreed with the need for this action, stating that Richard "being but a boy, did not hesitate, and granted what they [the foreigners of the court] requested." The chronicler then went on to describe how, on hearing of his chancellor's obduracy, the king "who had only the wisdom of a boy . . . in a spirit of anger . . . sent men to demand the seal from [Scrope]," and moreover that, "nobody dared to say anything openly about the matter, for fear of incurring the ill-will of the king's attendants, and because of the unreasoning youthfulness of the king himself." This was the first time Walsingham was openly critical of the king, and the first time responsibility for failure was laid squarely on the king's own shoulders. We are left in doubt as to Walsingham's explanation for the crisis: in the space of two short paragraphs, he alluded to the king's immaturity—his "boyhood"—on no fewer than four occasions.

We may question how much embellishment Walsingham used in this account, but there is no disputing the fact that Scrope was peremptorily dismissed or that the chancellor's office remained vacant for over two months.[161] It is this dismissal, of course, which holds significance for the present discussion, but it is also worth remarking on the extraordinary actions of the chancellor who had categorically refused to carry out the wishes of his sovereign. This provides a very clear insight into prevailing attitudes toward Richard II even after the minority councils had been abandoned, and of the very real sense in which the king continued to be viewed as holding a position in the polity that permitted the sort of paternalistic restraint that Scrope appears to have tried to impose. Richard was old enough to be allowed *some* freedom in the way he governed and in the choice of personnel he surrounded himself with, but he had not yet achieved the stature and position that protected his decisions and actions from the harsh censure and opposition of his critics. Whether or not the chancellor was justified in making this stand, it is perfectly apparent how this attitude, and specifically Scrope's actions in the summer of 1382, would have infuriated the king and driven him to the outer limits of total frustration. His dismissal of Scrope was an extraordinarily bold act. It was the clearest assertion a king could make that government served his needs, and that crown officials were there to be appointed—or dismissed—as he saw fit. Richard was not going to let a major practical consideration in the effective running of government stand in the

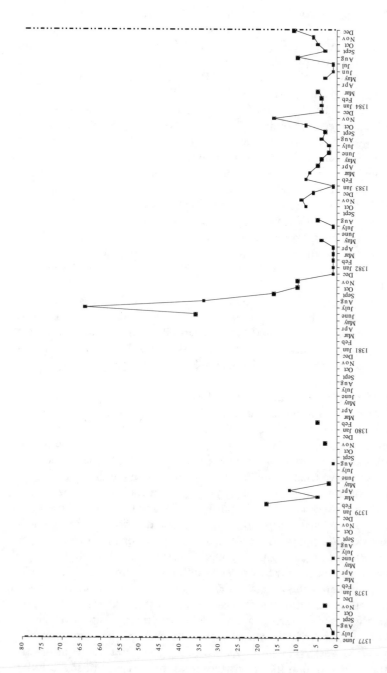

Figure 3.6 Letters Patent Warranted "By King," 1377–1384.

way of his desire to assert the principle that the chancery, and chancellor, should be instruments of his will. In terms of government, this act signified Richard's coming of age. The delay in finding an alternative to Scrope points to the fact that the decision to remove him had not been preplanned. Possibly it had not even been thought through, though it should be remembered that a recent precedent had been set just a year previously when the regime had coped without a chancellor for over eight weeks after the execution of Archbishop Sudbury at the height of the Peasants' Revolt. As in the summer of 1381, so too in the summer of 1382, government did not grind to a halt. This is demonstrated in figure 3.6 which shows the number of letters patent which were authorized by the king in person.[162] Indeed, it is evident from a strongly worded signet letter addressed to his treasurer, keeper of the privy seal and keeper of the chancery rolls that Richard was monitoring very closely what they were doing and had high expectations that in discharging their duties the king's interests above all else should be served. The letter, dated 26 August 1382, "expressed surprise that they who for a time have the keeping of the great seal have taken upon them to present John Scarle clerk of the chancery to the church of Newton Regis in Worcestershire, as if they had the power of the chancellor [whereas] the king has presented John Menhir chaplain of the household."[163] It went on to say that they "should make no presentation in future without the king's special command." This was the clearest statement yet of Richard's desire to exercise control over the distribution of patronage: if the chancellor were not available to do this for him, he would do the job himself. The episode shows very clearly the emerging personality of Richard II, as a strongly independent and authoritative young king.

CONCLUSION

The chapter has thus ended by providing a glimpse into the political turbulence of Richard's later years. The political community had been very anxious to see their king emerge from his youth—from his "unofficial" minority—and assume powers as a fully functioning adult king presiding over a peaceful and politically inclusive kingdom. Instead, what they got was a king who was headstrong and noncompliant, and who seemed to favor a small group of individuals who had no natural claim to be the king's foremost advisors and counselors. The problem was not that Richard was reluctant to take on the reins of government,[164] but that Richard was exercising his authority in a way that caused increasing disquiet among an important section of the political elite. The abandonment of the formal apparatus of "minority government" meant that power was more clearly and unambiguously focused on the person of the king and those whom he chose to surround himself with. It was perhaps only natural that Richard gravitated toward individuals such as Robert de Vere, earl of Oxford, Hugh, earl of Stafford, and Thomas Mowbray, earl of Nottingham, who were of his own generation or men such as Simon Burley or Michael de la Pole whose position in the polity was made primarily on the back of service to him rather than to his father or grandfather. Thus, almost as soon as the continual councils had been disbanded, the political community sought new ways of imposing checks and balances on the king's actions, as if the unofficial minority had been given a new lease of life to allow for the continuing deficiencies that the king was perceived to have. In the very parliament (November 1380) that appeared to signal the end of the period of caretaker government by discontinuing the continual councils, a new set of impositions were made on the king in the form of demands for a major enquiry "to survey and examine in all the courts and places of the king, both in his household as well as elsewhere, the state of the said household, and the expenses and receipts whatsoever incurred by any of his ministers."[165] The Commons also asked to have the five principal officers of state "elected and chosen" in parliament, and shortly after the assembly ended Sir John Cobham was appointed to oversee the workings of the household.[166] It was a pattern that was repeated the following year: several months after Richard had apparently led the kingdom from the brink of disaster by drawing the rebels of Essex away from London in June 1381, parliament demanded yet another household commission and imposed another two "guardians" on the king (the earl of Arundel and Michael de la Pole) to "accompany the person of the king, and belong to his household, to advise and govern his person, et cetera."[167] The fiction of Richard's adulthood had thus given way to the fiction of his youth, or at least an assertion that it was the king's youthful tendencies that disqualified him from taking on the full reins of government. We should remember that in France, throughout the 1380s, Charles VI—a king of comparable age to Richard II—was ruling with the aid of a much more formally constituted minority government, so the measures taken by parliament to rein Richard in during this decade may not have been regarded as unduly repressive or inappropriate, even if with hindsight they appear as such.[168]

Patronage, finance, and counsel were the issues that defined the conflicts of the late 1380s, but the origins of this conflict arguably lay in the first years of the reign when the political community had become conditioned into thinking that interference with, and management of, a king with adult status was a natural and acceptable state of affairs. The idea that the first years of Richard's reign created the conditions that would later lead to a catastrophic breakdown in political consensus is not, of course a new or obscure one, but whereas previous scholarship has tended to see this historical causation in terms of personalities—of the king, his advisors, and his opponents—this discussion points to failings of a more structural kind, in the way government was calibrated at the very outset of the reign. The underlying problem lay in the ambiguity attached to Richard's position, which generated a sense of uncertainty and suspicion, an absence of clear and decisive leadership, and a set of conflicting political imperatives. The situation is amply demonstrated by the contradictions inherent in the actions of the rebels in 1381. On the one hand, they self-consciously proclaimed their right to take up arms in the belief that Richard, as a young and innocent child, was defenseless against the machinations of his evil counselors; on the other hand, they looked to Richard—by seeking interviews and presenting petitions to him—to provide the leadership and direction necessary to resolve the kingdom's woes and save their own fortunes.[169] Richard was a child *or an adult* depending on particular political needs and circumstances. The political community was thus paralyzed in a state of uncertainty as to how to deal with the young king—power was given to him with one hand, in the belief that he was old enough to rule in his own right and that it was in the kingdom's best interests that he did so, only for it to be taken away by the other hand, in the belief that he was not quite competent enough to be trusted to exercise full and untrammeled authority, and that it was in the kingdom's best interests to impose safeguards to limit or monitor his exercise of power. The ambiguity surrounding Richard's status would have been increased by the fact that from the very start the king seems to have been exposed to the workings of government and may even have been directly and actively involved in discharging large volumes of government business in person. The matter of governing the realm had thus originally been conceived as a power-sharing exercise. With no formal end to this situation it was perhaps inevitable that Richard would never be allowed the breathing space to develop the political self-assurance and trust which were prerequisites to successful rule. Far from unifying the realm, Richard's acquisition of power exacerbated existing tensions and created new and deep-running fault lines within a political community that had become used to asserting a claim to active participation in politics and government.

It would be easy to judge these years harshly. If contemporaries believed that youth was inherently incompatible with successful kingship, because a boy king could not exercise "independent will," why did the political community not face the reality and formally install a minority government? In practical terms, at least, the answer may be found by questioning whether in fact there was any alternative system of government that was obviously better than the constitutional "fudge" of the early years of Richard II's reign. From 1380, Englishmen need only have looked across the channel to France to see how the appointment of a regent and a formal minority government created a whole set of different, and potentially far more divisive, political problems.[170] The constitutional settlement of October 1377 was built upon an impressive foundation of political unity because it was focused upon the person of the king; installation of a regency would have created clearer demarcation, in terms of delineating exactly where real authority lay, but it would have been far less effective in covering over political divisions, and dissent would consequently have been much more likely. This leads us to an important principle that informed political thinking at the time; namely, that there was no proper alternative to personal kingship, and that maintaining the façade of the king ruling in his own right was infinitely more attractive than an officially declared minority which had dubious claims to political legitimacy and representation. It is telling that there was no contemporary comment on the merits or otherwise of the decision to tackle Richard's youth in this way: the scant attention paid to government in the first years of the reign focused specifically on the performance and cost of the continual councils rather than on the more underlying issue of where power was or should be located.[171] It was universally accepted that all authority ought in theory, if not in practice, emanate from the king. Only the king could effectively represent and exercise the public authority with which his office was imbued. In itself, this approach to Richard's nonage was a success; the "minority" years were notable for the high level of "consensus politics" that was achieved. The difficultly lay in navigating a clear and acceptable path from this position, where a large measure of authority was exercised on Richard's behalf, to a position where Richard was exercising full authority in his own right, and in this respect the English polity singularly failed.

NOTES

1. I would like to express my gratitude to Alison McHardy for reading and commenting on an earlier draft of this chapter, and for generously allowing me to consult her sourcebook on the reign of Richard II ahead of publication (*The Reign of Richard II, 1377–1397: From Minority to Tyranny*, ed. A. K. McHardy (Manchester University Press, forthcoming).

2. *The St Albans Chronicle: The Chronica Maiora of Thomas Walsingham, I, 1376–1394*, ed. and trans. J. Taylor, W. R. Childs, and L. Watkiss (Oxford, 2003), 689–91. Walsingham was writing some time after the event, probably in the early 1390s, for which see ibid., xcvii–xcviii; and G. B. Stow, "Richard II in Thomas Walsingham's Chroniclers," *Speculum* 59 (1984): 68–102 (esp. 83–84).

3. For background, see *Victoria County History, Suffolk* (1975), 2:56–72 (esp. 64).

4. *St Albans Chronicle*, 691. Also cited in *Chronicle of Adam Usk, 1377–1421*, ed. and trans. C. Given-Wilson (Oxford, 1997), 7.

5. For the idea that Richard's youth informed much of the opposition to his rule, see A. Tuck, *Richard II and the English Nobility* (London, 1973), 89, 91; M. Bennett, *Richard II and the Revolution of 1399* (Stroud, 1999), 20–21, 197–98; C. M. Barron, "The Reign of Richard II," in *The New Cambridge Medieval History VI: 1300–c. 1415*, ed. M. Jones, 297–333 (Cambridge, 2000) (see esp. p. 311: "He behaved like a wayward teenager [in the 1380s] and was treated as such"); W. M. Ormrod, "Coming to Kingship: Boy Kings and the Passage to Power in Fourteenth-Century England," in *Rites of Passage: Cultures of Transition in the Fourteenth Century*, ed. N. F. McDonald and W. M. Ormrod, 47–48 (Woodbridge, 2004) and, most recently, C. Fletcher, "Manhood and Politics in the Reign of Richard II," *Past and Present* 189 (2005): 3–39 (esp. 31–39).

6. *The Westminster Chronicle 1381–1394*, ed. and trans. L. C. Hector and B. F. Harvey (Oxford, 1982), 229. The "heir" was possibly a reference to Thomas, duke of Gloucester who was believed to have had designs on the throne at this point. See N. Saul, *Richard II* (London and New Haven, 1997), 189–90.

7. *Westminster Chronicle*, 271; P[arliament] R[olls] O[f] M[edieval] E[ngland], ed. C. Given-Wilson, P. Brand, A. Curry, R. E. Horrox, G. Martin, W. M. Ormrod, and J.R.S. Phillips (Leicester, 2005), CD-version, parliament of 1388, part 3.

8. *PROME*, parliament of 1399, item 55.

9. See for example, Bennett, *Richard II*, 197.

10. *Chronicle of Adam Usk*, 7. Usk was a member of the committee that determined the grounds for Richard II's deposition and Henry's accession in September 1399.

11. See discussion by J. Watts, *Henry VI and the Politics of Kingship* (Cambridge, 1996), 27.

12. Printed in J. H. Harvey, "The Wilton Diptych: A Re-examination," *Archaeologia* 98 (1961): 1–28 (at 27–28). In another letter written at about the same time to the Byzantine emperor Manuel II, Richard declared how he thought that it was widely known "how some of our subject magnates and nobles, while we were yet of tender age and afterward also, have made many attempts on the prerogative and royal right of our regal state." See *English Historical Documents IV 1327–1485*, ed. A. R. Myers (London, 1969): 174–5.

13. A useful summary of the various interpretations of the king's youthful appearance in the Diptych is provided by D. Gordon, "The Wilton Diptych: An Introduction," in *The Regal Image of Richard II and the Wilton Diptych*, ed. D. Gordon, L. Monnas, and C. Elam, 20–22 (London, 1993). For important new light on the dating of the altarpiece, see S. Mitchell, "Richard II and the Broomcod Collar: New Evidence from the Issue Rolls," in *Fourteenth Century England II*, ed. C. Given-Wilson, 171–80 (esp. 179) (Woodbridge, 2002).

14. This was the phrase used by the Commons in 1377 to introduce the arrangements they proposed for the king's minority: *PROME*, parliament of October 1377, item 14.

15. See, for example, A. Steel, *Richard II* (Cambridge, 1941), 38–41, 174–75; V. H. Galbraith, "A New Life of Richard II," *History* 26 (1942): 223–39 (at 226) (Richard was "similar to the lonely boy at school . . . misunderstood by the masters [and] a misfit in his own class"); Saul, *Richard II* (the "effects of his upbringing are likely to have given him a powerful sense of uniqueness while leaving him inexperienced in the handling of relations with the great men of the realm."), 454; A. K. McHardy, "Richard II: A Personal Portrait," in *The Reign of Richard II*, ed. G. Dodd, 30 (Stroud, 2000) ("Richard's personality, and the problems which this caused, was formed in his childhood,"). And see most recently, A. Reitemeier, "Born to be a Tyrant? The Childhood and Education of Richard II," in *Fourteenth Century England*, ed. Given-Wilson, 147–58.

16. For a welcome note of caution, see G. B. Stow, "Stubbs, Steel, and Richard II as Insane: The Origin and Evolution of an English Historiographical Myth," *Proceedings of the American Philosophical Society* 143 (1999): 601–38. I have also benefited from reading an unpublished paper by Dr Brenda Carter, "Richard II on the Couch: History and Psychology."

17. See the recent discussion by W. M. Ormrod who argues that the commission of government set up in 1386, which accrued to itself all executive powers of the king, was justified in the eyes of the political community precisely because the king had not yet formally asserted his majority: "Coming to Kingship," 47–48.

18. *Westminster Chronicle*, 391–93.

19. J. B. Henneman, *Olivier de Clisson and Political Society in France under Charles V and Charles VI* (Penn., 1996), 129–30.

20. The declaration made by Richard to his council was followed by public declarations which did not couch his assertion of authority explicitly in terms of the attainment of majority rule, merely that "the king has taken upon his own person the governance of the realm, purposing to rule with deliberation of the council more prosperously than heretofore": *CCR, 1385–9,* 671.

21. See, for example, Saul, *Richard II,* chapter 3 entitled "Accession and Minority, 1377–81."

22. Steel, *Richard II,* 44.

23. See J. L. Watts, "When Did Henry VI's Minority End?," in *Trade, Devotion and Governance: Papers in Later Medieval History,* ed. D. J. Clayton, R. G. Davies, and P. McNiven, 116–39 (Stroud, 1994).

24. See Tuck, *Richard II,* 33.

25. On the Good Parliament, see G. Holmes, *The Good Parliament* (Oxford, 1975); G. Dodd, "A Parliament Full of Rats? *Piers Plowman* and the Good Parliament of 1376," *Historical Research* 79 (2006): 21–49 (esp. 27–30). On his treatment of London, see R. Bird, *The Turbulent London of Richard II* (1949), chaps 1–2; P. Nightingale, "Capitalists, Crafts and Constitutional Change in Late 14th-Century London," *Past and Present* 124 (1989): 3–35, esp. 5–24.

26. J. Dahmus, *William Courtenay, Archbishop of Canterbury 1381–1396* (Penn., 1966), chaps 3 and 4; A. Goodman, *John of Gaunt: The Exercise of Princely Power in Fourteenth-Century Europe* (Harlow, 1992), 241–44.

27. *PROME,* parliament of 1376, item 10. The names of the councilors are recorded in *The Anonimalle Chronicle 1333 to 1381,* ed. V. H. Galbraith (Manchester, 1927), 91.

28. Holmes, *Good Parliament,* 105, 158–59. The council lasted for about three months, between July and October 1376.

29. Tuck, *Richard II,* 36–37; Saul, *Richard II,* 28–31, and for one of the first expressions of this approach to the councils, see T. F. Tout, *Chapters in the Administrative History of Medieval England,* 6 vols. (Manchester, 1920–33), 3:324.

30. G. Holmes, "Latimer, William, Fourth Baron Latimer (1330–1381)," *Oxford Dictionary of National Biography* (Oxford, 2004), Online version.

31. W. M. Ormrod, "Knyvet, Sir John (*d.* 1381)," *Oxford Dictionary of National Biography* (Oxford, 2004), Online version. There is some uncertainty attached to his role on the council because no records exist of the payment of his wages. However, it is most likely that his remuneration was considered to be covered by the annuity of 200 marks granted to him in January 1377: Lewis, "Continual Council," 248.

32. P. Partner, "Wykeham, William (*c.*1324–1404)," *Oxford Dictionary of National Biography* (Oxford, 2004), Online version.

33. Saul, *Richard II,* 31–34.

34. R. Allen, "Cobham, John, third Baron Cobham of Cobham (*c.*1320–1408)," *Oxford Dictionary of National Biography* (Oxford, 2004), Online version.

35. R. Barber, *Edward, Prince of Wales and Aquitaine: A Biography of the Black Prince* (London, 1978), 50, 76, 153.
36. D. S. Green, "The Household and Military Retinue of Edward the Black Prince," Unpublished PhD Thesis, University of Nottingham, 2 vols. (1998), 1:58–59.
37. Ibid., 65.
38. Cf. C. J. Rogers, *The Wars of Edward III: Sources and Interpretations* (Woodbridge, 1999), 198–99.
39. In October 1365, Hales had participated as a knight of St John in the crusade of Pierre I of Cyprus to capture Alexandria: J. Sarnowsky, "Hales, Sir Robert (*d.* 1381)," *Oxford Dictionary of National Biography* (Oxford, 2004), Online version.
40. R. K. Rose, "Appleby, Thomas (*d.* 1395)," *Oxford Dictionary of National Biography* (Oxford, 2004), Online version.
41. For background, see A. J. MacDonald, *Border Bloodshed: Scotland and England at War 1369–1403* (East Lothian, 2000), 45–51.
42. *PROME,* parliament of October 1377, item 18.
43. For discussion, see G. Dodd, "Henry IV's Council, 1399–1405," in *Henry IV: The Establishment of the Regime, 1399–1406,* ed. G. Dodd and D. Biggs, 95–115, esp. 96, 102–3 (Woodbridge, 2003).
44. A point most effectively illustrated in the discussion of J. A. Tuck on the powers exercised by the treasurer: "Richard II's System of Patronage," in *The Reign of Richard II: Essays in Honour of May McKisack,* ed. F.R.H. Du Boulay and C. M. Barron, 1–20 (London, 1971).
45. These individuals normally formed the core of the administrative council when it met. In Henry IV's reign it was not unusual for the council to comprise just these officers and one or two of the king's advisors: Dodd, "Henry IV's Council," 105.
46. For example, see *PROME,* parliament of October 1377, item 22.
47. Saul, *Richard II,* 45.
48. *PROME,* parliament of October 1377, item 19.
49. Ibid., item 26.
50. For a useful discussion of the Great Council in the reign of Richard II, see A. L. Brown, *The Governance of Late Medieval England, 1272–1461* (London, 1989), 175; and A. Goodman, "Richard II's Councils," in *Richard II: The Art of Kingship,* ed. A. Goodman and J. L. Gillespie, 59–82 (esp. 76–82) (Oxford, 1999).
51. The existence of these warranty notes was recorded by Tout, *Administrative History,* 3:336, note 5. Tout points out that, "after the close of the parliament of 1377, there was, for some thirteen months, an almost constant stream of warranties by great council recorded both in the patent and close rolls," and more recently Saul, drawing on Tout's work, has suggested that "in 1379 meetings of the [Great Council] were held every few weeks" (*Richard II,* 46). Caution should be exercised before linking warranty notes with meetings of the Great Council: there could often be a period of some delay before chancery letters were

issued as a result of authorization by the Great Council so that a spread of warranty notes over an extended period of time may not in fact indicate the semi-continuous existence of this body.

52. For brief discussion, see C. Given-Wilson, *The Royal Household and the King's Affinity: Service, Politics and Finance in England, 1360–1413* (1986, New Haven and London), 213.
53. All these grants are in *CPR, 1377–1381*, 136.
54. The National Archives (TNA), C 81/1539/1.
55. TNA, C 81/1539/2.
56. TNA, C 81/1539/4. The other days for which lists survive are: 19 March (TNA, C 81/1539/3a), 26 March (TNA, C 81/1539/7); 10 May (TNA, C 81/1539/11); 30 May (TNA, C 81/1539/12); 9 June (TNA, C 81/1539/9a); 18 June (TNA, C 81/1539/9b).
57. Saul, *Richard II*, 28–29, 31.
58. *Westminster Chronicle*, 18–21.
59. *St Albans Chronicle*, 245.
60. Tuck, *Richard II*, 36.
61. *PROME*, parliament of 1379, item 5.
62. Commissions of array, "to resist hostile invasion and the destruction of the English tongue" were issued for Northumberland, Westmorland, Yorkshire; and commissions to "guard the shores of the sea" and to "array and equip [men] with arms" were issued in Devon, Kent, Norfolk, Suffolk, Surrey, and Sussex: *CPR, 1377–1381*, 359–60.
63. See below, pp. 125–6.
64. Possibly the closest we come to identifying the sorts of people who are likely to have attended such meetings lies in a petition presented by the "Commons of London" in December 1376 in which the names of those attending a meeting of the Great Council, in the "White Chamber near the Painted Chamber" of Westminster Palace, were provided in the endorsement. The individuals were John of Gaunt; the archbishops of Canterbury and York; the bishops of London, Durham, Lincoln, Bath and Wells, Worcester, Salisbury, and Norwich; the earls of March, Warwick, Stafford, Suffolk, and Salisbury; Lords Percy (later to become earl of Northumberland), Neville, Latimer, Basset of Drayton, Fitz Walter; and the chancellor, treasurer, keeper of the privy seal, and others. For this and another related petition see TNA, SC 8/59/2909 & 2908; see also *CPR, 1374–1377*, 387, 389.
65. *PROME*, parliament of 1379, item 5.
66. *CPR, 1377–1381*, 635–38.
67. TNA, SC 8/173/8639, 173/8632.
68. See G. L. Harriss, *King, Parliament and Public Finance in Medieval England to 1369* (Oxford, 1975), 509–17; ibid, "War and the Emergence of the English Parliament, 1297–1360," *Journal of Medieval History* 2 (1976): 35–56.
69. For an overview of the Good Parliament, see Holmes, *Good Parliament*, and Dodd, "A Parliament full of rats?"

70. *PROME,* parliament of 1378, item 23.
71. *PROME,* parliament of October 1377, items 18–20.
72. Ibid., item 17.
73. See E. H. Kantorowicz, *The King's Two Bodies: A Study in Mediaeval Political Theology* (Princeton, NJ, 1957), chaps 3–5; and Watts, *Henry VI,* 22–23.
74. "[T]he Crown, being something that concerned all, was not a private but a public inheritance," Kantorowicz, *King's Two Bodies,* 373.
75. *PROME,* parliament of October 1377, item 20.
76. Grants of taxation could only be demanded by the crown if a state of urgent necessity could be shown to exist, and specifically (but not exclusively) if the funds were required for the defense of the realm. The conditional nature of such grants inevitably exposed the crown's subsequent expenditure of this money to public scrutiny. On the principle of necessity, see Harriss, *King, Parliament and Public Finance,* 33–39; M. Prestwich, *English Politics in the Thirteenth Century* (Basingstoke, 1990), 114–17.
77. *PROME,* parliament of October 1377, item 27.
78. *PROME,* parliament of 1379, item 12.
79. *PROME,* parliament of October 1377, item 50.
80. The Commons included the chief justices of both benches, the chief baron of the exchequer, the treasurer of the household, the clerk of the privy seal, and the chief keepers of the forests in their list of officers to be appointed "by parliament." The crown agreed to have only the continual councilors, the chancellor, treasurer, steward of the household and chamberlain nominated by the Lords in the assembly, and it did not explicitly agree to have those appointments made outside parliamentary time ratified within the assembly.
81. For discussion, see G. Dodd, *Justice and Grace: Private Petitioning and the English Parliament in the Late Middle Ages* (Oxford, 2007), 166–71.
82. *PROME,* parliament of October 1377, item 26.
83. *PROME,* parliament of October 1377, item 56. The regard given to the acts of the Good Parliament was no doubt due to the high level of continuity of personnel between the two assemblies, and above all to the reappointment of Sir Peter de la Mare as Speaker in October 1377. For the re-election of MPs see, N. B. Lewis, "Re-election to Parliament in the Reign of Richard II," *EHR* 48 (1933): 364–94.
84. G. Dodd, "The Lords, Taxation and the Community of Parliament in the 1370s and 1380s," *Parliamentary History* 20 (2001): 287–310 (esp. 303–4).
85. An indication of the prevailing sense of national vulnerability is provided by a letter sent in February 1379 by Henry Wakefield, bishop of Worcester to the archdeacon of Gloucester requiring prayers for the king and realm because "the country is surrounded by such terrible enemies that human power is lessened and it is right to ask God's help that

the kingdom may be brought by laudable triumph . . . to tranquil and happy times, and that the enemy shall not succeed, nor shall the small plant from the royal stem lose his inheritance": *A Calendar of the Register of Henry Wakefield, Bishop of Worcester 1375–1395*, ed. W. P. Marett (Leeds, 1972), 152. For a broader context to these prayers, see A. K. McHardy, "The English Clergy and the Hundred Years War," *Studies in Church History* 20 (1983): 171–78.

86. *PROME*, parliament of October 1377, item 48. The poor financial standing of Woodstock is discussed by Tuck, *Richard II*, 45–46 and A. Goodman, *The Loyal Conspiracy: The Lords Appellant under Richard II* (London, 1971), 87–94.

87. On Woodstock, see Dodd, "Lords, Taxation and Community of Parliament," 301–2. For petitions from other lords, see TNA, SC 8/125/6231 (1380, Edmund Mortimer, earl of March); 125/6220 (1380, John Mowbray, earl of Nottingham); 109/5416 (1381, Thomas Arundel, bishop of Ely); 107/5317 (1377–81, Thomas Hatfield, bishop of Durham). On Gaunt's debts, see A. Goodman, "John of Gaunt," in *England in the Fourteenth Century: Proceedings of the 1985 Harlaxton Symposium*, ed. W. M. Ormrod, 67–87 (esp. 80–81) (Woodbridge, 1984).

88. See *CPR, 1377–1381*, 635–38.

89. Ibid., 340. London was singled out by Richard le Scrope in his opening address to the 1379 parliament when he reported that the king had pawned the crown jewels as a guarantee against the loans: *PROME*, parliament of 1379, item 5.

90. A common petition presented in 1379 complained that "various letters of credence under the privy seal were sent to various parts of the realm by certain knights and squires of the king's court, to request loans of silver for the king's use; which letters had blank seal-strips, and the said creditors of their own authority wrote the names of many persons on the seal-strips of the aforesaid letters, and delivered the letters to them, affirming that the king had sent them to them, and they demanded from them sums as great as they wished, and those who excused themselves from paying such sums they fiercely threatened on behalf of the king": *PROME*, parliament of 1379, item 30. The king's subjects were expected to provide interest free loans to the crown at times of great necessity, but the obligation was qualified by an understanding that the recipients of such requests could set the amount to be loaned themselves and they could excuse themselves on the grounds of poverty. For background, see G. L. Harriss, "Aids, Loans and Benevolences," *The Historical Journal* 6 (1963): 1–19, esp. 6, 12–17.

91. Watts, *Henry VI*, 21–31.

92. *PROME*, parliament of October 1377, item 14. For the rumors, see *St Albans Chronicle*, 99; and *Anonimalle Chronicle*, 104.

93. See discussion below, pp. 138–39.

94. See Saul, *Richard II*, 36–38.

95. The pair presented a joint petition in the parliament of October 1377 asking that four bishops, four earls, four barons, and four knights of the council be assigned to hear their right and their evidence "so that they can come to a suitable decision on the supplicants." The petition appears not to have been answered: TNA, SC 8/18/895.

96. *St Albans Chronicle*, 245.

97. Ibid.

98. R. H. Jones, *The Royal Policy of Richard II: Absolutism in the Later Middle Ages* (Oxford, 1968), 10–11; Steel, *Richard II*, 44; Saul, *Richard II*, 28; Goodman, *John of Gaunt*, 71.

99. *St Albans Chronicle*, 157.

100. Goodman, *John of Gaunt*, 15–17; *St Albans Chronicle*, lii-liii, lxxiii, lxxvi-lxxix.

101. N. H. Nicolas, ed., *Proceedings and Ordinances of the Privy Council of England*, 7 vols. (London, 1834–37), 3:234.

102. For the problems which could confront a regency government see D. A. Carpenter, *The Minority of Henry III* (London, 1990), esp. 53–54. Note Walsingham's comment that Gaunt's decision to "retire" from the court in 1377 was informed by his fear that "if anything bad happened to the king or the realm he would be blamed, and would receive little or no thanks for the good things he had done," *St Albans Chronicle*, 157.

103. For a similar dilemma faced by the political community in discerning (and checking) the influence of Humphrey, duke of Gloucester, on the young Henry VI in the 1430s, see Watts, *Henry VI*, 117–20, 155–58.

104. *PROME*, parliament of 1379, item 5.

105. Goodman, "John of Gaunt," 84.

106. Jones, *Royal Policy of Richard II*, 10.

107. An interesting parallel can be made with the circumstances of 1422 when Humphrey, duke of Gloucester, searched in vain to show that Gaunt had been made "governor of the realm" to substantiate his own claims to the title. All that could be found, however, was that "my lord of Lancastre hadde no such name of gouernor but oonly hadde his bretheren my lord of York and Gloucestre associed to hym for to surveye and correcte the defautes of them that were appointed for to be of the kingis counseil." See S. B. Chrimes, "The Pretensions of the duke of Gloucester in 1422," *EHR* 45 (1930): 101–3.

108. Cf. Tuck, *Richard II*, 40, note 5.

109. *The* Chronica Maiora *of Thomas Walsingham, 1376–1422*, trans. D. Preest and ed. J. G. Clark (Woodbridge, 2005), 63.

110. *PROME*, parliament of 1377, item 14.

111. *St Albans Chronicle*, 68–71. On the numbers of "Lancastrians" in parliament, see J. Wedgwood, "John of Gaunt and the Packing of Parliament," *EHR* 45 (1930): 623–25; S. Walker, *The Lancastrian Affinity 1361–1399* (Oxford, 1990), 239.

112. For the unhappy relationship between London and Gaunt, see Bird, *Turbulent London*, esp. 23–28.
113. *PROME*, parliament of 1377, item 23.
114. Watts, *Henry VI*, 21–31.
115. TNA, SC 8/84/4194; 85/4221; 93/4628; 102/5085; 103/5108; 103/5111; 104/5168; 146/7269/ 147/7347.
116. The importance of Scrope to the government of Richard's early years and his close ties to Gaunt have been stressed by Saul, *Richard II*, 50–51.
117. For the life and career of this war veteran see J. Sumption, "Angle, Guichard (IV) d', earl of Huntingdon (*c*.1308x15–1380)," *Oxford Dictionary of National Biography* (Oxford, 2004), Online version. Neither Saul nor Tuck ascribe any importance to d'Angle's position in the household, though it is possible that his presence there—and his absence from 1380, after his death—were important factors in shaping the political environment for the king in his early years of rule.
118. Cf. Goodman, *John of Gaunt*, 71. Such was the influence of Gaunt that as late as August 1384 the king's ability to reach a judgment on disturbances in London without the presence of his uncle was brought into question by the defendant in the case, John of Northampton, who is reported to have remarked, "I hope, my lord king, that you do not mean to proceed to judgment or to exercise jurisdiction in the absence of your uncle the duke of Lancaster." Needless to say Northampton's impertinence did not help his cause: he was promptly sentenced to a traitor's death by the king, only to be spared through the intercession of Queen Anne. See *Westminster Chronicle*, 93.
119. See, for example, Saul's comment that "it may only have been from late 1383 . . . that Richard involved himself in routine matters of government," *Richard II*, 110.
120. See, for example, Steel, *Richard II*, 44: "The king himself was, of course, too young to affect politics directly for at least four years to come [from his accession]."
121. *St Albans Chronicle*, 152–53; *Westminster Chronicle*, 414–17.
122. *PROME*, parliament of October 1377, item 26.
123. For an overview of the warranty note, see A. L. Brown, "The Authorization of Letters Under the Great Seal," *Bulletin of the Institute of Historical Research* 37 (1964): 125–56.
124. Saul, *Richard II*, 109.
125. *CPR, 1377–1380*, 6.
126. Ibid., 9.
127. Ibid., 12.
128. I.e. "per ipsum regem et consilium," or "per ipsum regem et magnum consilium."
129. For example, see *CPR, 1377–1380*, 102: confirmation of letters patent dated 12 February 1374 providing John de Surray with an annuity of £100 for life out of the farm of the city of London (warranted "by king and council").

156   Gwilym Dodd

130. Brown, "Authorization of Letters," 131–40. For further background, see J. F. Baldwin, *The King's Council in England During the Middle Ages* (Oxford, 1913), 257; B. Wilkinson, "The Chancery," in *The English Government at Work, 1327–1336*, 3 vols, ed. J. F. Willard and W. A. Morris, 3:179–83 (Cambridge, MA, 1930–40); W. M. Ormrod, "The Origins of the *Sub Pena* Writ," *Historical Research* 61 (1988): 11–20.

131. For Richard's itinerary, see Saul, *Richard II*, Appendix.

132. For further discussion on the administrative processes that lay behind the distribution of royal patronage, see G. Dodd, "Patronage, Petitions and Grace: the "Chamberlains' Bills" of Henry IV's Reign," in *The Reign of Henry IV: Rebellion and Survival, 1403–1413*, ed. G. Dodd and D. Biggs, 105–35 (Woodbridge, 2008).

133. The following references, dating to 1377, are in *CPR, 1377–1380*: July 20—Kennington Manor (p. 11); August 2—Windsor Castle (p. 14); August 19—Berkhamsted (p. 18); September 21—Bushey Manor (p. 21); October 28—Shene (p. 34); November 11—Shene (p. 58).

134. TNA, SC 8/103/5134.

135. TNA, SC 8/184/9180.

136. TNA, SC 8/215/10731 (ca. 1377–1378).

137. TNA, SC 8/18/891. The bill was also endorsed with the name of Simon Burley, the king's tutor and vice-chamberlain, a sure sign that it had initially been considered in the king's chamber; see Dodd, "Patronage, Petitions and Grace."

138. E.g. TNA, SC 8/18/891 (1378); 126/6252 (1377); 184/9180 (1377).

139. TNA, SC 8/18/883 (1377).

140. TNA, SC 8/19/908.

141. C. Given-Wilson, "Richard II and his Grandfather's Will," *EHR* 93 (1978): 320–37.

142. *PROME*, parliament of 1379, item 26 (the bill of 1378 was recorded in the parliament roll of 1379). Note Given-Wilson's view that Richard was as much responsible for the controversy surrounding Edward III's will as were his favorites, and especially Simon Burley: "Richard II and Grandfather's Will," 334.

143. Saul, *Richard II*, 28–29.

144. Tuck, *Richard II*, 42–43, 48–49.

145. Given-Wilson, *Royal Household and the King's Affinity*, 161–62.

146. *St. Albans Chronicle*, 93; Saul, *Richard II*, 51. See CPR, *1381–85*, 107 and 301 (14 March 1382 and 2 August 1383) for grants to Burley in recompense for the labor and expense he had gone to in bringing Anne from Germany.

147. For a recent discussion, see W. M. Ormrod, "In Bed with Joan of Kent: The King's Mother and the Peasants' Revolt," in *Medieval Women: Texts and Contexts in Late Medieval Britain: Essays for Felicity Riddy*, ed. J. Wogan-Browne, R. Voaden, A. Diamond, A. Hutchison, C. Meale, and L. Johnson, 277–92, esp. 279 (Turnhout, 2000).

148. TNA, SC 8/209/10448.
149. Cf. Comment by Walsingham, that the continual councils "drew from the king's treasury throughout the year a large sum of money, but achieved nothing or very little that was of benefit"; *St Albans Chronicle*, 345. Note also how the size of the continual councils diminished between 1377 and 1380, from twelve to eight individuals (see table on p. 112). For the constitutional problems caused by such councils, see Watts, "When did Henry VI's Minority End?" 119, and *Henry VI*, 85–86.
150. Note, however, that petitions addressed only to the council very quickly disappeared after 1380. Examples include, TNA SC 8/88/4394; 115/5722; 116/5774; 129/6449; 141/7046; 158/7865; 159/7941; 160/7982; 164/8164; 165/8243; 166/8273; 168/8398; 170/8490; 172/8587; 207/10324; 209/10409; 212/10591, 10593; 213/10619, 10647; 215/10715, 10750; 216/10770, 10771; 258/12867; 267/13301.
151. Ormrod, "Coming to Kingship," 35.
152. For a summary, see Saul, *Richard II*, 72; W. M. Ormrod, "The Peasants' Revolt and the Government of England," *Journal of British Studies* 29 (1990): 1–30, 20–21. Walsingham expressed dismay that not one of the royal knights or esquires who witnessed the humiliation of the Queen Mother in the Tower of London challenged "a single one of such disgraceful acts," whereas he attributed to Richard "a resourcefulness and courage beyond his years"; *St Albans Chronicle*, 425 and 439 (for discussion, see Ormrod, "In Bed with Joan of Kent," 285–87). The *Westminster Chronicle* (p. 9) described how "counsel perished from the wise" at the height of the rebellion, and how London "was without a clear view of what was to be done." Richard is then portrayed as an active and clear-headed leader boldly declaring to the rebels "I am your king, your leader, your captain. Those among you who support me are to go out at once into the open country" (11–13).
153. N. Orme, *From Childhood to Chivalry: The Education of the English Kings and Aristocracy, 1066–1530* (London, 1984), 5–6.
154. For discussion, see Ormrod, "Coming to Kingship," 38–39.
155. Fletcher, "Manhood and Politics," 31–39. However, Fletcher's contention that Richard's failure to campaign in person on the continent was above all due to restrictions placed on him by a political community reluctant to grant taxation is difficult to reconcile with the account in the *Westminster Chronicle* of a council meeting held early in 1385 which saw a serious altercation between Gaunt and the other councilors on exactly this topic. Gaunt strongly advocated a French campaign with the king at its head, but he was opposed by all the other councilors apart from his brothers. According to the chronicle, it was as a result of this disagreement that a plot was hatched to murder the duke. From this episode, at least, it is quite plain that the reluctance to see the king personally lead an expedition to France emanated from within the court, as

it was said that both the king and the "whole council" felt great displeasure at Gaunt's declaration that he would not assist Richard unless the latter meant to cross the channel: *Westminster Chronicle*, 110–13. Richard's reluctance to venture north of the Forth during his Scottish campaign later in the year, in the face of intense pressure from Gaunt, is similarly difficult to reconcile with the idea of a young king desperately keen to prove himself in battle: *St Albans Chronicle*, 762–73.

156. The use of the signet seal became a "political" matter later in the 1380s when the council installed by the Wonderful Parliament of 1386 sought ways of restricting Richard's initiative in government by having royal instructions to the chancellor directed via the privy seal office: Tuck, *Richard II*, 70; W. M. Ormrod, "Government by Commission: the Continual Council of 1386 and English Royal Administration," *Peritia* 10 (1996): 303–21, esp. 317–18.

157. Saul, *Richard II*, 110. I agree with Saul that too much "politics" can be read into the use of the signet seal, but the argument that its use was specifically the result of a new policy initiated by John Bacon, royal secretary, is less easy to sustain in light of the fact that his appointment occurred a full year before the signet seal came into use. I also disagree that the routine nature of the correspondence authorized by the signet seal meant that "it could hardly have arisen directly from the exercise of the king's will": Much of what kings did was, in fact, mundane and routine.

158. For the petitions "signed off" by Burley, see TNA, SC 8/18/891 (1378); 115/5709 (1384); 222/11083 (1377–87), 11097 (1384), 11099 (1382); 223/11139 (1383); 224/11154 (c. 1384), 11155 (c. 1382); 226/11268 (? C. 1384), 11269 (c. 1380- c. 1386), 11271 (1380); 236/11791 (1377–1383), 11793 (1379). For the petitions with de Vere's named recorded, see TNA, SC 8/223/11102 (c. 1381), 11135 (1380); 224/11168 (c. 1383).

159. For background, see Tuck, *Richard II*, 87–89.

160. *St Albans Chronicle*, 620–23.

161. See *CCR, 1381–1385*, 214–15.

162. In 1381, the Great Seal was placed in the household and traveled around with the king, hence the large number of direct warrants *per ipsum regem* ("by the king himself") shown in Figure 6 (for discussion, see W. M. Ormrod, "The Peasants' Revolt and the Government of England," *Journal of British Studies* 29 (1990): 1–30, esp. 21–22). In 1382, the Great Seal remained at Westminster, in the custody of the keeper of the privy seal and keeper of the chancery rolls, and was therefore used very much as it had been in more conventional times when the chancellor was in office.

163. *CCR, 1381–1385*, 214.

164. A view held by Barron, "Reign of Richard II," 302, 308.

165. *PROME*, parliament of January 1380, items 13–15.

166. Tuck, *Richard II*, 44.

167. *PROME,* parliament of 1381, item 38.

168. Charles VI was eleven years and nine months when he succeeded to the throne on 16 September 1380; Richard II was ten years and six months when he acceded on 21 June 1377. For background on Charles VI, see F. Autrand, *Charles VI: La Folie du roi* (Paris, 1986), 13–14, 19–21; Henneman, *Olivier de Clisson,* 103–19.

169. For example, note the *Anonimalle Chronicle's* account of the communication between the king and rebels in which the latter "sent replies [to Richard] by the said messengers that they had risen to save him and to destroy traitors to him and the kingdom"; cf. *The Peasants' Revolt of 1381,* ed. R. B. Dobson, 2nd edn. (London, 1983), 129.

170. Louis of Anjou, the oldest of the late king's brothers, was installed as regent, but political rivalries between him and the other royal uncles, together with widespread social revolt, very soon necessitated a modification to this arrangement so that authority was shared out on a more consensual basis throughout the 1380s: See R. Vaughan, *Philip the Bold: The Formation of the Burgundian State* (London, 1962), 39–42; Autrand, *Charles VI,* chap. 5; Henneman, *Olivier de Clisson,* 103–19.

171. *St Albans Chronicle,* 344–45.

CHAPTER 4

THE MINORITY OF HENRY VI, KING OF ENGLAND AND OF FRANCE

R. A. Griffiths

A king's minority is the antithesis of personal kingship. By a considerable margin, Henry VI is the youngest monarch ever to mount the English or British throne. Born at Windsor castle on 6 December 1421, there was no time in his conscious early life when he was not king of England, for Henry was hardly nine months old when his father, the lionized Henry V, died on campaign near Paris in the early hours of 31 August 1422, aged thirty-four. The child's subsequent minority accordingly lasted longer than that of all other young English kings. In addition, Henry VI became king during an intensive war whose ultimate aim was to substitute the English for the Valois monarch in France, thereby creating what became known as a "dual monarchy" of unprecedented ambition. In quite exceptional circumstances, therefore, Henry of Windsor undertook extraordinary responsibilities and obligations that in practice others would have to discharge for him for at least a decade and a half. The arrangements that were accordingly made in the autumn of 1422 had personal, political, and constitutional implications for England's kingship that were unique and arguably more significant than those arising from other royal minorities.

This chapter examines, first, the nature and effectiveness of those arrangements, which were devised in the expectation that the baby would survive into adulthood; second, the features of Henry's upbringing and early experience that prepared him, adequately or otherwise, for active kingship; third, the delicate matter of how the king's minority was brought to an end; and from time to time it notes the value of precedent and memory in comparing Henry VI's minority with the minorities of other young English kings. Together, these issues cast light on how the medieval English monarchy came to terms with Henry's[1] minority in order to sustain stable government in England and its dependent dominions, pursue ambitious claims and expensive war in France, and involve the social elite in the weighty responsibilities of ruling. Several substantial studies in recent years have illuminated relevant aspects of Henry VI's reign and minority: the king's biography from birth to death (and beyond); the political and governmental conventions of the age; the practical exercise of the king's authority by both Henry and others in his stead; the political and social worlds of the English shires and regions, and the dominions beyond the realm; and, in a few cases like that of the king's greatuncle, Henry Beaufort, the lives of some of the most influential figures.

In a codicil that he added to his last will just four days before he died, Henry V referred to his baby son as prince of Wales, an act calculated to remove any doubt that the dying king regarded his only child, whom he had never seen, as heir to the crown of England.[2] The title and status of prince of Wales had been inseparable from acknowledgement of the right to succeed to the English throne since 1301, when Edward I granted his Welsh territories to his eldest son, Edward of Caernarfon (later Edward II), "and his heirs kings of England in perpetuity" and styled him prince of Wales; the younger Edward was sixteen years old.[3] It is likely that the political discord and, then, the civil war of Edward II's later years allowed no opportunity for him to make his elder son, also called Edward, prince of Wales before the king was deposed in 1327 and the fourteen-year-old boy was acknowledged as king in his stead. Edward III, however, did create his eldest son and heir (later known as Edward the Black Prince) as prince of Wales in 1343, when the boy was barely thirteen years of age. Henry V could doubtless recall his own investiture as prince in October 1399, also at the age of thirteen, as well as the formal declarations that his father made in parliament in 1404 and 1406 to ensure that the crown should descend to Prince Henry and his heirs before any other members of the usurping Lancastrian family.[4] In each of these cases, the new prince of Wales was well on the way to adulthood. But on 1 September 1422, when Henry V's only son and heir was less than one year old, the situation was somewhat more precarious. During the previous week, as King Henry lay dying, his mind may have turned to another princely precedent, that of 1376. When the Black Prince died before his father, leaving a nine-year-old son, Richard, as heir to the throne, the elderly Edward III was prevailed upon to declare his grandson prince of Wales in order to remove any lingering uncertainty about the succession. Although there is no sign in 1422 that anyone other than the baby Henry was considered to be the most appropriate and rightful successor to Henry V, the dying king may have wished to reinforce this assumption by styling his son prince of Wales and recording the act in one of the codicils appended to his last will. There was certainly no time or opportunity for a formal and public investiture as in the past, but, as was made clear to parliament on Edward III's behalf in 1376, the making of a prince of Wales was the king's prerogative alone.[5] The creation of princes of Wales in the later Middle Ages was akin to, and replaced, the ceremonious procedure whereby twelfth-century English kings (and dukes of Normandy before that) had designated during their lifetime who their successors should be. Yet never had a designated heir been as young as was Henry of Windsor in 1422.[6]

On 21 October, less than two months after his accession to the English throne, Henry VI succeeded his maternal grandfather as king of France according to the terms of the treaty which Henry V had imposed on King Charles VI at Troyes in order that Henry himself should become the French king after Charles's death. Henry V had not bargained for "the Grim Reaper" for he died seven weeks before the fifty-three-year-old Charles. In May 1420, the treaty of Troyes had settled the crown of France, in the event of Charles's death, on Henry V "and our heirs for evermore," and soon afterward the English king married Charles's daughter Katherine of Valois. Henry's last codicils implicitly acknowledged that the couple's baby son would shortly succeed Charles VI, whose own son, the dauphin, was consequently disinherited.[7] In 1422, therefore, the awesome inheritance of the crowns of both England and France fell into a baby's cradle. Henry of Windsor was to be a child-king for the next fifteen years, the longest period of royal minority in English and British history.

There had been no child-monarch in England between the Norman Conquest and King John's death in 1216; but between 1216 and 1553 there were six of them. That may be taken to indicate that succession to the throne in the senior male line became established and was generally accepted. However, in each of the six cases the period of minority was bound to produce some uncertainties and potential instabilities in a polity in which the king ruled as well as reigned; at the same time, each period of minority rule provided some reference points for the future. These six minorities also contributed to certain constitutional and institutional changes in English governance. In 1216, there was no plausible or acceptable alternative to King John's only son, Henry (who was nine years old), even though England was in the throes of a civil war and a French army under a French prince was in the kingdom. There were no surviving children of either Henry II or Richard the Lion-heart available to claim the crown or the oversight of young Henry, while Louis, the eldest son of the French king, had the support of only part of the baronage. In recognition of his royal blood and *faut de mieux*, the nine-year-old Henry III was crowned within ten days of his father's death.[8] In 1327, the imperative was continuity at the perilous moment of Edward II's abdication and deposition; his fourteen-year-old elder son was immediately crowned as Edward III. In 1377, for the first time, a minor succeeded at a comparatively peaceful juncture, indicating that rule by a boy from the senior male line of English kings was now fully acceptable. When Edward III's eldest son, the prince of Wales, had died the previous year, there had been a *frisson* of unease that caused the elderly king to declare that the prince's only surviving son, Richard, should succeed him; soon afterward, Edward publicly created him prince of Wales. Although, in 1377, Edward III had three other mature, capable sons who in an earlier age might have advanced a plausible claim to the throne, there appears to have been no overt opposition to the accession of the ten-year-old Richard of Bordeaux, who was swiftly crowned king as Richard II.[9]

The accessions of these three minors—Henry III, Edward III, and Richard II—provided some sort of reassuring precedent for the succession of Henry V's baby son, though the circumstances of 1422 were significantly different in several respects. England itself may have been peaceful, but war was being waged at full throttle in France where Henry V died, and furthermore the new king was far younger than any of the earlier minors. However, as we have seen, the baby's grandfather, Henry IV, who had deposed Richard II in 1399, had circumspectly declared in parliament and in detail arrangements for the succession to his throne by seniority of birth within the royal family (regardless of age), something which Edward III and Richard II had not done so resolutely.[10] That all four youngsters were accepted as king by the political classes owed something, first, to English custom hardening into law whereby noble estates normally descended undivided to the eldest male heir; second, to the fact that all four were born after their fathers had been anointed king and so could be said to have inherited the royal and consecrated blood; and—more

importantly—to the realization in the later Middle Ages that the sophistication and complexities of royal administration and government
made it possible to conceive of the king as both an individual and an
institution, in other words that he had personal (or private) and public capacities that might be separately identified.[11] The exceptionally
young age at which Henry VI succeeded gives his minority unique
importance in perpetuating this particular, exquisite, fiction which has
characterized the British monarchy ever since and enabled a pragmatic (though not always peaceful) attitude to rulership. In contrast,
the canonical doctrine of the *rex inutilis*, the useless or incompetent
king, seems to have had little resonance in England, even in Edward
II's and Richard II's later years, and in any case this doctrine was not
regarded as applicable to legitimate kings incapable of ruling by virtue
of their minority.[12]

That it was the king who ruled, regardless of his age, was symbolized within weeks of Henry VI's accession when, at a meeting in the
king's chamber in Windsor castle on 28 September 1422, the great
gold seal of England was surrendered into the child's hands by his father's last chancellor, Thomas Langley, bishop of Durham. The great
silver seal had been taken abroad by Henry V; after it had been returned to England by 17 November, John Kemp, bishop of London
and formerly chancellor of Normandy, handed it to Henry VI so that
he could transfer to Bishop Langley as the baby's first chancellor.[13]

Henry VI's ensuing minority required careful, long-term arrangements by which this fiction could continue and at the same time the
realm could be effectively governed. On each occasion when Henry
V had led his armies to France, in 1415, 1417, and 1421, he made
what amounted to a new personal will, but the arrangements that his
father had made for the succession meant that he had no need to
concern himself unduly about the rule of England should he die on
campaign without an heir of his own body.[14] The birth of his son in
December 1421 created a new situation for the dying king. Thomas
Walsingham, the knowledgeable chronicler at St Albans abbey, understood this: He quickly appreciated the critical implications of
Henry V's death and the succession of a child-king, and the challenges that they might pose to a stable and successful government in
the immediate future. Referring to the well-known text from *Ecclesiastes*, 10.16–17:

Vae tibi terra cuius rex est puer et cuius principes mane comedunt
Beata terra cuius rex nobilis est et cuius principers vescuntur in tempore suo
ad reficiendum et non ad luxuriam

(Woe to thee, O land, whose king is a boy and whose princes feast [that is, squander their time] in the morning.
Blessed art thou, O land, whose king is of noble birth and whose princes eat at the appropriate time in order to refresh and not to indulge),

he did not question the hereditary right of the baby to succeed his father or necessarily contemplate the future with foreboding; rather did he stress the obligation of the king's subjects—first and foremost the nobility—to support their new king "by their actions and their good counsel collectively" (*indivisi*) during the long minority ahead.[15] This text was a familiar one in medieval instructional and sermon literature, and its cautions and precepts were particularly apt in the context of English royal minorities. It had appeared in Bartholomew Anglicus's popular encyclopaedia, *De proprietatis rerum* (*ca.*1245), and, perhaps more to the point, in John Trevisa's English translation of Bartholomew's work, completed in 1398.[16] In the circumstances of 1422, and in the light of Henry V's record of effective kingship, this was less a warning about the unsuitability of a child-king than a reminder to those who would bear responsibility for the king and his realm of what their obligations were during his ensuing minority. It is true that the first clause of the text, when taken in isolation, might be misinterpreted as a criticism of child-kings, and at Eastertide 1444 Thomas Kerver, a bailiff of the abbot of Reading, was accused of repeating the text, *Ve regno cui puer Rex est*, in English "in an enthusiastic (and malign) way" after hearing it mentioned in a sermon delivered by the prior provincial of the Dominican order in England before none other than Henry VI himself. But it was rather Kerver's more specific criticisms of Henry VI's adult rule and the recent conduct of the war in France that led to his trial and condemnation for treason, and it is worth noting that Henry VI personally granted Kerver a pardon of his life in August 1444. Kerver may have attracted unwelcome attention to himself initially by a precipitate and overly excitable reaction to a sermon that he had heard in the presence of the king.[17] In 1422, however, the English lords and bishops and Henry V's officers were at one with the St Albans chronicler in accepting their responsibilities as the Old Testament's precepts enjoined.

The sermon that greeted the lords and commons when parliament assembled at Westminster on 9 November also took its inspiration from the Old Testament and was scarcely less pointed in urging the cooperation of the lords in the government of the realm. It was delivered by Henry Chichele, archbishop of Canterbury, because Thomas Langley's re-appointment as chancellor of England, who would normally have been expected to deliver the opening address, would not occur until a week later.[18] The same general sentiment is the theme of the prose work, *The Serpent of Division*, composed by John Lydgate, the Lancastrian writer and publicist. At the same time as it warned of the dangers of civil strife and selfish ambition among "the lordes and prynces of renowne" and "the noblesse," as exemplified in the rivalry between Caesar and Pompey, it promoted the virtues of unity in the interest of good government.[19]

In the early years of the new reign, Henry V's surviving brothers, John, duke of Bedford and Humphrey, duke of Gloucester, the lords more generally and parliament seem to have shared these attitudes and taken such entreaties to heart. This is not surprising, since it was in no one's interest to exploit the situation created by the king's sudden death abroad: Not even Edmund Mortimer, earl of March, in whose name the failed plot of 1415 had been hatched, and who was among the companions of Henry V at Bois de Vincennes in August 1422, sounded a jarring note. Obligation and precedent as well as self-interest dictated that those with constitutional responsibility and political power should demonstrate a sense of responsibility after 1422. As for the Scots, who may have drawn wry satisfaction from the king's early death (they certainly did so later), they were unlikely to take advantage of a baby's accession because King James I had been in custody in England since 1406; moreover, the duke of Albany, the regent of Scotland, was content that he should stay there. In Wales, rebellion had fizzled out in Henry IV's reign and the policy of conciliation pursued by Henry V, partly to serve his war purposes, had removed the main causes of the unrest. These motives and circumstances doubtless explain the widespread degree of continuity shown in making appointments to royal offices both centrally and in the provinces and Wales—as had been a feature of the months following the violent removal of Edward II in 1327. To regard these reactions simply as a legacy of Henry V's rule is too narrow and immediate a judgment, though the continued peacefulness of the realm while the king had been waging war in France was undoubtedly an important factor in 1422.[20]

In the months that followed Henry V's death, the climate of opinion, formed by custom, precedent, and certain legal or biblical maxims, ensured that a collective effort was made to safeguard the interests of Henry VI and his realm during his minority. One of the codicils to his father's last will specified that the "principal guardianship (*tutelam*) and defence (*defensionem*)" of the king, and implicitly of his interests as king of England, should be assumed by Henry V's younger surviving brother, Humphrey, duke of Gloucester. None of the codicils made precise mention of the baby's inheritance as "heir and regent of the realm of France" (to quote the terms of the treaty of Troyes), although Henry V did make several priority bequests to the abbey of St Denis, near Paris.[21] However, the war and the immediate crisis confronting the high command of the large English army in France must surely have preoccupied the dying king and taken priority in his mind when he came to consider the future government of his conquests and especially their military administration. Even before the king's last illness, political circles in England had expressed some fears that this might prove to be so. Although the treaty of Troyes had specifically provided that England and France should each retain its own laws and administration, even though both kingdoms might soon be ruled by the same monarch, concern was expressed in the parliament which met on 20 December 1420 about the king's long absence in France (since 1417) and his habit of taking decisions relating to England while he was away. The commons in particular were uneasy, and at their request the statute of 1340, which declared that the English realm and people should never be subject to Edward III or any of his successors as kings of France, was pointedly confirmed by this parliament. When the next parliament met, in May 1421 in Henry V's presence, the terms of the treaty of Troyes were carefully explained and an effort was made to reassure the members.[22]

The wills that Henry V prepared prior to each of his journeys to France were essentially personal documents, and even that of June 1421, a year after the treaty of Troyes was sealed and when he may have known that his queen was pregnant, was concerned almost exclusively with his English interests. Nor did these wills, or the codicils which the king devised as he lay dying, make any stipulations about the government of England—let alone of France—in the event of his early death. After all, his father's statute had settled the succession in the house of Lancaster most recently in 1406, and there was precedent enough to guide his relatives, the lords, and parliament should his own offspring mount the throne while still a child. On the other hand, the king and his entourage at Bois de Vincennes in the last days of August could hardly have failed to discuss the practicalities of administration in both England and France in the event of the king's likely and imminent demise. His heir was safe at Windsor castle and the government of England had been placed in the charge of his younger brother, Humphrey, duke of Gloucester, in May 1422 when both Henry V and Humphrey's elder brother, John, duke of Bedford, who was then heir to the throne, crossed the channel. It was therefore convenient and predictable that Duke Humphrey should be entrusted with the guardianship of the baby and the defense of his interests in England when Henry V's death seemed in prospect. However, the relevant codicil that was added to his will on 26 August was couched in terms that invited more than one interpretation of the authority assigned to such a guardian. The learned king himself may have been responsible for the use of the civil-law term *tutela*, which could imply more than the mere physical care of the king's heir; though at Henry's bedside were two senior English bishops who may also have provided advice. John Kemp, bishop of London and chancellor of Normandy, was a highly trained civil lawyer, while the elderly John Wakering, bishop of Norwich, though a nongraduate, had been a long-serving civil servant in England and an experienced diplomat abroad; the king's secretary, William Alnwick, was also a civil lawyer. The terminology and concepts of civil law would have been familiar to all three.[23]

If it was not considered appropriate that these codicils should include provision for the civil and military administration of Normandy and the conquered territories in France, it does not mean that this crucial matter was not urgently discussed during the king's last days, and contemporary chroniclers make clear that it was. In the light of Henry V's priorities as heir to the French throne and the shock which his illness and impending death doubtless caused to those leading the military campaign, it was understandable—indeed, inevitable—that he and his entourage should look to Bedford and England's ally, Philip, duke of Burgundy, to control the volatile situation in France. It seems likely therefore that, in the event of the king's death, it was decided that Bedford should be made governor of Normandy and that the regency of France during the lifetime of the ailing Charles VI be offered to Burgundy. When Burgundy declined the offer in 1422, Bedford thereupon became regent of France as well as governor of Normandy, and he continued to be so until the young Henry VI himself arrived in France in April 1430 and was crowned at Paris in December 1431; after the king returned to England some months later, Bedford continued to rule in Lancastrian France in the king's place.[24]

It is tolerably certain that on his deathbed Henry indicated his wish that responsibility for the governance of England should be separate from the regency of France during the coming minority, so that Henry V's two brothers, Gloucester (in England) and the elder, Bedford (who was at hand in France), should rule in the new king's name. After Henry V's death, Bedford accordingly became governor of conquered Normandy and regent of the realm of France.[25] But it was soon realized that such deathbed dispositions as they applied to England were not desirable on either constitutional or political or personal grounds.

Even in 1216, when William the Marshal, earl of Pembroke had been appointed *rector regis et regni,* the meaning of this office was arguably more that of guardian, master, or director than that of regent, and the arrangement lasted only three years (when the king reached the age of twelve) and Pembroke was not replaced; meanwhile, a council of notables carried on the government on behalf of Henry III, whose great seal displayed him enthroned as a grown man.[26] In 1327 and 1377, no one was made *rector,* but again councils were appointed (and now in parliament) to govern on behalf of the two young kings, Edward III and Richard II, who had their own great seals to indicate that the kingship of England was indeed theirs.[27] These delicate theoretical and practical arrangements were not without their difficulties, prompted partly by an awareness among the political élite that one day, not too far ahead, a minor king would come to exert his own will, and partly by a growing realization on the king's part that the personal exercise of power could soon be within his grasp. Such considerations help to explain why the arrangements for Henry VI's exceptionally long minority were rather more precise than those made hitherto: They defined separate and specific responsibilities that were to be exercised collectively with the aim of securing wide acceptance and ensuring the continuation of stable rule.

These arrangements were made in the name of Henry VI, with the assent and advice of the lords in parliament, and with the assent (only) of the commons: They constituted a powerful assertion of the public *persona* of the king, despite his age, and they associated him in the initial acts of his minority and thereby gave them unassailable authority.[28] In the weeks after Henry V's death, the lords were reported to have examined precedents, especially those of 1377 if not of earlier minorities, while Humphrey, duke of Gloucester, paid special attention to the arrangements made in 1216; these were helpful to a degree but did not always point in the same direction.[29] As to Henry V's codicil assigning guardianship and defense of the king to Gloucester, and the king's evident wish that Bedford should undertake the regency of France, as the baby king's closest kinsmen, these dispositions were modified by the lords as far as England was concerned; in France, on the other hand, regents had been nominated in the past and Bedford proceeded to use the title—until Henry VI himself arrived in his French realm in April 1430. Accordingly, it was not until 5 December that, in the king's name, Bedford was appointed to the

more circumscribed positions of protector and defender of the realm
and the English Church and the king's principal councilor, but with
his brother Gloucester taking his place whenever he was out of the
kingdom.[30] Gloucester, however, continued to protest and eventually,
in March 1428, the lords in parliament had to make it plain that no
king by his last will "nor otherwyse" could determine arrangements
for the realm's governance after his own death, and also that birthright
of itself conveyed no right to powers of government (as perhaps it had
in earlier centuries). It was instead asserted that Gloucester's appointment had been advised and made by the infant king's authority, the
three estates of the realm assenting: The lords in parliament or in an
appointed council collectively had the ultimate authority to govern
during Henry's minority.

Parliament was crucial as the forum for deciding and recording the
lords' decisions during this minority. It met frequently (on average
there was a new parliament every sixteen months), its sessions were
busy rather than leisurely, and King Henry put in an appearance at
every parliament and thereby demonstrated the royal authority, with
the single exception of the assembly that met in 1431 when he was in
France.[31] The frequent, if brief, parliamentary meetings imply that the
lords, who were regularly summoned, were confronted with the business of government with some regularity; they also suggest that there
was a significant leaven of parliamentary experience available among
the elected knights of the shire and burgesses of cities and boroughs.
Both circumstances are likely to have emphasized the capacity of parliament to ensure administrative and political stability in the years after 1422. It is true that "continuous re-election [of knights of the
shire and burgesses] over even a short space of time was still, if not a
rare thing, at least unusual": the overlap of personnel from one parliament to the next stood at an average of one-fifth of the members during Henry VI's minority. Nevertheless, it is worth noting that as many
as a quarter of the elected members who sat in the second parliament
of the reign (1423) had also sat in the first. Moreover, in assessing
more general parliamentary experience, the indications are that in the
parliament of 1422, and indeed over all eleven parliaments from then
until 1437, those knights of the shire—the more influential group
among the commons—"with substantial parliamentary experience far
outnumbered those with none at all or even those who had but slen-
der acquaintance with Westminster as representative agents." Professor
Roskell's conclusions seem especially noteworthy: The shire-knights—
many of whom were lawyers—had "a keen professional appreciation
of the value of business-like procedure and of the significance of

precedent," and they (and some of the burgesses too) knew one another, were[32] often related to one another by family ties, and might be
"in frequent and close communication both in and between the times
of parliamentary session on matters of their lords' concern and their
own"—and, it might be added, those of the kingdom at a most critical juncture. To set the tone of the transactions of business in the first
parliament of the minority, the choice of Roger Flore, MP for Rut-
land, as the commons' speaker could hardly have been more appropriate and reassuring: He was a lawyer, a senior official of the duchy of
Lancaster, and was connected with Henry Chichele, archbishop of
Canterbury, and Richard Beauchamp, earl of Warwick, one of England's most distinguished and loyal commanders who was at Bois de
Vincennes in August 1422; and Flore had already been speaker three
times in Henry V's reign.[33]

The outcome was achieved with care, firmness, and a certain constitutional imagination. The lords in parliament effectively appointed
Gloucester (and the older and steadier Bedford whenever he should
be in the country) to be protector and defender of the realm, and the
king's chief councilor. These duties were more precisely defined and
delimited than were those of William the Marshal's office in 1216–19
and they involved no specific duty to take charge of the king's person
or to supervise his upbringing; moreover, a formal role was assigned
to a council which, "the king being in suche tendrenesse of age, rep-
resente his persone as toward execucion of the saide pollitique rule
and governaille of his land."[34] The lords who were nominated to this
council were as representative a group as might be expected to have
been assembled in the extraordinary and potentially unsettling situation that the lords and parliament faced in 1422. The conditions of
service under which the councilors operated were described with precision on several occasions from 1422 onward: They were individually
and publicly named; a sufficient number of them were required to attend in order to ensure sound decisions, with a majority of those
present carrying the day; and their responsibilities were emphasized
by the periodic publication of lists of the councilors as a body.[35] It
was only when Henry VI was crowned in November 1429, a month
before his eighth birthday, that the protectorate was formally ended,
although the council and the king's uncles, as alternately chief councilor in the realm, continued to discharge the practicalities of government in his name. It was a pragmatic solution that observed coherent
principles of collective noble responsibility, taking into account personal and political circumstances and the line of succession laid down
by Henry IV.

The council's appeals to John, duke of Bedford, in 1425–26 and 1433–34, when the king was too young himself to temper the friction between Gloucester and his uncle, Bishop (and, from 1426, Cardinal) Henry Beaufort, acknowledged the special authority that sprang from Bedford's unique position as Henry VI's presumed heir—an authority that was inevitably greater than that of his younger brother Gloucester. After all, the king might not survive childhood and in that eventuality Bedford would find himself king. He had been conscious of this special position since Henry V's death, both in England and in France, not (as he declared to the city of London in October 1422) out of "ambicion ner of desir that we might have of worldly worship" but rather because he was "next unto the coroune of England and havyng chief interesse after the king that is oure souverain lord."[36] As such he helped to moderate disputes within the English council while continuing to govern Lancastrian France; despite the ending of his formal regency while Henry VI was in France, Bedford continued to exercise powers of government there in the king's name until his death in 1435.

THE UPBRINGING OF THE KING

As St Anselm had explained several centuries earlier, a child's upbringing is formative: A king's was no less so. Whatever the preferences of Henry V (and despite the precedent of 1216), the lords in 1422 separated the guardianship and upbringing of the person of Henry VI from the office of his protector and defender and his chief councilor. This may have been partly because of a baby's needs; but also English law recognized the capacities of children only when they emerged from infancy at about the age of seven.[37] As he lay dying, Henry V directed his uncle, Thomas Beaufort, duke of Exeter, an utterly loyal and dependable nobleman, to take formal charge of his son, and he assigned two senior members of his household, Sir Walter Hungerford and Henry, Lord FitzHugh, who were equally staunchly devoted to Henry V and the dynasty, to organize initially the household that even a baby king required. It could hardly have been envisaged that these mature soldiers and royal servants would play a significant part in the child's upbringing. In the meantime, Henry VI lived with his widowed mother, Katherine of Valois, during his earliest years and was cared for in his daily routine by nurses and women.[38]

The position of Queen Katherine was unusually sensitive because of her youth (she was not quite twenty-one at the time of her husband's death) and, according to one chronicler, her inability "to curb her carnal passions." The arrangements of 1422 might be threatened if she were to remarry injudiciously or form imprudent relationships, and so the parliament of 1427–28 that explicitly redefined Gloucester's position as protector also forbade Katherine's remarriage without the king's consent: This may have been Gloucester's *quid pro quo,* for the queen's name was being linked at this juncture with that of Edmund Beaufort, the young nephew of Gloucester's uncle and rival, Cardinal Beaufort.[39] Meanwhile, in the 1420s, Katherine and Henry lived at Windsor or at the queen's residences not too far away, and as part of the public demonstration of her son's kingship she accompanied Henry to parliament and on other formal occasions—until, that is, the queen astonished everybody (and offended some) by marrying without public announcement, in about 1430, a modest Welshman, Owen Tudor, who found himself in deep trouble as a result; but at least he was not a powerful noble who might upset the minority settlement.[40] Thereafter Henry, who was no longer an infant, saw less of his mother and enjoyed the companionship of no other close family beyond his mutually antagonistic uncles, Bedford and Gloucester, and his great-uncle, Cardinal Beaufort. By contrast, Henry III had had three siblings, although his mother retired to France two years after King John's death; whilst the mothers of both Edward III and Richard II played a prominent part in their sons' lives as they grew into their mid-teens. Rather was provision made for Henry VI's upbringing as a boy in his own household under the supervision of the earl of Warwick, Richard Beauchamp, a former companion of Henry V. This distinguished soldier of high chivalric reputation was formally appointed as Henry's guardian and master at a meeting of the great council on 1 June 1428; the king himself formally made the appointment, which wisely included protection for the earl in the event that he felt moved to correct or punish his royal charge.[41] This period, then, when Henry had reached the age of about seven, marked an important rite of passage.

In one important facet of his young life, one that was of great potential significance for the future of his dynasty, Henry VI's experience was little different to that of earlier minor kings. Royal marriages had critical political and diplomatic implications, and suggestions of possible brides were made at an early stage, in the cases of Henry III and Edward III well before they succeeded to the throne. It should cause no surprise, therefore, that a proposal for the marriage of Henry VI to Margaret, the six-year-old daughter of King James I of Scotland, should have figured in negotiations with the Scots by 1430, or that a match with a daughter of Charles VII of France should be offered as a bargaining counter by the English ambassadors at the peace congress at Arras in 1435. Neither proposal was fruitful: England's military and diplomatic situation had deteriorated by the 1430s and suitable brides elsewhere seem to have been in short supply.[42] Moreover, the marriage of a reigning monarch who was a child was an even more delicate matter, especially when Queen Katherine was no longer pivotal to Henry VI's upbringing. As young kings, both Edward III and Richard II were strongly influenced by their mothers at the time they were married, respectively, to Philippa of Hainault in January 1328 and Anne of Bohemia in January 1382; it may not be a coincidence that both Henry III and Henry VI, whose mothers came to have little influence on their young sons as king, did not in fact marry until they were well into their twenties, the former in January 1236 when he was twenty-eight and the latter in April 1444 when he was twenty-three. Aside from the formidable challenge of securing the agreement of Bedford, Gloucester, and Cardinal Beaufort to a suitable bride for Henry VI, the marital experiences of both his uncles may not have fitted them particularly well to negotiate a marriage for their nephew.[43] The lack of a supportive wife in the latter stages of his minority may have accentuated his familial isolation.

Henry's education during his first fifteen years seems to have been varied and appropriate, and in accordance with the regimen common in noble households: from courtesy, manners, and good behavior with some physical activity in childhood, to letters and languages (including French) and knightly exercises in boyhood, and all in a pious Christian environment overseen by chaplains and a personal confessor.[44] This second phase in his upbringing had been heralded as early as May 1426 when his uncle John, duke of Bedford, knighted him publicly during a meeting of parliament, and this ceremony was followed by his own act of knighting a large group of young nobles; all this was rather earlier than the experience of Henry III, who was knighted at the time of his accession at the age of nine.[45] According to most of those contemporaries who commented on the young king, Henry was a healthy, alert, and intelligent child, who gradually showed an awareness of his unique position to the extent that he needed to be gently restrained from time to time—like all young teenagers—though Warwick came to find that a ticklish task. On the occasion of his coronation in Westminster abbey in November 1429, he was observed looking about him "sadly and wisely"—whatever that might mean at the age of almost eight. After the ceremony, Gloucester in parliament divested himself of his office of protector and defender. Henry also stood up well to his visit to France in 1430–32

ultimately for his coronation there in December 1431; his arrival in
his French realm caused the suspension of Bedford's office of regent.[46] He was evidently taught to take his exceptional responsibilities
seriously, and when the duke of Burgundy took the critical decision in
1435 to withdraw his allegiance from the Lancastrian king and return
to the Valois fold, the fourteen-year-old Henry realized its momentous significance. According to the Burgundian chronicler, Enguer-
rand de Monstrelet, when he received a letter from the duke omitting
the customary address to Henry as his sovereign lord, tears welled up
in the young king's eyes—and the sense of betrayal still rankled two
decades later.[47] If there was something missing from an upbringing
that was designed to complement the complex governmental arrangements for the minority regime and to prepare Henry for active kingship, it was the creation of an environment in which he could develop
sound, independent judgment that would eventually free him from
the tutelage of his uncles and his councilors.

Like Richard II, Henry VI had several uncles or great-uncles who
could claim a prominent position during the king's minority and,
indeed, Henry V had recognized this before he died. Of the two surviving legitimized sons of John of Gaunt, duke of Lancaster, by his
mistress Catherine Swynford, Thomas Beaufort, duke of Exeter was
trusted by Henry V, who gave him immediate charge of his baby son
in 1422. Thomas's elder brother, Henry Beaufort, bishop of Winchester, was an astute and highly capable figure, no less devoted to
Lancastrian interests but with ambitions in both Church and state
that made others wary of him—even Henry V who denied him a car-
dinalate in 1417. Henry's surviving brothers, John, duke of Bedford
and Humphrey, duke of Gloucester, neither of whom had a legitimate
child, were successively the baby king's heirs. None of these figures
(not even Exeter, who in any case died in 1426) could be said to have
played a consistent role in educating the young king prior to the
coronation expedition to France in 1430; but their relations with one
another were tense as they sought to assert their own influence in
government and in the conduct of the French war. Gloucester and the
bishop were especially antagonistic and in 1425–26 Bedford had to
return from France to impose a settlement on them—though in reality he seems to have sympathized with Beaufort and after both men
sailed to France in March 1427 it was Bedford who invested the
bishop with his cardinal's hat at Calais.[48]

The progress from boyhood to adulthood occurred rather earlier
in a king than in the generality of his subjects because it signified the
passage from the formal possession of kingly authority to the antici-

pated realities of personal rule; nevertheless, in the fifteenth century no customary age had been established at which this transformation should take place.[49] It could hardly be otherwise in view of the number and range of competing influences that were inevitably exerted on a young king, and his own consciousness of his duty and obligations as well as the opportunities of his powerful position: This had been the experience of Henry III, Edward III, and Richard II (albeit in Richard's case with displays of frustration).[50] The precedents of 1216 and 1377 (if not of 1327) had been examined after Henry V's death, and it is reasonable to suppose that minds would turn sooner or later to the stages by which Henry III's minority was brought to an end and to the turbulent circumstances (which would be best avoided) of Richard II's emergence as an adult ruler. In Henry VI's case, there are hints that his uncles and councilors began to adjust to the developing personality of the king after he returned from France in January 1432, when Henry was only ten; however, they continued to recognize that certain decisions affecting him personally must await the end of his minority some years hence.[51] Although Dr Watts goes so far as to assert that "Henry VI's minority ended when he was ten," that would have been far earlier than in the case of all other young English monarchs. Rather was the realm re-united and re-acquainted with a king whose own will would need to be taken gradually into account in the years ahead.[52]

It was in the 1430s, as the king entered his teenage years, that his uncles and their allies sought to influence the king's mind and control his behavior; the queen was less frequently at his side. They created about him an atmosphere of political bitterness, even of personal hatred: When they quarreled openly in his presence, as Gloucester and Bedford did in 1434 during yet another attempt by the latter to calm a major political storm, it was at best unedifying and unsettling for the boy. After Bedford's death in September 1435, Cardinal Beaufort and Duke Humphrey were left in direct confrontation with one another.[53]

THE TRANSITION FROM MINORITY
TO MAJORITY KINGSHIP

Toward the end of 1432, the king's guardian, the earl of Warwick, reported that Henry was "growen in yeers in stature of his persone and also in conceyte and knoweleche of his hiegh and royale auctoritee and estate," as any self-conscious child might be; at the same time, the earl had become concerned at the sinister influences being brought to bear on the eleven-year-old monarch (who was "sturred . . . frome his lernyng and spoken to of divers matiers no behovefull")—probably and especially by Gloucester, who earlier in the year (in February and March) had dismissed senior officers of state and of the king's household in a ruthless act of political butchery to coincide with the king's return from France and to strengthen his own position. After Bedford returned to England in 1433, at the formal invitation of the king but doubtless at the prompting of the council, the duke and Cardinal Beaufort were able to reassert their influence and restore some balance to the competing interests swirling around the king; it may have helped matters that Henry traveled to the abbey of Bury St Edmunds, in Suffolk, on 24 December and stayed there for almost three months. When, after the king's return to Westminster in April 1434, Gloucester openly attacked his brother's record in France and Bedford replied with undisguised bitterness, the king was moved, either by his own feelings of alarm or by the other councilors, to intervene personally and beg his uncles to stop quarrelling.[54] With the king only twelve years of age, it is unnecessary to regard these appeals as "a deliberate repudiation of the king's personal exercise of his powers in the interests of political harmony at the centre."[55]

The return of Bedford to France in July 1434 for the last time removed his restraining hand from the attempts to manipulate the young king. In November 1434, Cardinal Beaufort was among those councilors who expressed concern at the way in which Henry was being encouraged by unspecified persons to alter the arrangements for conciliar government: They acknowledged the "grete understanding and felyng, as evere thei sawe or knewe in any Prince, or other persone of his age," but they were forthright in advising the thirteen-year-old that he should "not lightly to agree him or assente therto." In view of his recent argument with Bedford, Gloucester is the most likely person to have been responsible for this intervention.[56] Henry's upbringing as a teenager, then, was marked by intense personal pressures from his uncles and their supporters among the councilors, even if he became aware of the political implications of these pressures only gradually.

In several important respects, the ending of Henry's minority occurred during 1436–37 and was formally complete by November 1437 when the king was almost sixteen. It is perhaps significant that Henry assumed personal responsibility for ruling just when the future of the dual monarchy was brought into question politically, militarily, and financially. This legacy of Henry V's was the most persistently important and increasingly troubling preoccupation of the minority regime, and by the mid-1430s the future of Lancastrian France sharply divided English opinion as to whether to seek peace with the Valois and Burgundy or to continue the war. As a young adult, Henry VI seems to have become attracted by the prospects for peace: The death of his uncle Bedford in the Norman capital, Rouen, on 15 September 1435, and more immediately the Burgundian siege of Calais in June 1436 and the Scottish siege of Roxburgh castle early in the following August, focused his and others' minds. There even seems to have been a suggestion that the fourteen-year-old king should be placed at the head of an army intended to relieve Calais. Henry was also concerned about the long-standing dispute between the Pope and the Church Councils that continued to divide Christendom. His strong sense of Christian morality, nurtured since boyhood by his chaplains and confessors, was deeply scandalized, and Pope Eugenius IV's emissary in England, Piero da Monte, the papal tax-collector, appealed to the king in person and elicited his strong support for Eugenius's position.[57]

It was a sign of the developing role of the king that, after eight years in the progressively taxing post of king's guardian and tutor, the earl of Warwick laid down his charge in May 1436 and turned his attention to his estates and to preparing to return to service in France.[58] The king's exercise of his royal authority is apparent from the summer of 1436 onward, to judge by the language and procedures used in authenticating and registering expressions of his own will, especially by means of his sign manual or signature, and by the nature of the grants of patronage that he made. He is recorded as making a number of grants on his own authority and attending several meetings of the council, without causing any adverse reaction among his uncles and other councillors.[59]

This did not, however, necessarily imply that Henry, from the age of fourteen, was preparing to dispense with the body of councilors that had hitherto exercised his authority for him. To have done so would have been rash or, at the very least, unwise when there were several more years in prospect before the king might be regarded as a mature monarch. That had certainly been the case with Henry III and Richard II in the past. But straws in the wind that indicated that an adjustment in Henry's and the council's roles would be likely in the next few years were apparent to well-placed observers. On 10 September 1436, Hue de Lannoy, one of the duke of Burgundy's prominent and far-sighted advisers, sent his master a long memorandum about the prospects of peace between Burgundy, France, and England: He noted that although Henry VI "is young, too young to rule . . . it is probable that, everything considered, they [the English] are tired of war and will gladly embrace a more reasonable policy, the more so now than ever before, since the king will be fifteen on St Nicholas's day." De Lannoy was writing from Ghent, whose merchants and other citizens were in constant communication with London and the southeast and were a ready source of intelligence for the Burgundian court. Both Gloucester and Cardinal Beaufort were intimate witnesses—and erstwhile managers—of the increasing pace of the king's intermittent official activities. By the early spring of 1437, when Beaufort was contemplating a visit to the continent, he declared at a great council in April that King Henry had reached such an age "that he may the better absente him" from England. It is worth noting, too, the deaths of both the king's mother and his grandmother at this juncture: Queen Katherine of Valois died on 3 January 1437 after a long illness, and Queen Joan of Navarre on 18 July. Although neither seems to have been particularly close to Henry during the 1430s, their deaths served to underline the increasing isolation of the king's position within royal circles.[60]

As in Henry III's case, there may have been no formal declaration that Henry VI's minority was ended; even the willful Richard II did not take the initiative to announce publicly his majority until 1389 when he was well past his twenty-first birthday.

The formal declaration of November 1437 acknowledged that certain appointments, pardons, and matters of grace—in short, the king's exercise of his patronage—were henceforward to be at Henry VI's personal disposal, while his council (which was re-appointed) should continue to discuss and conclude more public matters, though the more important of these should be referred to the king for his advice. This seems to have been a practical and rational arrangement, made with the king's agreement as he approached his sixteenth birthday; it might well avoid the kind of resentments and disagreements felt by both Richard II and his nobles in 1383, when there appears to have been no formal declaration of how the king's government should be conducted as he moved toward adulthood. The lords in 1422 had examined the precedent of Richard's minority when they devised the arrangements for Henry VI's, and they are likely to have noted at the same time the difficulties encountered when Richard began to assert his regal will in the early 1380s. In 1437, therefore, "It seems that the purpose behind the continued existence of the Council was the provision of a safe environment in which [Henry VI] could feel his way into his job."[61]

The passage of a king into adulthood and toward an active role in government was bound to be one of the most delicate and tense stages of his minority, whatever the level of his intelligence and the quality of his education. In addition to pressures from individuals, there was plenty of considered advice available to Henry VI—especially around 1436–38—which was designed to influence him in discharging his public and private roles as king. For example, the "Libelle of Englysche Polycye" was an emotionally charged verse-essay in political economy whose arguments and assertions sought to persuade his councilors (and doubtless wider opinion) of the urgent need to protect Calais and the narrow seas and, thereby, English commerce at a time when they were threatened especially by the duke of Burgundy and his subjects.[62] In a similar, general vein were two works that Humphrey, duke of Gloucester commissioned from the Italian humanist, Titus Livius Frulovisi, whom he patronized: the poem "Humfroidos," which celebrated Duke Humphrey's own accomplishments, and, shortly afterward (in 1437), the Life of Henry V, which was dedicated to Henry VI and which described Henry V's triumphs in France and especially Duke Humphrey's part in them.[63] From this time, too, is datable the tract "On the rule of princes," a moral and religious work written specifically for Henry VI and presented to him probably by one of his inner circle of chaplains. It rehearsed the personal and other traits desirable in a ruler and the moral and religious precepts that he ought to follow, while at the same time taking sage advice.[64] This last tract described the qualities of a spiritually minded prince, stressed the dignity and responsibilities of kingship and the importance and pitfalls of receiving counsel, and it urged the merits of peace with France. The advice it contained was especially appropriate for the maturing Henry VI at this juncture in his life and reign, and such advice seemingly weighed heavily with him as he embarked on a sixteen-year period of more personally active rule—before he was laid low by a severe mental collapse at the beginning of August 1453.[65]

Just as the political elite in 1422 made themselves aware of events in 1216 and 1377, so the circumstances of Henry VI's minority, and in particular the disputes that then arose among the king's councilors and his uncles, may have directly influenced what took place after Edward IV died on 9 April 1483. But the arrangements that were made for the second Yorkist king and his government worked far less successfully than did those of 1422. This may seem surprising because King Edward's elder son, Edward, was twelve years old and had been prince of Wales for almost as long. Dominic Mancini, an Italian visitor in England at the time of the king's death, reported a rumor that Edward IV in his will had made his brother Richard, duke of Gloucester (later Richard III), "protector of his children and realm," but it is more than likely that the queen and the late king's councilors in London envisaged the swift coronation of the new monarch on 4 May, after the manner of Richard II (aged ten) in 1377, in order to obviate the need for a protector. In any case, sixty years earlier, Henry VI's councilors had made it plain that the wishes of a dead king could not determine the arrangements to be made for his successor's minority. The boy was already in the care of members of Queen Elizabeth's Wydeville family and the expectation was that the crowned king would thenceforward rule merely with the advice of a council.[66] Richard, duke of Gloucester, who was in Yorkshire, far from London, at the time of his brother's death, was not party to these plans and he evidently believed that, as Edward IV's only surviving brother, he should be accorded a special position among the young king's councilors; he specifically instanced the roles of protector and chief councilor of the uncrowned Henry VI that the duke of Bedford and Humphrey, an earlier duke of Gloucester, had been accorded— whatever King Edward's will may have said. The likelihood that, following the precedent of Henry VI's coronation in November 1429, Richard of Gloucester's protectorate would end with Edward V's crowning, and the possibility that the guardianship of the young king as well as his council would be dominated by Richard's enemies, led the duke to enforce the postponement of the coronation and then to seize the throne for himself.[67] Events in 1483 starkly revealed the practical difficulties and dangers inherent in royal minorities—and the fragility of the political and constitutional arrangements that needed to be made in the context of personal relationships and ambitions, and whatever lessons might be drawn from the past. The outcome of the arrangements on this occasion—the deposition and murder of Edward V—was disastrous for the English monarchy.

When Henry VIII died in January 1547, his only son was nine years of age; although he had been proclaimed duke of Cornwall at his christening, the king had never brought himself to declare him prince of Wales. However, the minority of 1422 evidently came into some people's minds in 1547, and the new king, Edward VI, according to his personal *Chronicle*, became interested in Henry VI.[68] Yet there were significant departures from the precedents of 1422 and 1483 that caused a number of problems. Although Edward's coronation on 20 February quickly followed his father's death, a protector of the king's realms was nevertheless appointed and on terms that included governance not only of the realm but of the king's person too, albeit with advice provided by a council. This arrangement—in some ways reminiscent of William the Marshal's position as long ago as 1216—proved to be a prelude to vicious faction when Edward died in 1553, the second English king not to survive his minority.

A century later still, in 1653, politicians, soldiers, and constitutional thinkers gave even less—indeed, scant—attention to precedent for rule during a republic, except in one respect. A protectorate was created for the last time in British history, but it had only titular resemblance to that of 1422. It was designed for Oliver Cromwell, and after his death in 1658 it was continued by his son Richard. On these two occasions there was no king and no independent or designated council to whom the protectors might be answerable, at least formally—and that had fatal consequences.[69] By contrast, the arrangements made for Henry VI were resourceful and lasting and met contemporary expectations. Whatever the tensions that underlay them and which, it must be admitted, grew serious as the years passed, these arrangements resulted in arguably the most successful of the minority regimes that were required periodically to sustain England's personal monarchy during the later Middle Ages.

NOTES

1. Among the more prominent of these studies are Bertram P. Wolffe, *Henry VI*, 2nd edn (New Haven and London: Yale University Press, 2001); John Lovatt Watts, *Henry VI and the Politics of Kingship* (Cambridge: Cambridge University Press, 1996); Ralph Alan Griffiths, *The Reign of King Henry VI: The Exercise of Royal Authority*, 2nd edn (Stroud: Sutton Publishing, 1998); Simon J. Payling, *Political Society in Lancastrian England: The Greater Gentry of Nottinghamshire* (Oxford: Oxford University Press, 1991); Christine Carpenter, *Locality and Polity: A Study of Warwickshire Landed Society, 1401–1499* (Cambridge: Cambridge University Press, 1992); Helen Castor, *The King, the Crown, and the Duchy of Lancaster: Public Authority and Private Power, 1399–1461* (Oxford: Oxford University Press, 2000); Gerald L. Harriss, *Cardinal Beaufort: A Study of Lancastrian Ascendancy and Decline* (Oxford: Oxford University Press, 1988).
2. Patrick Strong and Felicity Strong, "The Last Will and Codicils of Henry V," *English Historical Review* 96 (1981): 99. A near-contemporary copy of seven codicils, dated 26 August 1422, was rediscovered in 1978 among the archives of Henry VI's foundation of Eton College (Eton College Records 59 fol. 6v-7v).
3. *Reports from the Lords Committees Touching the Dignity of a Peer of the Realm*, (London: Record Commission, 1829), 5: 9, summarized in *Calendar of Charter Rolls, 1300–1326* (London: HMSO, 1908), 6. The grant of the lands was made on 7 February; by 1 March the king's son

was being referred to as prince of Wales: *Calendar of Patent Rolls, 1292–1301* (London: HMSO, 1895), 578.

4. For comment, see John Goronwy Edwards, *The Principality of Wales, 1267–1967: A Study in Constitutional History* (Caernarfon: Carnarvonshire Historical Society, 1969), 16–17; Ralph Alan Griffiths, "The Sense of Dynasty in the Reign of Henry VI,", in *Patronage, Pedigree and Power in Later Medieval England,* ed. Charles Derek Ross, 15–16 (Gloucester: Alan Sutton, 1979), reprinted in Ralph Alan Griffiths, *King and Country: England and Wales in the Fifteenth Century* (London: Hambledon Press, 1991), 85. On the second occasion, in 1406, Henry IV's declaration was enshrined in a statute: *Statutes of the Realm,* 11 vols. (London: 1810–28) Statute Roll, 2: 151.

5. *Rotuli. Parliamentorum,* II, 330, with comment in Nigel Saul, *Richard II* (New Haven and London: Yale University Press, 1997), 17. It may have helped in removing any question relating to the succession that Henry V's next brother and heir, John, duke of Bedford, was with the king when he died, as also was Edmund Mortimer, earl of March, whose Plantagenet lineage had posed a threat to the Lancastrian dynasty only seven years before, as one element in the earl of Cambridge's conspiracy, for which see Thomas Brynmor Pugh, *Henry V and the Southampton Plot of 1415* (Southampton: Southampton Records Series XXX, 1988).

6. John H. Le Patourel, "The Norman Succession, 996–1135," *EHR,* 86 (1971): 235–40; and most recently, George Garnett, *Conquered England: Kingship, Succession and Tenure, 1066–1166* (Oxford: Oxford University Press, 2007), 147–52, 156.

7. *Foedera,* IV, iii, 179–80, translated in Alec R. Myers, ed., *English Historical Documents,* IV (London: Eyre and Spottiswoode, 1969), 225–26; with comment in Griffiths, *The Reign of King Henry VI,* 16–17.

8. David A. Carpenter, *The Minority of Henry III* (London: Methuen, 1990), 12–13; above chap. I am grateful to my colleague, Ifor Rowlands, for help in elucidating the interesting events of 1216.

9. For the circumstances (and speed) of the accessions of 1327 and 1377, see above chaps. 2 and 3.

10. For evidence of disputes about the succession later in Richard II's reign, in 1397–99, see Saul, *Richard II,* 396–97.

11. On the personal and abstract crown by the mid-twelfth century, see George Garnett, "The Origins of the Crown," in *The History of English Law: Centenary Essays on 'Pollock and Maitland,'* ed. J. Hudson, especially 210–14 (Oxford: Oxford University Press, 1996). For a general discussion and in relation to Henry VI's minority, see Watts, *Henry VI and the Politics of Kingship,* 22–29, 117–22.

12. Edward Peters, *The Shadow King: Rex Inutilis in Medieval Law and Literature* (New Haven and London: Yale University Press, 1970), 27. However, William Huse Dunham Jr. and Charles T. Wood are inclined to infer an awareness of the doctrine in 1327 and 1399, in "The Right

to Rule in England: Depositions and the King's Authority, 1327–1485," *American Historical Review*, 81 no.4 (1976): 739, 744.

13. The silver seal, rather than the gold seal, seems to have been the great seal habitually used during Henry VI's reign; both were recast to signify the new monarch: The National Archives, E404/40/29, translated in Frederick Devon, ed., *Issues of the Exchequer, Henry III-Henry VI* (London: Record Commission, 1837), 382; Henry C. Maxwell-Lyte, *Historical Notes on the Use of the Great Seal of England* (London: HMSO, 1926), 314; *CCR, 1422–1429* (London: HMSO, 1933), 26, 46, 49; and Griffiths, *The Reign of King Henry VI*, 13–14 (with references cited).

14. This was so even if (as Wolffe, *Henry VI*, 28, suggests) Henry V realized that his wife, Queen Katherine, was pregnant when he departed for France in June 1421.

15. Thomas Walsingham, *Historia Anglicana*, ed. Henry Thomas Riley, 2 vols (London: Rolls series, 1864), 2: 344 ("Vae, 'Salomonis metuentes, cujus terra rex puer est, etc.,'" followed by his commentary on the implications, sub anno 1422). The full quotation is from the Vulgate, with the translation here adapted from the King James version of the Bible.

16. Malcolm C. Seymour, ed., *On the Properties of Things: John Trevisa's Translation of Bartholomaeus Anglicus, De Proprietatis Rerum: A Critical Text*, 2 vols. (Oxford: Oxford University Press, 1975), 1: 320 (Book 6, "On lordship and bad lordship"): "Woo is ye lond yat hath a childe kinge and princes yat etith erliche." In the mid-twelfth century, it had also been quoted by William of Malmesbury in relation to the accession of the infant William the bastard to the duchy of Normandy (1035) with the acquiescence of the Norman nobility, and in full by John of Salisbury in his *Polycraticus:* William of Malmesbury, *Gesta Regum Anglorum: The History of the English Kings*, ed. Roger A. B. Mynors, R. M. Thomson and W. Winterbottom, vol. 1 (Oxford: Oxford University Press, 1998), 426–27; John of Salisbury, *Polycraticus: Of the Frivolities of Courtiers and the Footprints of Philosophers*, ed. Cary J. Nederman (Cambridge: Cambridge University Press, 1990), 70–71 (book V, chapter 6), references I owe to Ifor Rowlands. On the "protective aura" provided by the Norman nobility in 1035, see Garnett, *Conquered England*, 148.

17. Later generations faced with royal minorities, and modern historians, also seem to have displayed a partial knowledge of Ecclesiastes. See Cecil A. F. Meekings, "Thomas Kerver's Case, 1444," *EHR*, 90 (1975): 331–46, for a full discussion of the legal aspects of the case, though without specifically addressing Kerver's use of the biblical text. That Henry VI did not take amiss Prior John Courteys's use of the text in his sermon is indicated by Courteys's continued popularity as a preacher and his continuance as prior provincial until at least 1453: Alfred B. Emden, *A Biographical Register of the University of Oxford to AD 1500*, 3 vols (Oxford: Oxford University Press, 1956–9), 1:504.

186   R. A. Griffiths

18. *Rot. Parl.*, IV, 169, taking Exodus, xviii, 12–27, as its text; with comment in John S. Roskell, *The Commons in the Parliament of 1422: English Society and Parliamentary Representation Under the Lancastrians* (Manchester: Manchester University Press, 1954), 100–102.

19. John Lydgate, *The Serpent of Division*, ed. Henry Noble MacCracken (London and New Haven: Oxford University Press and Yale University Press, 1911). Walter F. Schirmer, *John Lydgate: A Study in the Culture of the XVth Century*, trans. Ann E. Keep (London: Methuen and Company, 1961), 82–88, is inclined to accept that it was written in December 1422 for Henry VI's uncle, Humphrey, duke of Gloucester, but Derek Pearsall, *John Lydgate* (London: Routledge & Kegan Paul, 1970), 138–39, reasonably cautions against such precision; see also Nicholas Perkins, "Representing Advice in Lydgate,", in *The Lancastrian Court*, ed. Jenny Stratford, 182–84 (Donnington: Shaun Tyas, 2003). Gerald Harriss, *Shaping the Nation: England, 1360–1461* (Oxford: Clarendon Press, 2005), 604, goes so far as to interpret Lydgate in 1422 as promoting rule by a single person, "probably Gloucester," one of the poet's patrons (though certainly not the only one).

20. Griffiths, *The Reign of King Henry VI*, 155; Michael Brown, *James I* (Edinburgh: Canongate Academic, 1994), 17–24; for the years after 1327, see William A. Morris and James F. Willard, eds., *The English Government at Work, 1327–1336*, vol. I (Cambridge, MA: The Medieval Academy of America, 1940), passim. For insistence on Henry V's "legacy," see Christine Carpenter, *The Wars of the Roses: Politics and the Constitution in England, c. 1437–1509* (Cambridge: Cambridge University Press, 1997), 77 and passim, followed by Harriss, *Shaping the Nation*, 595.

21. Strong and Strong, *EHR*, 96 (1981): 99–100. The bequests to St Denis were the first to be mentioned in the codicils, after those to his young son.

22. John S. Roskell, Linda Clark, and Carole Rawcliffe, *The History of Parliament: The House of Commons, 1386–1421*, 4 vols (Stroud: Alan Sutton Publishing, 1992), 1: 114–15; *Rot. Parl.*, IV, 127, 129, 135; Christopher T. Allmand, *Henry V*, 2nd edn (New Haven and London: Yale University Press, 1997), 161, 376–77.

23. *Oxford DNB* (sub nomine); Harriss, *Cardinal Beaufort*, 115 (for the suggestion of Alnwick's role). For the possible interpretation of *tutela* in Roman law, see Stanley Bertram Chrimes, *English Constitutional Ideas in the Fifteenth Century* (Cambridge: Cambridge University Press, 1936), 37–38 n. 1.

24. For interpretations of the chronicle accounts of the dispositions at Bois de Vincennes, see especially James Hamilton Wylie and William Templeton Waugh, *The Reign of Henry the Fifth*, 3 vols (Cambridge: Cambridge University Press, 1914–29), 3: 415–21, revised by John S. Roskell, "The Office and Dignity of Protector of England, with Special Reference to its Origins," *EHR*, 68 (1953): 200, reprinted in idem,

Parliament and Politics in Late Medieval England, 3 vols (London: Hambledon Press, 1981–3), 1: chap. 7, 200; Griffiths, *The Reign of King Henry VI,* 16–19; Wolffe, *Henry VI,* 29–30. For the acceptance of regency in France (in contrast to England), see Peter S. Lewis, *Later Medieval France: The Polity* (London: Macmillan, 1968), 97.

25. Despite Bedford's publicly declared intention to reunite Normandy and the French realm after Charles VI's death, in reality the duchy's independent administration continued, as did Bedford's governorship. Christopher T. Allmand, *Lancastrian Normandy, 1415–1450: The History of a Medieval Occupation* (Oxford: Clarendon Press, 1983), 22, 127–29.

26. Frederick William Maitland, *The Constitutional History of England* (Cambridge: Cambridge University Press, 1909), 200, gives a succinct account. David Crouch, *William Marshall: Court, Career and Chivalry in the Angevin Empire, 1147–1219* (London: Longman, 1990), 119, is also cautious about describing Marshal as regent. The obverse of the great seal was altered only in minor detail in each new reign after William II, thereby reflecting the continuity of the English monarchy. There was no special seal for a royal minority. Paul D. A. Harvey and Andrew McGuinness, *A Guide to British Medieval Seals* (London: British Library and Public Record Office, 1996), 27–29. For a description of the new seal of 1218, see Carpenter, *The Minority of Henry III,* 94.

27. These seals, suitably modified, were based on their predecessors' matrices: Walter de Gray Birch, *Catalogue of Seals in the Department of Manuscripts in the British Museum,* 6 vols (London: British Museum, 1887–1900), 1: 21–23, 28–29.

28. *Rot. Parl.,* IV, 174–76. The fundamental studies of the arrangements made in 1422 are Stanley Bertram Chrimes, "The Pretensions of the Duke of Gloucester in 1422," *EHR,* 45 (1930): 102–3; Roskell, *EHR,* 68 (1953): 193–234; and Strong and Strong, ibid., 96 (1981): 79–102. Subsequent detailed commentary is in Wolffe, *Henry VI,* chs. 2–3; Griffiths, *The Reign of King Henry VI,* chs. 1–5; Harriss, *Cardinal Beaufort,* chs. 6–10; and Watts, *Henry VI and the Politics of kingship,* chap. 4. The essential documents are conveniently assembled in Stanley Bertram Chrimes and Alfred L. Brown, eds., *Select Documents of English Constitutional History, 1307–1485* (London: Adam and Charles Black, 1961), 245–61.

29. The different conclusions possible are indicated in *Rot. Parl.,* IV, 326–27, and Chrimes and Brown, *Select Documents,* 260–62 (when the powers of Duke Humphrey were re-defined, 3 March 1428); with comment in Griffiths, *The Reign of King Henry VI,* 20–24.

30. Chrimes and Brown, *Select Documents,* 249–50, from *Rot. Parl.,* IV, 174. Prior to 5 December, Gloucester had no special standing, other than as the only one of the baby's two surviving uncles who happened to be in England; his commission as guardian (or *custos*) of the realm had lapsed with Henry V's death. On 5 November, he was authorized to preside at the parliament. This could hardly have been intended by

R. A. GRIFFITHS

the lords as a slight, though Gloucester may have taken it as such while
discussions about the minority regime continued. Chrimes and Brown,
Select Documents, 246–47, from *Proceedings and Ordinances of the Privy
Council of England*, ed. Nicholas Harris Nicolas, 6 vols (Record Com-
mission: London, 1834–7) 3: 6–7; contrast Watts, *Henry VI and the
Politics of Kingship*, 113 n. 41.

31. *Rot. Parl.*, IV, 326–27, records the lords' assertion in 1428 of the principles which defined Gloucester's powers. See Watts, *Henry VI and the
Politics of Kingship*, 111–22, though whether these "concepts" were as
plain to the lords and others at the outset of the reign as they became after several years of minority government is a moot point. Anne Curry,
" 'A game of two halves': Parliament, 1422–1454," in Linda Clark, ed.,
Parchment and People: Parliament in the Middle Ages (Edinburgh: Edinburgh University Press, 2004), 74–99, provides a valuable analysis.
For parliament as the ultimate authority for what was done in 1422, see
Watts, *Henry VI and the Politics of Kingship*, 116. Interestingly, there
was a body of opinion in France that also held that the king could not
alter succession to the throne: Malcolm G. A. Vale, *Charles VII* (London: Eyre Methuen, 1974), 32.

32. Roskell, *The Commons in the Parliament of 1422*, chap. 3 (with the quo-
tations on pp. 38, 43, 44, 85). The general experience of the burgess-
members seems not significantly less. It will be possible to test these
conclusions in greater detail when the History of Parliament Trust has
completed its studies of the parliamentary commons during Henry VI's
reign.

33. John S. Roskell, "Roger Flore of Oakham," *Transactions of the Leices-
tershire Archaeological and Historical Society*, 33 (1957), 36–44, reprinted
in idem, *Parliament and Politics in Late Medieval England*, 3: chap. 12,
supplemented by Roskell, Clark and Rawcliffe, *House of Commons,
1386–1421*, 3: 91–94.

34. *PPC*, 3: 233–34; Chrimes and Brown, *Select Documents*, 259. This description of the council's role was included retrospectively in the councilors' declaration to the dukes of Bedford and Gloucester on 28
January 1427.

35. John Lovatt Watts, "When did Henry VI's Minority end?" in *Trade,
Devotion and Governance: Papers in Later Medieval History*, ed. Dorothy
J. Clayton, Richard G. Davies, and Peter McNiven, 121 and n.24, 26,
27 (Stroud: Alan Sutton, 1994); for the periodic definition and record-
ing of the councilors' responsibilities during the 1420s, see Griffiths,
The Reign of King Henry VI, 28–32.

36. Watts, *Henry VI and the Politics of Kingship*, 116, 118, 121; see *PPC*, 4:
95. The letter to London is in Chrimes and Brown, *Select Documents*,
245, and may not have been Bedford's only reminder to contemporaries
of his position.

37. See, for example, Deborah Youngs, *The Life Cycle in Western Europe,
c.1300–c.1500* (Manchester: Manchester University Press, 2006), 41.

38. Griffiths, *The Reign of King Henry VI*, 51–52. It had been one of Henry V's last wishes that his baby son should live with his mother: Strong and Strong, *EHR*, 96 (1981): 99. For Exeter (who died in 1426), Hungerford and FitzHugh (who died in January 1425), and the king's early household, see Griffiths, *The Reign of King Henry VI*, 34, 51–57 (and references cited there).

39. Ralph Alan Griffiths, "Queen Katherine of Valois and a Missing Statute of the Realm," *Law Quarterly Review*, 93 (1977): 248–58, reprinted in idem, *King and Country: England and Wales in the Fifteenth Century*, 104–13, and noting two subsequent comments by Geoffrey Hand and George O. Sayles. The contemporary chronicler's comment is in *Incerti Scriptoris Chronicon Angliae de Regnis Trium Regum Lancastriensium Henrici IV, Henrici V et Henrici VI*, ed. John Allen Giles (London: D. Nutt, 1848), pt. 4, 17.

40. Ralph Alan Griffiths and Roger Stuart Thomas, *The Making of the Tudor Dynasty*, 3rd edn (Stroud: Sutton Publishing Limited, 2005), chap. 3. That the marriage was private but legal is suggested by BL, Add. MS.15, 644 (a reference I owe to Michael Bennett). See Michael Bennett, "Table Tittle-tattle and the Tudor View of History,", in *People, Places and Perspectives: Essays on Later Medieval and Early Tudor England in Honour of Ralph A. Griffiths*, ed. Keith Dockray and Peter Fleming, 155–66 (Stroud: Nonsuch Publishing Limited, 2005), for the later fascination with Katherine's and Owen's story. Gerald L. Harris (*Cardinal Beaufort*, 178 n. 34) muses that their first-born was given the name of Edmund because the child's father was Edmund Beaufort, not Owen, and finds it an "agreeable possibility that Edmund 'Tudor' and Margaret Beaufort were first cousins and that the royal house of 'Tudor' sprang in fact from Beauforts on both sides"!

41. *CPR, 1422–1429*, 491–92; *PPC*, 3: 294–95. For the family circle of the earlier minor kings, see Carpenter, *Minority of Henry III*, 153; William Longman, *The History of the Life and Times of Edward the Third*, 2 vols (London: Longmans, Green and Co., 1869), 1: 40 (noting how Edward III visited his mother two or three times a year after her "honourable confinement" in 1330); Saul, *Richard II*, 51.

42. Griffiths, *The Reign of King Henry VI*, 159–50, 198; Michael Brown, *James I* (Edinburgh: Canongate Press, 1994), 110; Jocelyne Gledhill Dickinson, *The Congress of Arras, 1435: A Study in Medieval Diplomacy* (Oxford: Oxford University Press, 1955), 131. For marriages suggested for Henry III and Edward III before their accessions, see Frederick Maurice Powicke, *King Henry III and the Lord Edward: The Community of the Realm in the Thirteenth Century* (reprinted Oxford: Oxford University Press, 1966), 159; W. Mark Ormrod, *The Reign of Edward III: Crown and Political Society in England, 1327–1377* (New Haven and London: Yale University Press, 1990), 6.

43. Saul, *Richard II*, 83. For Gloucester's turbulent marriages with disastrous diplomatic consequences in the 1420s and 1430s, see Kenneth H. Vickers,

Humphrey, Duke of Gloucester (London: Constable and Company, 1907), chaps. 4 and 5, and Ralph Alan Griffiths, "The Trial of Eleanor Cobham: An Episode in the Fall of Duke Humphrey of Gloucester," *Bulletin of the John Rylands Library,* 51 (1969): 381–99, reprinted in Griffiths, *King and Country: England and Wales in the Fifteenth Century,* chap. 15. Five months after the death of his wife, Anne of Burgundy, in November 1432, Bedford married the seventeen-year-old Jacquetta of Luxemburg, causing a rupture with Anne's brother, the duke of Burgundy (Jenny Stratford, *The Bedford Inventories: The Worldly Goods of John, Duke of Bedford, Regent of France (1389–1435)* (London: The Society of Antiquaries of London, 1993), 17–18). Neither Gloucester nor Bedford produced a legitimate heir from their respective marriages.

44. For details, see Wolffe, *Henry VI,* 36–38, 45–47; Griffiths, *The Reign of King Henry VI,* 52–54.

45. Ibid., 80 and n.70 (for chronicle reports of about three dozen new knights, who evidently attracted much attention).

46. Griffiths, *The Reign of King Henry VI,* 52–53, 231; Wolffe, *Henry VI,* 48–49. The most recent account of the king's expedition to France is Anne Curry, "The 'Coronation Expedition' and Henry VI's Court in France, 1430 to 1432," in *The Lancastrian Court,* ed. Jenny Stratford, 29–52 (Donnington: Shaun Tyas, 2003).

47. Dickinson, *The Congress of Arras,* 177; Griffiths, *The Reign of King Henry VI,* 817.

48. Of these four, only Henry Beaufort has a full-scale and sympathetic study written about him (Harriss, *Cardinal Beaufort,* especially chaps. 8–9 for the quarrel and its aftermath); Ethel Carleton Williams, *My Lord of Bedford, 1389–1435* (London: Longmans, 1963), is a charming, if dated, biography, and Stratford, *The Bedford Inventories,* concentrates on Bedford as collector and patron of the arts; apart from studies of his literary interests, Vickers, *Humphrey, Duke of Gloucester,* is the only comprehensive portrait of Gloucester, while Exeter merits more attention than he has hitherto received.

49. Charles T. Wood, *Joan of Arc and Richard III: Sex, Saints and Government in the Middle Ages* (New York and Oxford: Oxford University Press, 1988), 36–37, has interesting remarks on the gradual emergence of kings from their minority.

50. As Richard ruefully recalled at the time of his declaration of majority at the age of twenty-two: see *The Westminster Chronicle, 1381–1394,* ed. and trans. Leonard C. Hector and Barbara F. Harvey (Oxford: Clarendon Press, 1982), 390–93; and above chap. 3.

51. For Henry III's gradual introduction to active kingship between the ages of sixteen and twenty-one, and Richard II's awkward and resented emergence as an adult king between the same ages, see Carpenter, *Minority of Henry III,* 321–23, 389; Saul, *Richard II,* chap. 6; and above chap. 1.

52. Watts, in *Trade, Devotion and Governance,* 131; idem, *Henry VI and the Politics of Kingship,* 118–19, though in common with a number of

modern writers he is reluctant to allow any development of will power in the young king.

53. *PPC*, 4: 110, 210–13; James Gairdner, ed., "Gregory's Chronicle," in *The Historical Collections of a London Citizen* (London: Camden Society, 1876), 158, 160.

54. Griffiths, *The Reign of King Henry VI*, 44, 196, and references cited there; Watts, in *Trade, Devotion and Governance*, 123 and n. 43. Aside from his usual appearance at parliament, the king seems to have been brought to the council on several occasions during Bedford's stay in England: ibid., 124 and n. 55. For Gloucester's continuing hostility toward Beaufort, and Bedford's period in England in 1433–34, see Harriss, *Cardinal Beaufort*, chaps. 11–12. Henry's visit to Bury is vividly recorded in the illuminated *Lives of Sts Edmund and Fremund*, which John Lydgate, monk of Bury, was commissioned to produce for presentation to the king. Kathleen L. Scott, *Later Gothic Manuscripts, 1390–1490*, 2 vols (London: Harvey Miller Publishers, 1996), 1: 225–29; A.S.G. Edwards, ed., *The Life of St Edmund King and Martyr: John Lydgate's Illustrated Life Presented to Henry VI* (London: 2004). The length of the visit is probably to be explained by the severe outbreak of plague around London which may also have caused the dissolution of parliament at Westminster on 21 December 1433, rather than as a cost-saving measure for the royal household or a sign of the king's irrelevance. Friedrich W. D. Brie, ed., *The Brut or the Chronicles of England*, pt. 2 (London and Oxford: Early English Text Society, 1908), 467.

55. Watts, in *Trade, Devotion and Governance*, 124.

56. *PPC*, 4: 132–37, 287–89; *Rot. Parl.*, V, 433–34, 438. See Griffiths, *The Reign of King Henry VI*, 41–44, 58–60.

57. Ibid., 162, 203, 231, 233; A.N.E.D. Scofield, "England and the Council of Basel," *Annuarium Historiae Conciliorum*, 5 no. 1 (1973): 84ff; compare Harriss, *Cardinal Beaufort*, 298 ("there can be no doubt that Henry VI himself desired peace with all the ardor and idealism of his years and religious temperament"). For the suggestion that Henry VI should lead the force to Calais, see Watts, *Trade, Devotion and Governance*, 125.

58. Alexandra Sinclair, ed., *The Beauchamp Pageant* (Donnington: Paul Watkins, 2003), 42–46, with the touching, late fifteenth-century illustration of the earl receiving his sealed commission in 1428, and symbolically taking the young king in his arms, on pp. 140–41.

59. TNA, E28/57/92; *CPR, 1429–1436*, 601. For his grants to both Gloucester and Beaufort in late July-early August 1436, see Griffiths, *The Reign of King Henry VI*, 231–32, supplemented by Watts, *Trade, Devotion and Governance*, 125–26 and n.68–70 (which mistakenly places the former grant in TNA, E28/58).

60. Richard Vaughan, *Philip the Good: The Apogee of Burgundy* (London: Longmans, 1970), 104–5; *PPC*, 5: 9, quoted by Watts, *Henry VI and the Politics of Kingship*, 131. For the relationship between Henry and the queens, see Griffiths, *The Reign of King Henry VI*, 60–63.

61. *PPC,* 6: 312–15; the great council at which the declaration was made was prefaced by an interesting two-month tour of the midlands and west country, for which see Mabel E. Christie, *Henry VI* (London, Constable and Company, 1922), 376–77. For comment, see Griffiths, *The Reign of King Henry VI,* 237–38, 275–78, and, by contrast, John Lovett Watts, "The Counsels of King Henry VI, *c.* 1435–1445," *EHR,* 106 (1991): 286–88 (with the quotation on p. 289). John Watts believes that Henry VI was not himself capable of contributing to any such initiative and that his councilors were responsible for involving him in decision-making in this way, even though Henry was not yet sixteen and younger than earlier minor kings in taking a role in government. On the other hand, the argument that Henry continued to be introduced gradually to active kingship for a further year and more is persuasive (p. 290, and Watts, *Henry VI and the Politics of Kingship,* 130–43).

62. Sir George Warner, ed., *The Libelle of Englysche Polycye: A Poem on the Use of Sea Power, 1436* (Oxford: Clarendon Press, 1926), with comment in George A. Holmes, "The Libel of English Policy," *EHR,* 62 (1961): 193–216, and Griffiths, *The Reign of King Henry VI,* 225, 236–37. A number of manuscripts of the "Libel" were in circulation.

63. Ibid., 224–25, 237. For Titus Livius, see Antonia Gransden, *Historical Writing in England, II: c. 1307 to the Early Sixteenth Century* (London: Routledge & Kegan Paul, 1982), 210–13; and for "Humfroidos" and its context, James A. Doig, "Propaganda, Public Opinion and the Siege of Calais in 1436," in *Crown, Government and People in the Fifteenth Century,* ed. Rowena E. Archer, 102 (Stroud: Alan Sutton Publishing, 1995).

64. The tract exists only in one copy, and the volume of which it is a part formerly included a portrait of the king and was presumably intended for presentation to him: Jean-Philippe Genet, ed., *Four English Political Tracts of the Later Middle Ages* (London: Royal Historical Society, Camden Society fourth series, 18, 1977), 40–173 (from BL, Cotton MS., Cleopatra A.XIII fol. 4r-135v). The tract specifically refers at the outset (p. 53) to the sieges of Calais and Roxburgh in 1436. For further discussion, including of possible authors in the king's circle, see Griffiths, *The Reign of King Henry VI,* 239–40 and n. 47.

65. For the sudden onset of the king's illness, which is likely to have blighted his life thereafter, ibid., 715–18.

66. Below chap. 5; *The Usurpation of Richard III: Dominicus Mancinus ad Angelum Catonem de Occupatione Regni Anglie per Riccardum Tercium Libellus,* 2nd edn., ed. and trans. Charles A. J. Armstrong (Oxford: Clarendon Press, 1969), 60–61.

67. Charles Derek Ross, *Richard III,* 2nd edn (New Haven and London: Yale University Press, 1998), chap. 4, and Rosemary Horrox, *Richard III: A Study of Service* (Cambridge: Cambridge University Press, 1989), chap.2, provide detailed accounts. See below chap. 5.

68. Jennifer Loach, *Edward VI*, ed. George Bernard and Penry Williams (New Haven and London: Yale University Press, 1999), 6, 33, 98, and chap. 4 for Edward VI's coronation.

69. See Roskell, *EHR*, 68 (1953): 227–30, for the Cromwellian protectorates.

CHAPTER 5

A Story of Failure:
The Minority of Edward V

Michael Hicks

The minority of Edward V is a story of failure: nothing less, and very little more. Edward V was twelve years old when he acceded to the English throne on 9 April 1483. Ten weeks later, on 25 June 1483, he was deposed by his paternal uncle Richard Duke of Gloucester, King Richard III. One of the two Princes in the Tower, the ex-king disappeared and was probably murdered. It is his brief reign that best highlights just how perilous royal minorities were. Whilst Richard III's ambition was important and most probably he sought the crown from the start, it was actually divisions within the minority regime that made his usurpation possible. Richard was not the prime mover. The dire consequences of the failure of this minority included the resumption of civil war, a successful invasion, the bloody defeat and death of his usurper, and a change of dynasty. For centuries the fate of the Princes was the most terrible warning against political ambition. It remains the stuff of legend today.

Minorities had happened before, as we have seen. The most relevant precedents were those in 1377 of Richard II and in 1422 of Henry VI, respectively ten years and nine months old at their accessions, and both therefore a good deal younger than Edward V in 1483. In the first case, John of Gaunt, the young king's eldest paternal uncle did not bid for the regency. In 1422–23, it appears, Henry VI's two paternal uncles did, but both were rebuffed by the lords, who decided on collective rule and devised for the resident royal duke the title of protector only, which did not carry with it the right of rule, and confided the person of the king successively to other custodians.[1] It is certain in 1483 that Richard of Gloucester approved this precedent and sought the limited powers of protector:[2] Probably others agreed. Most likely this was also what King Edward IV had intended. However, another precedent had been created in 1429, when Henry VI went to France. He was crowned, nominally came of age, and his protectorate ceased, power being exercised thereafter on his behalf during the fiction of his adult rule by a council headed by a royal duke as chief councilor. Edward V was already older in 1483 than Henry VI had been in 1429. This was the precedent first applied in 1483, when it was decided that Edward should be crowned and come of age. There was also a bid for power, not this time by the young king's paternal uncle, but by the queen and her kindred (the Wydevilles). The precise relationship between the decisions to crown the young king, to declare him of age, to dispense with a protectorate, and to pass rule to the Wydevilles remains unclear. What is certain is that these decisions were the key to everything that followed. If Edward IVs death undoubtedly inaugurated the whole cycle of events, it was the Wydeville coup d'état that broke the consensus, prevented collective rule, and fuelled the factional infighting that made a usurpation possible.

Edward V had been born at Westminster on 2 November 1470. He was the eldest son of King Edward IV and his consort Elizabeth Grey (née Wydeville), who were married sometime before 20 September 1464. Queen Elizabeth was crowned on 26 May 1465. To our knowledge, no doubts were raised about the validity of the prince's parents' marriage or his own legitimacy between his birth and his accession.[3] As the eldest legitimate son of a reigning monarch, Prince Edward took precedence by primogeniture over all his other siblings, both his younger brothers and sisters, and his three elder sisters Elizabeth (b.1466), Mary (1467–81), and Cecily (b.1469). He superseded the eldest, Elizabeth of York, hitherto heiress apparent, in the Yorkist line of succession. At his birth, when the throne was briefly usurped by the Lancastrian King Henry VI (1470–71), Prince Edward's mother Queen Elizabeth was in sanctuary at Westminster and his father King Edward was in exile. The infant Edward's status and significance were indeterminate. In May 1471, the Lancastrian regime was destroyed and Edward IV recovered his throne, reigning without interruption for a further twelve years. Henceforth there was no question that Prince Edward was heir apparent. Indeed at a great council at Westminster on 3 July 1471, 47 notables swore allegiance

on him and promised on his father's death to "take and accept you as
true, very and righteous King of England." On 11 July following
Prince Edward was created Prince of Wales, Duke of Cornwall, and
earl of Chester: the traditional patrimony of the king's eldest son.
From Michaelmas 1472, he was granted the actual possession and
revenues of these honors, estates, and jurisdictions, which was managed for him by a council that came to be dominated by his mother's
Wydeville kindred.[4] Again when parliament next met in autumn
1472, his status and possessions were confirmed, and at yet another
great council on 9 November 1477 all the peers present did homage
to him. Amongst those swearing ostentatiously and attesting on each
occasion was his youngest paternal uncle Richard Duke of Gloucester.[5] Following Edward IV's death on 9 April 1483, the succession of
Prince Edward as King Edward V was therefore automatic. There is
no reason to doubt that any of the initial contenders for power, the
royal household, civil service, or the Wydevilles, were other than loyal
to the new king. Indeed, Crowland wrote, "all who were present [at
the royal council] keenly desired that this prince should succeed his
father in all his glory."[6] Despite what followed and whatever secret intentions, Duke Richard repeatedly, publicly, and obsequiously pro-
fessed as much.

Yet Edward V was a minor aged twelve years and five months. Even
allowing for the accelerated majorities at sixteen of the Yorkist royal
dukes and of previous kings, such as Edward IV himself at nineteen,
several years had to pass before he could rule effectively himself. Although still only 42 at his death and certainly not expecting to die,
Edward IV had foreseen the possibility that his son might succeed
whilst still under age in 1471, in 1475,[7] and no doubt on other occasions. Edward IV's last days were used not only to repent, to compose
himself, and to settle accounts on earth, on the most extravagant scale
as befitted his notorious sins, but also to prepare for his son's accession, albeit too late and apparently ineffectively. King Edward had tolerated and controlled the rivalry at court between his chamberlain
William Lord Hastings on the one hand and his queen, her Wydevilles
brothers, and her sons by her first marriage, Thomas Marquis of Dorset
and Lord Richard Grey. Although Hastings was a distant cousin of the
queen, the reluctant stepfather-in-law of Dorset, and participant with
him in the late king's vices, he was also the Wydevilles' foe, each apparently contriving dirty tricks to discredit the others.[8] Now, however,
Edward IV reckoned that continued feuding might destabilize the
new regime of his son. The peace that he imposed on them on his
deathbed[9] proved to be merely formal, for neither faction trusted the

other. Most probably Edward gave other instructions for implementation after his death, but we cannot know what they were. In 1475, he had left his queen in charge,[10] because he was taking both royal dukes with him on his invasion of France. Unlike 1454,[11] not even the queen herself seems to have considered that she should be regent, but King Edward may well have intended the Wydevilles to have custody of the young king. Edward IV may now have nominated his brother and his son's sole surviving paternal uncle Richard Duke of Gloucester as protector, as Rows was to report, or at least to govern, as Mancini stated.[12] Edward IV had no opportunity to tender his blessing or last advice to his heir, since the young prince was far away in Ludlow in a household dominated by his maternal uncle Anthony earl Rivers and half-brother Lord Richard Grey, respectively the queen's eldest brother and younger son. Apparently Edward IV foresaw that political unity and common purpose, a collective sharing of responsibility, and government by consensus was essential if his son's rule was to work. There were at least three distinct interests to be accommodated: Gloucester; the Wydevilles and their dependants; and Hastings and his allies within the royal household and central administration. Maybe there were more, since minorities were a time for the lords in the provinces to assert their majority opinion and overwhelming power. We do not know if any such instructions from the dying king were observed. That even his will went unproven, to the eternal damage of his soul, suggests not: the executors who declined the administration certainly included members of the minority council.[13]

A king's power died with him. Once dead, implementation of the wishes of the late king depended on current circumstances and on the unpredictable interplay of constitutional principle and personal advantage.

On 16 April 1483, the new king wrote under his signet from Ludlow to the burgesses of King's Lynn.

And where it hath pleased [God] to take out of this transitory life the most victorious Christian prince of famous memory King Edward the iiijth our king, loving lord, and father, whose soul God of his infinite mercy pardon. The lamentable and most sorrowful tidings thereof was showed unto is the xiiijth day of this present month . . . We intend . . . to be at our city of London in all convenient haste to be crowned at Westminster.[14]

By 14 April, therefore, Edward V knew that he was to be crowned at once. Perhaps he also knew the date, 4 May. It had already been decided to follow the precedent of 1429, of coronation and immedi-

ate majority, rather than that of 1422, a protectorate. Since any protector would inevitably be Gloucester, it was his claims that were
shelved. These decisions were not taken at Ludlow, but at Westminster. Edward IV had died in the early hours of 9 April. Allowing time
for the news to travel from Westminster to Ludlow, where it had arrived on 14th, the royal council had to make these decisions that day
or very soon afterward. That Henry VI had been crowned aged eight
may have been a precedent difficult for anyone, however loyal and
committed to the young king, to resist his coronation at twelve. Lord
Hastings and the Crowland chronicler, who were so committed, may
not instantly have recognized the implications. Possibly it was that the
1429 precedent was simply being applied. Moreover, the passing of
the outgoing king, his elaborate funeral arrangements, and the
breakup of his household may well have preoccupied Hastings as head
of that household. It is tempting to suppose that the queen's family
had realized all this, had checked the constitutional precedents and
options, and had planned for these eventualities during the days since
Edward IV first fell ill—his death had been reported prematurely
at York on 7 April.[15] Queen Elizabeth attended in person, overshadowed the meetings of Edward V's council, and was apparently attended disproportionately by courtiers, officials, and churchmen
rather than magnates of real substance. The 18 adult lay peers at the
late king's obsequies included only three of comital rank.[16] Mancini
reports the queen's son Dorset as saying that "We are so important,
that even without the king's uncle we can make and enforce these
decisions."[17]

What happened therefore on the first day or first days of Edward
V's reign was tantamount to a Wydeville coup d'état. Rather than
the collective rule that had worked so well in Henry VI's minority,
the queen and her family were set to dominate and to rule. In lieu of
consensus, the door was opened to renewed faction-fighting, although the Wydevilles intended to prevent that by asserting the
prestige of the queen-mother and their control over the young king.
To oppose Edward V was disloyal, treasonable, and hence impossible. To stand any chance, therefore, their rivals needed to wrest
away control of the young king, whose person became a key prize of
politics. The decisions taken by the council were fateful and carried
grave and potentially permanent consequences. No doubt all parties
wanted only the best for the young king, as interpreted by themselves, which certainly included the continuance of their own role
at the center of affairs. Hastings spoke for those who wanted the
Wydevilles utterly excluded from control of the young king:[18] an

uncompromising stance allowing only for complete victory or absolute defeat. It is possible of course that the Wydevilles had no malign intentions toward their rivals, but Hastings, who knew them best, believed that they had. He thought they posed a threat to him personally that he was desperate to avert. As far as we can tell, there was no such threat to Gloucester, who was merely deprived of the decisive role that he thought his due, but he also had interests that might have been thwarted. With so short a deadline, it was impossible for anyone—the rest of the Lords or Gloucester himself—to reverse the king's immediate majority and its implications constitutionally or indeed any way other than by force. The Wydeville coup may therefore have set Gloucester at odds with the Wydevilles with whom hitherto, it appears, he was on good terms.[19] If he was denied any say, some councilors observed, "the duke could accede only reluctantly, and perhaps might upset everything."[20] Rather than ensuring stability, which was doubtless intended, these precipitate and unrepresentative decisions may have set in motion the whole chain of disasters in motion. At the very least, they were the prerequisite for Gloucester's own first coup d'état on 1 May, which would not have been necessary had no decision been made. And Gloucester's first coup, as we shall see, did much more than merely postpone or thwart the coronation.

We know that there were further heated discussions in the council that are reported by the contemporaries Crowland and Mancini. These accounts have much in common, but also significant and irreconcilable differences. Mancini implies at least two meetings, at least one located after both Edward IV's funeral at Windsor (19 April),[21] and the receipt of letters from Gloucester in which he asserted his claims to rule—not necessarily explicitly for the protectorate.[22] That discussion, however, had been preempted by the earlier decision on an immediate coronation and was no longer feasible. Crowland reports a heated debate merely on the size of the escort required for the ceremonial progress of the new king to his capital for his coronation—a detail unlikely to have been decided at the inaugural council of the new king. Underlying this triviality was the issue who should rule. If the young king brought "an immoderate number of horse" assembled in the Wydeville interest, it would predetermine the nature of the regime and ensure their dominance. "The more foresighted" councilors, among whom Crowland evidently numbered himself, "thought that the uncles and brothers on the mother's side should be absolutely forbidden to have control of the person of the young man." Those objecting included Hastings himself, who rightly regarded the Wydevilles as his enemies. Unable to win the argument, he secured a smaller escort by threatening to flee from court:[23] presumably to his military command of Calais, an action which, on precedents of 1459–60 and 1469, risked civil war. The queen gave way. Custody of the young king and ascendancy over him after all surely sufficed to get her way, even unsupported by military force. Hastings was satisfied, so Crowland states, as he expected the two dukes of Gloucester and Buckingham to bring as many.[24] Undoubtedly Hastings kept Gloucester informed of developments. Mancini went further and (perhaps with hindsight) attributed to Hastings the plan to intercept Edward V before he reached London and to seize those opposed to themselves.[25] This was indeed what happened in Richard's first coup. Was Hastings rather than Gloucester the planner? Hastings may well have trusted that Gloucester was as loyal to the young king as he was himself: perhaps wrongly. Any such plan could have been thwarted if earl Rivers had brought the young king directly to London, via the Thames Valley rather than via Grafton Regis (Northants.), the route he took deliberately in order to ' meet up with the Duke of Gloucester.[26] Gloucester was somewhere in the North when Edward IV died. Allegedly he presided over a requiem mass in York Minster.[27] En route to London for the coronation, Gloucester arranged to meet up first with his political ally Buckingham and then with the king, whose governor Earl Rivers did not recognize the two dukes—both his brothers-in-law—as enemies. After a convivial evening (30 April) at Stony Stratford in Northamptonshire, Gloucester struck. Proceeding to Rivers's nearby seat of Grafton Regis where the king was staying and protesting his loyalty and his desire to protect him against evil councilors (the Wydevilles), Richard seized control of King Edward V, incarcerated Rivers and Grey, and dismissed his escort.[28] This was his first coup d'état. To Queen Elizabeth, this was Gloucester's first step to his own usurpation, but she was in a minority in her perception, unable to enlist support for a counter coup, and hence took sanctuary with her other children in Westminster Abbey. Wydeville power depended on control of the young king and dissolved when it was lost. Most people at the time accepted Gloucester's protestations of loyalty to the young king and willingly took the oath of allegiance that he expected of them. "Because this promised best for future prosperity," Crowland reports, "it was performed with pride and joy by all."[29] If Duke Richard's power depended on his possession of Edward V, his control was veiled, Edward being easily accessible at the bishop of London's palace by St Paul's cathedral, and the duke scrupulously observing all the marks of respect due to a king.[30] The 500 men that the dukes brought with them were insufficient to enable them to dictate and removed most apprehensions about their intentions.

That of course was after the king and the two dukes arrived at London on 4 May, the very day designated for the coronation, which therefore did not take place. This eventuality was presented neither as a change of plan for the future government, nor as a lengthy postponement, but merely as a delay. A new date was set for midsummer (24 June),[31] at which point the implication was still that the formal minority would cease. What was required for the intervening six weeks was therefore a temporary or interim arrangement. It was with this time limit that Gloucester was appointed as Lord Protector by the great council.[32] This title, created for Henry VI's uncles and three times applied to Gloucester's own father in 1454–60, gave the duke priority in defense, but did not bestow him the powers of a regent, at least theoretically. In practice however, with the approval of the council, "he exercised this authority with the consent and good-will of all the lords," wrote Crowland, "commanding and forbidding in everything like another king."[33] Plans were made for the coronation and for a parliament to accompany it. "Everyone [said Crowland] hoped for and awaited peace and prosperity in the kingdom."[34]

Quite apart from preparing for the coronation and parliament, the government that Gloucester led faced plenty of problems—diplomatic, military, and financial. England had been at war with Scotland for three years and still was. Maintaining the defenses, especially of Berwick and Calais, was a heavy charge. Edward IV was considering another war with France. Although there was no external risk to the regime, the late king's coffers were almost empty—there was insufficient money to pay for his funeral—and his supposed treasure was a myth. It was difficult to finance Dorset's fleet and even more so to confront it almost immediately afterward. Insight into the hand-to-mouth week-by-week management of governmental expenses is revealed by the unique survival of a volume of administrative memoranda.[35] Rather than fighting Dorset's seamen, Gloucester suborned them: a much cheaper option. Apparently he courted popularity by showing himself frequently in public, afforced his household, and on 5 June was joined by his duchess. Gloucester's short-lived protectorate apparently provided effective government. However it was an interim arrangement destined to expire and it was far from obvious what would happen next. A further crisis loomed.

The power that Gloucester had taken was temporary and did not amount to a decisive or permanent victory over the Wydevilles. Gloucester had wanted to destroy them. He had denounced them as evil councilors, whose interests did not coincide with those of the king or the public good. He may have accused them of destroying the ancient royal blood of England. He had presented his own first coup as a preemptive strike that forestalled their own intended attack on himself and Buckingham. Four wagons of rusty weapons blazoned with the arms of Wydeville and Grey had been produced as evidence.[36] Gloucester also charged them falsely with seizing the king's treasure.[37] Hence he had sought the condemnation (and thus execution) of Rivers and Grey as traitors, unsuccessfully. "But this he was quite unable to achieve, because there appeared no certain case as regards the ambushes, and even had the crime been manifest, it would not have been treason, for at the time of the alleged ambushes he was neither regent nor did he hold any other public office." The great council had therefore refused.[38] Gloucester had to concede the point openly, but Rivers and Grey remained in prison and were to be eliminated later. Putting off the coronation moreover merely postponed the decisions about the nature of government once Edward V was crowned and officially came of age.

What came next was a source of apprehension for Gloucester, Buckingham, and Hastings, who intended their control to continue, albeit less formally. How was this to be achieved? When parliament decided on Edward V's government, it would be attended by all parties, not just by Gloucester and his allies, but also their foes. If the great council dared to thwart his wishes, parliament was still less manageable. Gloucester could not expect it to condemn the Wydevilles. On past precedents, indeed, it could be expected to seek a balanced council on which all interests were represented. Certainly Elizabeth herself, who had committed no crime, could be expected to emerge from sanctuary and return to public life. The king's mother, stepbrothers, and maternal uncles could not be sidelined. Moreover pro-Wydeville inclinations could be expected once the young king came of age, who had shown himself committed to his Wydeville kin at Gloucester's coup.[39] Whatever Gloucester's relations hitherto with the Wydevilles, that coup had made them his enemies, with diametrically opposed objectives. With the queen in sanctuary, Rivers and Grey in prison, and Dorset at sea, the Wydevilles were neutralized, but only in the short term. Apart from Wydeville partisans, there were others—including Crowland, for instance—who were concerned that "the king's relatives and servants" remained in prison and that insufficient respect was shown to the queen. He was under pressure to come to terms with her.[40] We cannot know the negotiating position of either side. Presumably Gloucester's maximum terms offered less than Elizabeth's minimum terms or whatever she expected from parliament.

The speech that the new chancellor, Bishop Russell, composed for the opening of parliament argued that the new king should not take over government even after he was crowned. The burden of rule must needs "be borne and supported by the right noble and famous prince the Duke of Gloucester, protector of this realm. In whose great puissance, wisdom and fortunes resteth at this season the execution of the defence of this realm, as well against the open enemies as against the subtle and faint friends of the same." He ended with a highly apposite quotation from Psalm 22: "Uncle, I am glad to have you confirmed in this place, you to be my protector in all my businesses."[41] Even should Gloucester succeed in prolonging the minority beyond the coronation, however, he could not expect the untrammeled sway of the last few weeks. There was also to be "a certain number of wise and noble men to have power under him in all causes": evidently a continual council to be confirmed in parliament.[42] Gloucester's possible protectorate would still be time-limited—it would expire whenever Edward V came of age, probably at sixteen—and whatever power Gloucester exercised was bound to diminish as the king grew up, decisions were deferred to him, and suitors counted on the reversion. In the short run, Gloucester was probably safe from the revenge of the Wydevilles, but his personal interests need not prevail. After the death on 4 May of his ward George Neville, his tenure of his key northern estates dwindled to life only. Gloucester needed to adjust the original partition of the Warwick inheritance at the expense of Clarence's son Warwick. The latter's guardian, who intended Warwick for his daughter, was highly unlikely to agree: As he was the queen's son Dorset, he was well placed to prevent any such resettlement.[43]

Gloucester did not wait for parliament to decide, but staged his second coup on Friday 13 June. Lord Hastings was arrested for plotting his destruction in concert with the queen and he was summarily executed.[44] This falling out of allies came as a bolt out of the blue. The preceding Tuesday and Wednesday Gloucester had ordered armed forces to be levied to defeat a plot by the Wydevilles against himself, Buckingham, and the "old royal blood of this realm."[45] Whilst the Wydevilles might well have wished to assassinate the dukes, the approach of parliament surely rendered it unnecessary. Gloucester's countermeasure, which was timed not to produce results for a fortnight, appears not particularly appropriate.[46] Although there were probably others, we know only of two letters carried by Sir Richard Ratcliffe to the city of York and Lord Neville, both members of

Gloucester's own connection in the North, and both authenticated by his own signet and signature rather than any of the royal seals:[47] circumstances that indicate that they were issued under his personal authority rather than that of the royal council. If Hastings knew of these missives, he could be expected to approve. He had been thrilled by what had been achieved thus far, so Crowland said, with "only so much bloodshed . . . as might have come from a cut finger."[48] Hastings had transferred successfully to the chamberlainship of the household of a second king, and his enemies were discredited and disarmed. Surely Gloucester was essential to the continuation of his objectives? If however Hastings was also plotting against the dukes, still more in concert with his foes the Wydevilles and they with him, as Duke Richard alleged on 13 June, it can only have been because the young king, to whom all agree both parties were committed, was under threat. This was the interpretation preferred by all the contemporary narratives. Since Gloucester was the source of all these stories and no confirmatory evidence has been ever found, it is far more likely that the plot was the duke's own invention and merely a pretext to destroy Hastings. Bereft of their head, Hastings's followers proved as impotent as the Wydeville faction had been once Dorset, Rivers, and Grey were neutralized. It is difficult to interpret Gloucester's second coup as other than a preliminary to usurpation.

However, it was not seen in this way at the time. Up to this point, it appears, Duke Richard's professions of loyalty were generally believed, by the primate, Hastings, Crowland, and Canon Simon Stalworth, the great and continual councils, the corporation of London, and "the ignorant crowd" alike.[49] However, the necessary preconditions had been set for Edward V's reign to be terminated and for Richard III to take the crown. Both the court factions, of Hastings and the Wydevilles, had been decapitated, the two key councilors Rotherham and Morton incarcerated, and on 16 June the second prince Richard Duke of York joined Edward V in Gloucester's power within the Tower. Gloucester and Buckingham already had more manpower to hand than the peers they had summoned to parliament. Initially expected rather than present and perhaps more impressive in theory than in practice, Richard's northern army gave him all the force he needed to impose his will, albeit just in the short term. It was in this atmosphere of crisis that both parliament and coronation were deferred for five months (2 Nov.),[50] and Gloucester's protectorate thereby prolonged until at least then. No change of king was yet implied and it is just possible that none had been decided, in which case a change of mind occurred very shortly afterward. According to

Richard this was an act of conscience, the result of his discovery that Edward V was disqualified from kingship and that he himself was rightful heir to the house of York. This was because Edward V and his siblings were illegitimate; the children of the next brother Clarence were disqualified also by the duke's attainder.[51]

It seems unlikely that Richard experienced a sudden conversion because the charge that Edward V's parents had never been married was nothing new. Earlier efforts were apparently made to discount it both in 1464 and 1469. Related within the third degree of affinity—one of the prohibited degrees[52]—Edward and Elizabeth had married clandestinely. In 1464, according to More's somewhat garbled account, Edward IV's mistress Elizabeth Lucy (probably actually Margaret Lucy) was examined to establish whether she had been contracted to Edward first, but she regretfully denied the allegation.[53] Reluctantly the Reading great council had conceded that the union could not be impugned.[54] Charges of sorcery preferred against the queen's mother in 1469 were apparently intended to establish her illicit influence on the king and hence to invalidate her daughter's marriage, but a change in ministry forced the charges to be withdrawn.[55] The year 1483 thus witnessed a third attack on the marriage, the old charges of secrecy and sorcery being reiterated with unfounded promises of substantiation, but this time the key charge was that the king had not been free to marry because of an earlier binding contract with Eleanor Talbot, the widow of Sir Thomas Butler (d. ca.1460). Eleanor, who had died in 1468, had said nothing at the time, but now the story had been revealed,[56] supposedly by some northerner, but actually according to Crowland by someone well-known to have been in London at the time.[57] A decade later, the Burgundian Philippe de Commynes named the source as the Yorkshireman Robert Stillington, Bishop of Bath and Wells,[58] who as keeper of the privy seal at the time was well-placed to know any such story. However credible in view of Edward's other adventures, there is no conclusive evidence now nor was there then to confirm that Stillington was the source, or that the story was true. Although feasible, there is no more substance to the oft-repeated allegation of Edward's own bastardy.[59]

Such justifications were an essential component to Richard's usurpation. Codified in the so-called petition *Titulus Regius,* they were accepted both by the 1483 assembly and the parliament of 1484.[60] Constitutional lawyers ensured that King Richard's inauguration ceremonies mirrored those of 1399 and 1461. Might alone was not right. It was insufficient for Richard to usurp the throne because he could. Kings ruled by election and conquest as well as hereditary right. Edward V had been accepted as king by both the royal council and great council and had received oaths of allegiance from everyone that mattered. Constitutionally it is doubtful whether deficiencies in his hereditary title really debarred him from the crown, especially since he had already attained the throne. In practice, the English did not accept the legitimation of bastards by the Church as grounds for inheritance. Politics certainly could not wait on the convenience of the Church to rule on the validity of a royal marriage. To the complaint that allegiance had been tendered irrevocably to Edward V, Richard's answer was such oaths had been tendered in error, on the basis that the young king had been legitimate.[61] Deposition and usurpation followed quickly, on 25 June, when Edward V's replacement by Richard III was approved on the precedents of 1461 by a select assembly of his partisans, which Richard described on 28 June as the "lords spiritual and temporal and the commons of the land":[62] A properly convened parliament, as in 1460, might have refused. Most historians of his own time and since have rejected his arguments as mere pretexts. More important, they were rejected also by the Yorkist establishment, the adherents of Hastings and the Wydevilles, who rebelled wholesale on behalf of Edward V in October and acknowledged his sister by Christmas.[63] If not already dead, such expressions of disbelief and commitment are explanation enough of why the ex-king could not be allowed to live. The momentary dominance that Richard established in London in June and July 1483 and which enabled him to depose Edward V was insufficient to keep him on his throne in the longer term. He never gained acceptance and destroyed not just his nephews, himself, and his dynasty, but also domestic peace.

Although Edward V's reign falls within the protracted instability that historians have named the Wars of the Roses, internecine strife had ceased in 1471 and neither Edward IV nor Edward V had anything to fear from the Lancastrians or foreign powers. That a revolution should occur in 1483 was, therefore, unexpected. What made it possible? Clearly the death of Edward IV created a new situation and unleashed a new series of events, but there was nothing inevitable about what ensued. The failure of the minority of Edward V is usually blamed on the wickedness of his uncle Richard III, who aspired to the throne most probably from the start. Although Richard's actions created for him dangerous enemies in any future regime, he was not driven to usurp either by fear or by conscience. None of his actions could have availed had collective rule been agreed to on the models of 1377 and 1422. It was the abortive Wydeville coup that labeled the queen's kindred, not Richard, as hungry for power and vengeance and as the disturbers of the peace, their coup that enabled Richard's own two coups to be accepted as the public interest, and that caused him to be regarded as necessary for stability as late as 16 June.[64] That there was no effective king, a minority in which power was contested, gave to all parties opportunities that they all missed.

NOTES

1. J. S. Roskell, "The Office and Dignity of Protector of England with Special Reference to its Origins," *English Historical Review* lxviii (1953): 193–226.

2. D. Mancini, *The Usurpation of Richard III*, 2nd ed., ed. C.A.J. Armstrong (Oxford, 1969) [hereafter Mancini].

3. However the marriage was apparently impugned in 1469–70, Michael Hicks, *Edward V. The Prince in the Tower* (Stroud, 2003), 52; and see below.

4. Ibid. 57–58; *The Rolls of Parliament*, ed. C. Given-Wilson, 16 vols (Woodbridge, 2005), 14:24–36.

5. Hicks, *Edward V*, 61–63; *The Rolls of Parliament*, 14:24–39.

6. *The Crowland Abbey Chronicles 1459–86*, ed. N. Pronay and J. C. Cox (Gloucester, 1986) [hereafter *Crowland*], 152–53.

7. Hicks, *Edward V*, 58, 69; *Excerpta Historica*, ed. S. Bentley (London, 1833), 369.

8. M. A. Hicks, *Richard III*, 2nd edn. (London, 2000), 51.

9. T. More, *History of King Richard III*, ed. R. S. Sylvester (New Haven, CN, 1963), 10–11; Mancini, 62–63.

10. *English Historical Documents 1327–1485*, ed. A. R. Myers (London, 1969), 273.

11. Hicks, *Edward V*, 68–69.

12. A. Hanham, *Richard III and his Early Historians 1483–1535* (Oxford, 1975), 118; Mancini, 72–73.

13. *Registrum Thome Bourgchier*, i, ed. F. R. H. Du Boulay (Canterbury and York Society cxxi, 1948–50), 52–53. Those present may or may not have been the executors.

14. *Historic Manuscripts Commission 11th Report Appendix III, MSS of the Corporations of Southampton and King's Lynn* (1887), 170.

15. *The York House Books*, ed. L. Attreed, 2 vols (Richard III and Yorkist History Trust, Stroud, 1991), 1:282.

16. The services at Westminster Abbey on 17th were attended by Archbishop Rotherham, 11 bishops, Dorset, the earls of Huntingdon and Lincoln (a minor), Viscount Berkeley, and 12 barons (Abergavenny, Audley, Cobham, Dacre of the South, Dudley, Ferrers, Hastings, Howard, Lisle, Morley, Stanley, and Welles). Present at Windsor on 18th/19th were Rotherham, 3 bishops, Dorset, Huntingdon, Lincoln,

Berkeley, and 12 barons (Abergavenny, Audley, Cobham, Delawarr, Ferrers, Fitzhugh, Hastings, Howard, Lisle, Maltravers, Stanley, and Welles), *The Royal Funerals of the House of York at Windsor*, ed. A. F. Sutton and L.Visser-Fuchs (Richard III Society, London, 2005), 18–25.

17. Mancini, 74–75.
18. Crowland, 152–53.
19. C. Moreton, "A Local Dispute and the Politics of 1483: Roger Townshend, Earl Rivers and the Duke of Gloucester," *The Ricardian* 107 (1989).
20. Mancini, 72–73.
21. Sutton and Visser-Fuchs, *Royal Funerals*, 18–25.
22. Mancini, 72–73. However, Mancini reports that Gloucester was to be chief councillor, on the pattern of 1429; ibid. 71–72.
23. Crowland, 152–55.
24. Crowland, 154–55.
25. Mancini, 72–73.
26. M. A. Hicks, *Richard III and His Rivals. Magnates and Their Motives During the Wars of the Roses* (London, 1991), 227; Mancini, 74–75.
27. Crowland, 154–55.
28. Mancini, 74–79.
29. Crowland, 156–57.
30. Ibid. 156–57; Mancini, 76–77, 80–83.
31. Mancini, 123.
32. Mancini, 82–85; Crowland, 156–57. There are no surviving records of this great council, but the administration of Edward IV's will at Baynards Castle on 11 May was attended by both archbishops, 8 bishops, Buckingham, Gloucester, Arundel, Hastings, Stanley, "and many other nobles," presumably mere barons, *Reg. Bourgchier*, 52–53.
33. Crowland, 156–57.
34. Crowland, 158–59.
35. "Financial Memoranda of the Reign of Edward V," ed. R. E. Horrox, *Camden Miscellany* xxix (Camden 4th ser xxxiv, 1987), 200–44.
36. Mancini's statement that the weapons had been prepared for the Scottish war (Mancini, 82–83) is credible, both because Rivers and Sir Edward Wydeville served on it and because Grafton was the obvious place for them to be stored.
37. Mancini, 119; Hicks, *Richard III*, 126–27.
38. Mancini, 84–85.
39. Ibid. 76–77.
40. Crowland, 158–59.
41. S. B. Chrimes, *English Constitutional Ideas in the Fifteenth Century* (Cambridge, 1936), 177–78.
42. Ibid. 172.
43. Hicks, *Richard III and His Rivals*, 275–56. Among Dorset's property seized by Richard by 9 June 1483 may have been Warwick, who was

placed in the custody of his aunt Duchess Anne, *Stonor Letters and Papers 1290–1483*, ed. C. L. Kingsford (Camden 3rd ser xxix, xxx, 1919), ii.159; Mancini, 88–89.

44. Mancini, 90–91; Crowland, 158–59; More, *Richard III*, 46–47.
45. *Richard III: The Road to Bosworth Field*, ed. P. W. Hammond and A. F. Sutton (London, 1985), 103–4. It seems likely that all such letters were directed to Richard's adherents in the north.
46. Ibid. The army's progress to London was timed to coincide with the coronation, parliament, and the usurpation, see Crowland, 158–59.
47. Hammond and Sutton, 103–4.
48. Crowland, 158–59.
49. Crowland, 156–59; Mancini, 88–91; *Stonor L & P*, 2:161; see also Hicks, *Richard III*, 112–16.
50. Mancini, 123.
51. Hammond and Sutton, 157.
52. Through Elizabeth's mother Jacquetta's first husband John Duke of Bedford, a grandson of John of Gaunt and through Edward's mother Cecily, Gaunt's grand-granddaughter of Gaunt.
53. More, *Richard III*, 64–65; Hicks, *Edward V*, 34.
54. *Calendar of Milanese State Papers*, ed. A. B. Hinds (London, 1902), 1:113–14; Hicks, *Edward V*, 47–48.
55. *Calendar of Patent Rolls 1467–1477*, 190.
56. Hammond and Sutton, 155–56; see also J. Ashdown-Hill, "Edward IV's Uncrowned Queen: The Lady Eleanor Talbot, Lady Butler," *The Ricardian* 139 (1997).
57. Crowland, 160–61.
58. P. de Commines, *Mémoires*, ed. J. Calmette (Paris, 1925), 2:232, 305.
59. Hicks, *Edward V*, 26.
60. Hammond and Sutton, 155–59.
61. *Letters and Papers Illustrative of the Reigns of Richard III and Henry VII*, ed. J. Gairdner, 2 vols. (Rolls Series, London, 1861–63), 2:11–12.
62. Ibid., 12; see also C.A.J. Armstrong, "The Inauguration Ceremonies of the Yorkist Kings and Their Title to the Throne," *Transactions of the Royal Historical Society*, 4th ser xxx (1948), 51–73.
63. Hicks, *Richard III*, 153–64.
64. *Cely Letters 1472–1488*, ed. A. Hanham (Early English Text Society 273 [1975]), 185; Hicks, *Richard III*, 114.

CHAPTER 6

"HAVE NOT WEE A NOBLE KYNGE"?
THE MINORITY OF EDWARD VI

Charles Beem

As they considered the tragic fate of Edward V, the first two Tudor kings had every right to feel apprehensive about the prospect of a royal minority.[1] Both Henry VII (1485–1509) and Henry VIII (1509–47) faced the prospect of a minority succession in the final years of their reigns. In the case of the latter the prospect became a reality. Prior to his own death and in marked contrast to his Yorkist grandfather, Henry VIII exercised considerable political foresight concerning the inevitability of his son's minority reign. Once he became king, at age nine, Edward VI followed the historical path trod by Henry III, Richard II, and Henry VI, as he made the gradual transition to his majority reign, only to be struck down by a fatal illness three months prior to his sixteenth birthday.

At the epicenter of this minority is a figure often obscured in the histories of this reign, the young king himself.[2] Arguably the best educated monarch ever to sit on the English throne, Edward VI's influence on the course of the Edwardian Reformation, and his relationship to the affairs and direction of his government, remain hot topics among Tudor-era scholars. Edward left a significant body of literary remains, in the forms of his political chronicle, letters, rhetorical exercises, and administrative memoranda, which has formed the basis of widely varying historical interpretations concerning their relationship to the minority governance of his kingdom.[3] The extent and volume of these sources dwarfs that of any previous English royal minor, and complicates any assessment of Edward's historical agency as a minority king. This chapter joins the fray following a completely different methodological path. In previous chapters of this volume, the forms and legacies of five previous royal minorities have been examined, as well as their historical relationship with each other. The nature and form of Edward's minority shall also be subjected to the same comparative approach, in an attempt to provide a fresh perspective on the still difficult historical questions arising from the study of his reign.

Edward's was the final English royal minority. While the continuities of the medieval past were considerable, the sixteenth-century Tudor state significantly altered both the rationale and the means by which a minority government was constructed. Between the Battle of Bosworth (22 August 1485), which placed the parvenu Tudor dynasty on the throne, and the moment Henry VIII drew his final breath sixty-two years later (28 January 1547), monarchical government in England had increased in sophistication and scope, in its executive and administrative functions, its relationship with parliament, in the formation and implementation of religious policy, and the means by which royal power was represented to the kingdom.[4] If the five previous minorities were located historically in the high and later "middle ages," Edward VI's was "early modern," a reign, according to G. R. Elton, somewhat at odds with the supposed political realities of the mid-sixteenth-century Tudor state.[5] As critics of the Eltonian "Tudor revolution" stress the continuities with medieval practices and precedents, such as the role of the court, the final English royal minority represents the blending of centuries-old responses coupled with the modernizing trends of the Tudor monarchy.[6]

THE HOUSE OF TUDOR

During the first half of the sixteenth century in England, the prospect of a minority reign was a disturbing possibility. The rise of the Tudor dynasty itself was only made possible by the disappearance and probable deaths of Edward V and his younger brother. While Henry VII and his queen Elizabeth of York symbolically united Lancaster and York, and worked hard to provide for the Tudor succession, the prospect of a minority reign materialized with the death of their fifteen-year-old eldest son, Arthur, Prince of Wales, in 1502. This situation left the Tudor dynasty hanging by the thread of Henry's second, and only other surviving son, ten-year-old Henry, duke of York. While the future Henry VIII was, by all accounts, a strapping, robust lad, when Henry VII was apparently enduring a spate of ill health in 1503, a discussion held by supposedly loyal subjects in Calais mentioned both Edward Stafford, duke of Buckingham, and Edmund de la Pole, earl of Suffolk, but not the twelve-year-old prince, as the most likely successors to Henry VII.[7] This morsel of hearsay suggests a distaste and uncertainty that early sixteenth-century Englishmen may have felt toward the prospect of a minority king, twenty years after the disaster of Edward V's brief and traumatic reign. Yet, Henry VII took no steps to further ensure the succession of his heirs, after executing the earl of Warwick in 1499, and gaining custody of the renegade earl of Suffolk in 1506, other than keeping his eye on the other various male descendants of the House of York.[8]

It did not occur to Henry VII to ask his later parliaments for any form of statutory protections for his underage heir, nor did he compose a formal council of regency for the possibility of a minority succession. Henry VII's first parliament had recognized Henry's heirs, male and female, capable of inheriting at any age, while Henry also sought a papal bull confirming his kingship and the rights of his heirs to inherit.[9] His final will contained no clauses whatsoever relating to his heir's future government, which made his death in April 1509, just a few months shy of his heir's eighteenth birthday, his final dynastic victory.[10] Like his predecessors in England and contemporaries in Europe, Henry VII, in default of any other positive actions, ultimately recognized that the succession was subject to the hazards of ill fortune, or the will of God, and considered his own stable hold on power the best guarantee for the next reign.[11] Henry VII had tamed his aristocracy, and had reasonable expectations that their loyalty would pass directly to his successor.

For the most part, this was exactly what happened. J. S. Gunn has argued that Henry VIII's accession was shrouded in secrecy; Henry VII's trusted councilors concealed Henry VII's death and delayed Henry VIII's proclamation as king until the tower could be secured, and the council purged of Richard Empson and Edmund Dudley, efficient fiscal taskmasters for Henry VII, in a scenario highly reminiscent of the events surrounding Henry VIII's own death in January 1547.[12] But once Henry was proclaimed, the party began. In contrast to his austere and tightfisted father, the teenaged Henry VIII was wildly popular upon his accession, plundering his father's largesse at an alarming rate. To his subjects, Henry was a vision of virile, adult kingship; at six foot two he probably looked like an Olympic athlete. To his father's councilors, however, Henry was an overgrown boy-king in need of supervision and training, whom they delicately subjected to a form of *de facto, quasi*-minority. While the new king cut a dazzling image for public consumption, his initial royal council, which virtually duplicated that of Henry VII's final council, took the lead in charting the initial course of the new reign, in much the same *ad hoc* fashion that councils had come together spontaneously upon the accessions of Richard II, Henry VI, and Edward V.[13]

Henry's councilors well knew that this period of transition would be brief, but they did succeed in prompting Henry to honor his father's last wishes, and marry his brother's widow, Catherine of Aragon. It is unclear how they counseled Henry on the arrests of Empson and Dudley, who were both beheaded sixteen months after Henry's accession. But they were definitely lukewarm toward Henry VIII's dream of resurrecting the Hundred Years War, as both Catherine and later Thomas Wolsey acquired influence over the foreign policies of the maturing king.

As Catherine's influence waned by the 1520s, Wolsey, by then Lord Chancellor, archbishop of York, Cardinal, and papal legate, was reaching the apex of power under Henry. Henry had little interest in the administrative details of his administration, at least in the first half of his reign. In fact, he often played the part of an "articulate puppet," reading Wolsey's speeches to his royal council.[14] Ultimately, Wolsey's fate was linked with Catherine's, whose inability to bear sons, and the resulting divorce case initiated in 1527, help bring his career to an ignominious end, as his departure paved the way for the brilliant career of his secretary, Thomas Cromwell, whose vision and talents were instrumental in transforming the divorce into the English Reformation. Henry did have a daughter with Catherine, Mary, born 1516, but he was resistant to a female succession, and set his mind to obtaining an annulment from his first marriage so he could marry his mistress, Anne Boleyn.

Anne Boleyn also suffered from the same dynastic failure as Catherine; only wife number three, Jane Seymour, provided Henry with the male heir he most desperately wanted, Edward, born October 1537. Unfortunately, Jane died of complications shortly after giving birth, while Henry's three subsequent wives failed to produce heirs. Quite unlike all previous English royal minors, there was no queen mother to exert influence during Edward VI's minority. While Isabella of France and Elizabeth Wydeville had aimed for *de facto* power and influence, English royal minorities hold the historical distinction of not a single woman *de jure* regent, quite unlike the experience of continental monarchies, notably France. As king, Edward VI's royal contemporaries included Mary of Guise, later a *de jure* regent in Scotland on behalf of her daughter, Mary, Queen of Scots, whom he entertained royally in 1551, while Queen Catherine de Medici was waiting in the wings for her long and momentous career as a regent and major player in the wars of religion that plagued France for much of the second half of the sixteenth century.[15]

It is more than ironic that the king who was the father to England's first regnant queens was decidedly ambivalent to the concept of female rule. For the first six years of his life, prince Edward was his father's *only* recognized legitimate heir.[16] From the moment of his birth, Edward's survival was of singular dynastic importance; his health, upbringing, and education were top priorities for Henry's government. So was planning for the possibility of a royal minority. Henry probably had no illusions of a repeat of 1422, in which the lords temporal and spiritual came together both spontaneously and corporately to guide the government and protect the young king's interests. The element of spontaneity present in the events of 1483, however, which eventually resulted in Edward V's deposition, was an element Henry was undoubtedly keen to avoid.

Even before Edward was born, Henry VIII and Cromwell had already decided that a conciliar regime was the best bet for a royal minority government. This form of minority government had worked well enough during the early years of Richard II's minority, which provided the historical models for the royal councils of Henry VI's long minority reign. Reflective of these positive historical precedents, parliament's enactment of a Second Act of Succession (1536) empowered the king to compose a council of regency to rule for a minor king or queen, leaving open the possibility of the king's (or queen's) mother having a role in the education and guardianship of the minor monarch.[17]

Parliamentary planning for the form and function of a minority regime in advance was unprecedented. Henry, in close cooperation with Cromwell, had used parliamentary statutes as the means to separate the English Church from Rome, recognize the king as supreme head of the church, settle (and resettle) the succession, and take possession of England's monastic wealth. It was a small stretch to use statutory authority to devise in advance the formation of a regime that strongly mirrored the most successful of previous minority regimes. At the same time, Cromwell also labored to streamline the effectiveness of the Privy Council, which assumed its corporate form and function following his fall in 1540. Whether it was planned or not, by the end of Henry VIII's reign, the Privy Council emerged as an ideal form of regency capable of emulating the corporate nature of Richard II and Henry VI's regency councils.

By 1544, when it seemed clear that Henry's days of child begetting were over, a third Act of Succession restored the king's daughters Mary and Elizabeth as statutory heirs, with qualifications, after Edward, while the king was empowered to provide for further heirs, and compose a minority government in his final will. Henry's will, or wills, rather, have been the subject of much discussion and debate.[18] If we accept the 30 December 1546 document as a valid and legal reflection of what turned out to be Henry's last wishes, the will designated a body of sixteen executors who would function as a privy council during Edward's minority, assisted by another group of men termed "assistant executors." The will stipulated that Edward would achieve his full majority at age eighteen, and allowed him to annul any statutes or acts taken by his government during his minority following the achievement of his majority. What these stipulations seem to represent was Henry VIII's probable desire to render Edward's minority government as *conservative* as possible, in terms of forging policy, religious and otherwise, with built-in enticements for the executors to formulate policies in accordance with the maturing consent of the king himself.

PREPARING FOR JOSIAH

By the time he began composing his last will in December 1546, Henry VIII had already put much effort into paving the road to his son's eventual succession. The outlines of Edward's life prior to his accession betray an enormous amount of attention paid to the upbringing and lifestyle of a future minority king. A number of these policies strongly resemble positive attempts to minimize mistakes made in previous royal minorities.

Most importantly, consciously or not, Henry VIII prevented any faction present at his court from establishing a personal relationship with Edward. Until his accession, Edward remained mostly out of London and away from court, with visitation rights jealously handed out only to the most important personages. While Edward's health was a major factor in this decision, Henry also kept Edward completely away from the factional strife that dominated his court in the period 1540–47. This was in marked contrast to the experience of Edward V, whose deposition was directly connected to his perceived sympathy for his mother's family.

Was this close planning on Henry's part? Edward VI's closest male relative on his mother's side, his uncle Edward Seymour, created earl of Hertford in 1536, had risen steadily in the ranks of Henry VIII's

service in the final decade of his reign. In Henry VIII's final weeks of
life, Hertford stood in effective control of the government and the
court, as Henry handed over physical custody of his will directly to his
brother-in-law. Yet Hertford had been kept completely away from
Edward's tutelage, quite unlike Anthony Wydeville in the previous minority. Keeping Edward away from the possibility of factional affinities
may also have been behind Henry's decision to create Edward Prince
of Wales literally on the brink of his death. Again, Edward V provides
the salient contrast. Created Prince of Wales at the age of six months,
a year later Edward went to Wales at the head of his household and
council, with Anthony Wydeville, Earl Rivers, as governor and ruler,
and John Alcock, bishop of Rochester, as president of the council. Inevitably, Edward's whole life was spent in the bosom of the Wydeville
family. How close Edward V and Rivers actually were is difficult to
determine, but the appearance and belief of factional affinity between
them proved fatal to both.[19]

As he shielded his heir from factional influences, Henry also kept
Edward physically close to the capital. In keeping with this policy,
Henry declined to utilize his son as a figurehead for any form of regional administration in the northern or western marches, as he did
for his daughter Mary in the late 1520s.[20] In fact, Edward was never
more than one day's journey from London during his father's final
years, perhaps in case of an unexpected succession. Finally, Henry
never trotted Edward out for the kind of frequent and public mass
oaths of allegiance that the future Edward V was repeatedly subjected
to, even as an infant.[21]

Henry VIII also managed to avoid other problems of earlier minorities. The future Edward VI never became a "spoiled" child, in the
manner of historical descriptions of the youthful Richard II, fawned
over by his father's household men and his aristocratic circle of youthful companions; like Henry VI before him, Edward was subject to discipline and corporal punishment.[22] When Edward VI ascended the
throne, he was serious, sober, and already in possession of a youthful
but kingly *gravitas*. He immediately inherited a working privy council, mostly united in outlook, none of whom had any form of personal
relationship with him, with the exception of his godfather, Thomas
Cranmer, archbishop of Canterbury.

Edward's upbringing and the construction of a minority regime
suggest a thorough tutelage in the history of previous minority
regimes. A true Renaissance prince, Henry VIII had direct access to a
large body of historical works to guide him. Henry, in fact, used history, as it was understood in the sixteenth century, as a means to help

solve a number of his own contemporary problems. In the early 1530s, the compilation of the *Collectanea satis copiosa*, a composite of historical sources of varying accuracy, lent scholarly legitimacy to the concept of a *historical* royal supremacy of the Church. While we cannot say conclusively that Henry actually read any of the historical literature that was readily available to him (although he did annotate his copy of the *Collectanaea*), it is much more probable that Cromwell *did*. The desirability and feasibility of a minority conciliar regime was one significant policy that survived Cromwell's fall from grace and execution in 1540.

After Cromwell's fall, Henry VIII remained keen on obtaining works of history. In the early 1540s, Henry commissioned one scholar, the poet and antiquary John Leland, to look far and wide in the former monastic lands and gather together as many literary works, including histories, for his royal library.[23] Leland's dedication of his efforts in 1545 "prescribed the acts of your most noble predecessors, and the fortunes of this your realm," with one obvious historical purpose, to assist the process of guaranteeing the "succession in kingly estate, of your dere and worthily beloved son prynce Edward . . ."[24]

Henry would have also obtained knowledge of previous minorities from literate popular culture. Histories such as Polydore Vergil's *Anglica Historia* (1534), dedicated to Henry VIII, and Thomas More's *The History of King Richard III,* composed between 1513 and 1518, were boiled down for popular consumption in works such as Edward Hall's *The Union of the Noble and Illustre Famelies of Lancastre and York,* first published in 1542, which provided historical narratives of Henry VI's and Edward V's royal minorities for the consumption of a highly literate Tudor political society.[25] While Hall's narrative was unabashedly pro-Tudor, the successes and failures of the three previous minorities were duly recounted; the spoiled and undisciplined Richard II, and good Duke Humphrey, who later battled for control of Henry VI's minority with his archenemy and uncle, Cardinal Beaufort. Hall also did a superlative job of blackening Richard III's historical reputation to Shakespearean proportions, as a warning against unbridled aristocratic desires to take advantage of the uncertainties of a royal minority.[26]

The specter of the unstable fifteenth century, as recounted in Hall's chronicle, filled with unscrupulous overmighty subjects, haunted Henry VIII, who seemed to perceive a potential Richard III in virtually every nobleman with Plantagenet blood in his veins. In 1513, Henry executed his Yorkist cousin Edmund de la Pole, prior to one of his continental military escapades, while eight years later Henry's

Lancastrian cousin Edward Stafford, duke of Buckingham, was convicted and executed for treason on hearsay evidence alluding to his status as a potential heir to the throne. There had been whispers of Buckingham's royal pretensions since the beginning of the reign, but by the 1520s, Henry, now in his thirties and without a male heir, became markedly more sensitive to the words and actions, alleged and otherwise, of his various aristocratic cousins.[27] In the late 1530s, Henry destroyed the Pole family, descendants of the Yorkist prince George, duke of Clarence, over their alleged treasonable activities; only the exile Reginald and the informer Geoffrey escaped the block, perhaps the most notorious of Henry's judicial murders. At the end of Henry's reign, Thomas Howard, duke of Norfolk, became embroiled in the activities of his heir, the earl of Surrey, who had quartered the royal arms with his own, and was reported to think that the Howard's aristocratic stature made them the natural, and historical, protectors of prince Edward.

Surrey's folly signaled the final purge of executors included in the working version of Henry's final will. If Norfolk and Surrey were eliminated for summoning the ghost of Richard III, Bishop Stephen Gardiner of Winchester gave all indications for causing the same kind of trouble attributed to his fifteenth-century counterpart, Cardinal Beaufort. While Norfolk and Gardiner were religious "conservatives," who had opposed any moves toward Protestantism since Cromwell's fall, it is unlikely that their ouster from the list of executors was due *primarily* to their religious predilections.[28] As far as Henry was concerned, everyone in his court was a good Henrician Catholic, dutifully obeying the injunctions set out in the Act of Six Articles (1539) and the King's Book of 1543; Gardiner himself maintained this pretence well into Edward's reign. Henry's was *not* a collaborative supremacy, which he kept tightly in his fists. What form Edward's minority supremacy would take was not described in the will. While the Hertford coterie in the Privy Council possessed, for the most part, reformist Protestant beliefs, they enjoyed Henry VIII's favor primarily due to their perceived loyalty to Edward and ability to work productively together, and not to their religious beliefs, which they would not have discussed candidly with the king while he lived.

It was equally unlikely that Edward's tutors were chosen primarily for their proto-Protestant beliefs also. Just prior to his final continental military escapade in 1544, Henry VIII reorganized Edward's household, and appointed former Eton headmaster Richard Coxe, already Edward's tutor, as his almoner, perhaps through the influence of his good friend Archbishop Cranmer, who probably advised him to keep his proto-Protestant beliefs out of Edward's classroom. The brilliant scholar John Cheke, regius professor of Greek at Cambridge, who had the majority of personal instruction time with Edward, assisted Coxe. These men, along with Roger Ascham and the French Huguenot John Belmaine, all emerged as Protestants during Edward's reign. But during Henry's reign they were highly regarded as humanist scholars of the first rank. Henry wanted state-of-the-art Renaissance educations for all his children; the fact that Edward and Elizabeth's schoolmasters later revealed pronounced reformist views had little to do with their intellectual credentials, the best money could buy. Only after Henry VIII was dead could his English subjects "go public" with their reformist beliefs; as Cranmer and Gardiner squared off for theological control over a *minority* supremacy of the church.

Yet the fact remains, as Diarmaid Macculloch has observed, that the people closest to Henry in his final years were evangelical in sympathy.[29] However, the salient questions, what religious direction did Henry want England to pursue, and how aware was Henry of Hertford or Cheke's reformist sympathies, are difficult to answer conclusively. We can weigh a doubt against a certainty; as he contemplated the possibility of his own death, Henry VIII was not necessarily looking forward to a Protestant England.[30] What he was definitely looking forward to was a kingdom fully united behind and devoted to his heir.[31] By the time he died, Henry VIII had formulated and implemented a number of strategies and policies concerning Edward's eventual minority reign. A furious educational regimen, conducted outside the influence of the royal court, rendered Edward VI, on the eve of his accession, an ideal figurehead whom all his subjects could offer their allegiance to. The conciliar regime, modeled on those of previous minorities, and filled with men whom the king "trusted and loved above all other specially," was the most feasible solution to a minority that Henry could devise.[32] Whether Henry VIII knew he was going to die or not, or whether his will was a work in progress or a final testament, he had seemingly taken every possible precaution for the smooth and uncontested accession of his heir.[33]

There has been much debate concerning whether Henry VIII's will was disregarded, or even a legal document.[34] In comparison to its historical antecedents, however, the will was remarkably effective and durable. The wills of Henry V and Edward IV were much more concerned with the disposing of the estates of their kingships, rather than their office, as both kings hastily added codicils to deal with an imminent minority succession as they lay dying.[35] Prior to their deaths, there was no thought or time to provide statutory force for their codicils outlining their wishes for the form and personnel of a minority regime. In 1422, the lords in parliament threw out the portions of Henry V's wishes concerning the role of Humphrey of Gloucester, because those parts of his will relating to the affairs of the kingdom had not received the assent of parliament.[36] In 1483, Edward V never even made it to his first parliament.

Henry was not about to wait for Edward's first parliament to bestow an *ex post facto* blessing on his will, Edward's kingship, and the legitimacy of his minority government; he had his *own* parliament do that. In composing his royal will, which was empowered by the Third Act of Succession (1544), Henry pursued three strategies. First, he refused to name the members of the regency council until the final version of the will was read on 26 December 1546, which removed Norfolk and Gardiner from the list of executors. Second, the will provided for a legally sanctioned government to exist at the moment Henry VIII died, when Edward VI assumed the body politic of kingship. Finally, Henry sought to empower a group of councilors who he hoped would corporately and consensually offer their loyalty and support to his son's minority regime. When Edward's first parliament met, in November 1547, 10 months after his accession, it was no longer necessary to exercise the historical function of legitimizing the acts of an *ad hoc* minority government. Instead, Edward's first parliament faced a fully functioning, legitimate minority government headed by a Lord Protector.

THE PROTECTORATE

Henry may not have wanted a protector, but he could not have been ignorant about the historical significance of this role to previous royal minorities. Historically, the model of a protectorate was not an easy fit for Henry's projected minority government. The two salient examples, the fifteenth-century dukes of Gloucester, Humphrey and Richard, both argued against the appointment of a protector.[37] Humphrey's protectorate was terminated following Henry VI's coronation in 1429, when that young king was seven years old, two years younger than Edward VI upon his accession. The experience of Richard's 1483 protectorship remained a sufficient historical warning against the appointment of a powerful lord protector.

Fortunately for Henry, there were no adult royal males to capitalize on the precedent of a "traditional" aristocratic right to dominate the governance of a royal minority. In the achievement of the consensus of purpose Henry hoped his will would create, the recognition of a "first among equals" was bad policy, a clear invitation to the political community to gravitate toward the "rising sun" of a future *quasi-monarch*. This reasoning was part of the rather complicated dialogue included in the Second Act of Succession, and was basically the same argument Elizabeth I frequently used in response to repeated requests to name her own successor.[38] Henry had no desire to know his own winding sheet either, but the decision not to designate a formal protector had nothing to do with the summit of power and influence that Henry had allowed Edward's uterine uncle Hertford to achieve.

Henry, in fact, had already paved the road to Hertford's position of leadership within the Privy Council and at court prior to his death. Imperial Ambassador Van der Delft was certainly aware of Hertford's lofty status, writing to Emperor Charles V that he was the obvious choice to assume a position of leadership in the new government.[39] With the fall of Norfolk and Surrey, Hertford was the preeminent nobleman in Henry's court and government. This situation had much to do with the state of the peerage at the end of Henry's reign. In 1547, there were precious few adult males of the old nobility at all in England to lay claim to a traditional right to participate in a minority government; only one nobleman of the "old blood," the earl of Arundel, was included in Henry's projected minority government, and only as an assistant executor. Episcopal influence among the executors was also limited; those few bishops named were much more valued for their administrative or diplomatic expertise than their command of theology, with the notable exception of Cranmer. Undoubtedly, Hertford was the leader of a Wydeville-like faction, as the representative of Edward's uterine family. But unlike the Wydeville's of 1483, who faced stiff competition from Edward IV's household men and brother, Hertford had come to dominate in both court and Privy Council at the end of Henry VIII's reign; so Henry's death was perfect timing, as far as Hertford was concerned. While some scholars have suggested Hertford doctored Henry's will, he was reasonably assured of a dominant position within the regency council prior to Henry's death.[40]

Edward VI's accession was smooth and uncontested because all the major players, including the king, were swiftly able to gather together in London to accomplish regime change. This had not occurred in a minority reign since the accession of Richard II in 1377; in August 1422, upon the death of Henry V, roughly half the nobility and prelates were in Lancastrian France, while in April 1483, upon the death of Edward IV, both Edward V and Richard, duke of

Gloucester, were equidistant from London in Wales and Yorkshire respectively. The initial royal councils of Henry VI and Edward V operated under rather unprecedented circumstances; in the former, devising a means to signify the assent of an infant, and in the latter the lack of the physical presence of the king to offer his personal assent to their proceedings.

In marked contrast, nine-year-old Edward VI was well prepared to step immediately onto the center stage of Tudor kingship, entering London on 31 January 1547, three days after his father's death. He did so in Hertford's custody. Hours before Henry's death, on the 28th, Hertford and William Paget, the two most able and trusted of the king's councilors, paced the galleries outside the dying king's chamber, where they agreed that Paget would support Hertford's bid to become Lord Protector during the minority, while Hertford promised to be guided in all things by Paget's counsel. Once this was agreed upon, Hertford rode off in the night to Hertfordshire to fetch the new king. Hertford did not immediately inform Edward of his father's death, but waited until they reached Enfield, where Elizabeth was in residence, to inform him he was now king of England.[41] In these actions, Hertford followed the most durable of precedents relating to royal minorities, as he secured physical custody of the king's person prior to his bid to become protector.

Meanwhile in London, the remaining privy councilors kept the news of Henry's death secret. Parliament was in session and Chancellor Wriothesley informed the members of the king's passing on the morning of the 31st. Hertford and the young king arrived in the capital later that day, to the wild exaltation of the Londoners. That same afternoon the executors met together and unanimously approved Hertford as Protector of England and governor of the king's person because of his popularity, his leadership qualities, and, as Edward VI later put it, "because he was the king's uncle on his mother's side."[42] In turn, it was agreed that Hertford would govern with the advice and consent of his fellow executors, who would function as Edward's Privy Council.

In contrast to Richard of Gloucester's difficult and violent endeavor to achieve these very objectives in 1483, Hertford's coup was a quickly sustained and bloodless victory. But did it overturn the will as a legal source of the minority government's legitimacy? The will did contain an enabling clause, allowing the executors the flexibility to deal with unforeseen circumstances. The executors immediately put the clause to use as a means for the regime to have a single figurehead besides the person of the king, especially to treat with foreign governments.[43] Other executors thought the regime needed a sole executive; Sir Anthony Browne, Henry VIII's master of the horse and executor, remarked that a protectorate was "both the surest kind of government, and most fit for the commonwealth."[44] More recently, David Loades has remarked that Henry's executors "were perfectly entitled to believe that Henry had left an indeterminate situation rather than a determinate one, and that it was up to them to give the regency government a workable form."[45] Indeed, Hertford's initial protectorate was along the lines of Humphrey of Gloucester's; a first among equals, in the sense that Somerset would govern consensually with the other executors. It is perhaps more than a coincidence that contemporary historians such as Polydore Vergil, Edward Hall, and later Richard Grafton described the fifteenth-century Humphrey, duke of Gloucester, as a powerful lord protector, unhindered by the restraints of a royal council or parliament, in marked contrast to the actual and considerable restraints placed upon his prerogative.[46]

Hertford's protectorate (February 1547–October 1549) has been subject to a good deal of scholarly debate in the last forty years. Interpretations range from "the good duke," committed to the social and economic benefit of the lower orders, to an arrogant blunderer whose fatal mistake was his inability to forge a personal relationship with the king.[47] His protectorate was, nonetheless, momentous. He and his fellow executors had barely offered the new king their homage before Paget revealed the details of the much discussed "gift's clause" of Henry VIII's will.[48] As this information had been transmitted orally, the will could not be used to legitimize the package of creations that made Hertford duke of Somerset, John Dudley earl of Warwick, and Somerset's younger brother Thomas Baron Sudeley, so Edward's own authority as king was invoked. The king invested the new peers in an impressive ceremony on 17 February 1547. This event was followed by the king's coronation on 20 February, the first Protestant one in English history, which symbolically presented Edward as fully possessed of the body politic of kingship.[49]

Over the course of Somerset's tenure as Lord Protector, Henry VIII's will existed in a state of suspended animation as he employed Edward's own royal prerogative as king to legitimize the acts of his protectorate. While some historians have argued that the creation of the initial protectorate itself overthrew the will, others have argued that what finally overthrew the will, at least temporarily, were the letters patent issued 12 March 1547, which used the king's prerogative to create for Somerset a *quasi*-regal protectorship, with full control over the royal prerogative and the composition of the Privy Council.[50] But none of these events permanently disabled the will's statutory authority. In October 1549, the Privy Council cited the authority of the will as they revoked Somerset's protectorate.[51] As Dale Hoak has argued, the will provided the legitimacy for Somerset's Privy Council to abolish the protectorate, create new councilors, and govern corporately for the rest of the reign.[52]

These events were the end results of Somerset's inability to negotiate successfully the perils of an unfettered regency, rife with conflicting legal definitions and uses of legitimate royal authority. While Edward III and Richard II enjoyed the legal fiction of reigning as adult kings, Edward VI, like Henry III and Henry VI, was recognized as a minor in law. Nevertheless, as Somerset formulated policies completely independent of the king, he had little choice but to use Edward's authority to give his policies the full weight of royal will. This process was especially crucial in wielding the royal supremacy of the church.

Edward's minority supremacy was the chink in the government's armor that Princess Mary, Edward's heir, and the bishop of Winchester, both opponents of religious change, sought to exploit. With Henry VIII no longer able to hold his fingers in the dyke, England officially rejoined the Protestant Reformation under Somerset's protectorate. Somerset's path toward constructing an English Protestant church was deliberately cautious, and invoked Edward's full possession of kingly prerogative as its justification. While Somerset enjoyed *quasi*-regal power, he was not king, Edward was. Indeed, Somerset issued large numbers of royal proclamations in the king's name over the course of his protectorate; the key one of 1547 was the "Injunctions," which nudged the church only slightly in a more reformed direction as it ordered the placement of Erasmus's *Paraphrases,* Cranmer's *Homilies,* and an English bible in every parish.[53] Cranmer himself headed the commission to make sure the injunctions were observed in all dioceses.

Ultimately, Edward's royal supremacy was exercised corporately in the Privy Council and in Parliament. By the time Edward's first parliament met in November 1547, a variety of pressures came together to shape the pattern of religious change. A number of conservative bishops remained on the Episcopal bench, such as Gardiner, Bonner of London, and Tunstall of Durham, under pressure to conform to the moves toward Protestantism. At the same time, London was the hotbed of a furious clamor for rapid doctrinal change.

Edward's authority as supreme head was paramount and indispensable to the processes of religious reform. Exercising the supremacy of the church was perhaps the most slippery of slopes for Somerset to climb; reforming efforts needed to have the personal sanction of a *quasi*-sacred king. But how to cast Edward in the role of a *bona fide* supreme head, when it was clear to his contemporaries that he did not personally exercise the more temporal aspects of his royal prerogative? The answer was found in the Old Testament. Comparisons to Josiah, boy-king of the ancient kingdom of Judah, who banished idolatry as he reestablished the observance of Deuteronomic law, were made explicit at Edward's coronation in Cranmer's address.[54] Indeed, historical comparisons to Josiah (or Josias) proved very useful in constructing an image of Edward as a king capable of collaborating in the further reform of the English church, and offering his assent as supreme head.[55] Two and a half years later, in 1549, Somerset wrote to Reginald Pole, defending his collaboration with the king in the exercise of the royal supremacy,

You fear because the king is a child. But, with the help of God and faithful councilors and subjects, he has defended his own as none of any age has done before. Josias and Solomon at his best were not old.[56]

The same year, Hugh Latimer put the best possible face on Edward's minority, in the second of his Lenten sermons of 1549, wagging his finger at the "nay-sayers" as he recounted the progress of Edward's kingly tutelage:

What people are they that saye, the kynge is but a childe? Have not wee a noble kynge? Was there ever kynge so noble? So Godleye? Broughte up with so noble counsaylours? So excellent and well learned Scholemaisters? I wyll tell you thys, and I speake it even as I thynke. Hys majesty hath more godlie wytte and understanding, more lernynge, and knowledge at thys age, then xx. of his progenitors . . . . [57]

John Foxe later carved this image of providential power into historical orthodoxy, writing how Edward "removed and purged the true temple of the lord, [as] Josias restored the true service and worship of God . . ."[58] Ultimately, the image of Josiah, perceived as an active historical agent even as a child, was grafted onto Edward's public image as a king capable of divinely inspired religious reform, in collaboration with his council and his parliaments, within the structures of an essentially corporate royal supremacy.

Armed with his Josiah, Edward's first parliament was a showcase for the full presentation of Somerset's protectorship. At the same time, it was equally a display for the increased range and competence of parliament's role in the governance of a royal minority *and* in the exercise of the royal supremacy.[59] The king presided at the opening, while Somerset enjoyed the special seat denied Humphrey of Gloucester in the previous century. With one stroke, parliament repealed Henry VIII's treason laws, including the Act of Six Articles and the censorship prohibitions, appropriated the chantries, and authorized the mass to be administered in both kinds. Parliament also modified Henry VIII's will by repealing the clause allowing Edward to annul any acts when he achieved his majority.

Somerset dominated this first parliament in a dazzling light of power and popularity, hot on the heels of his victory over the Scots at the battle of Pinkie (10 September 1547). As M. L. Bush has argued, subjugating Scotland was the centerpiece of Somerset's protectorate, and, ultimately, the cause of its ruin.[60] Somerset had other pressing problems. In the pursuit of his domestic and religious policies, Somerset managed to alienate both his government and wide segments of the population. Somerset's agrarian policy, while noble, enraged the gentry classes who successfully thwarted his anti-enclosure policy. While peasants may have been pleased with Somerset's efforts to ease their plight, they were loath to embrace his religious changes. Edward's second parliament (November 1548–March 1549) passed an Act of Uniformity (2 and 3 Edward VI, c. 1), and authorized Cranmer's first *Book of Common Prayer* as the uniform liturgy and doctrine of the English Church. By the summer of 1549, the government gained a clear picture of the lower order's attachment to more traditional forms of religion.

At the same time, Somerset alienated the young king and the Privy Council with his cold and imperious nature. In addition to the protectorship, Somerset also had possession of Edward VI's person, whose household was under the effective control of his brother-in-law, Michael Stanhope. Somerset kept up the king's studies, but kept him on a rather short fiscal leash, a policy exploited by his younger brother Thomas Seymour, lord Sudeley, in his own efforts to create a personal relationship with Edward. Unlike his refined and distant brother, Sudeley was charming, reckless, and perhaps mad. Still a bachelor upon Edward's accession, Sudely had impetuously married Henry's widow Catherine Parr, and later abused Elizabeth's reputation before his wife's death. (7 September 1548). Viewing himself in historical comparison to Humphrey of Gloucester in 1422, Sudeley conspired to gain Edward's guardianship.

The method to Sudeley's madness was to bribe the king, employing an intermediary, John Fowler, to give the king gifts of cash, which were eagerly accepted and used to reward the king's favored clerics and other royal servants. Sudeley had little trouble convincing the king that he would make a better guardian than Somerset; Edward reportedly said, "it were better for him [Somerset] to die before."[61] Sudeley's machinations came to a head at the end of January 1549, following his arrest and month-long interrogation by the Privy Council. On March 10, a bill of attainder was passed. Sudeley's reckless behavior thrust Edward fully into the harsh realties of Tudor politics, fostering a royal reserve that historians have often characterized as frosty; following Sudeley's execution (20 March 1549), Edward simply remarked in his chronicle, "also the lord Sudeley, Admiral of England, was condemned to death the March ensuing."[62]

The trauma of the Sudeley ordeal was followed by the revolt of the common people in the summer of 1549. Two major causes fueled the revolts, religious changes, in Cornwall and Devon, and oppressive agrarian practices in Norfolk. In his efforts to quell the rebellion, Somerset's authority as lord protector turned out to be a less than sufficient substitute for royal leadership. Ethan Shagan has recently argued that Somerset attempted to minimize the instability of his quasi-regal protectorate by befriending the commons, assuming the role of religious reformer, and playing "an aggressive game of popularity politics."[63] At the rebellion's onset, Somerset, in an attempt to save military resources for his Scottish enterprise, was seen to have colluded with the rebels, in a series of letters that, to his contemporaries, offered an astonishing level of leniency. When push came to shove, however, there was no alternative but to invoke Edward's personal authority to help quell the rebellion. In a message to the Devonshire rebels, a letter written in Edward's name emphatically declared,

We are your rightful king, your liege lord, your king anointed, your king crowned, not by our age, but by god's ordinance, not only when we shall be of 21 years, but when we are 10 years. We possess our crown, not by years, but by the blood and descent from our father king Henry the Eighth.[64]

This definition of Edward's kingship was radically different from the one Somerset described to Reginald Pole at virtually the same time; here Edward was not a participant in a collaborative royal supremacy, but the font of royal power. When necessary, Edward's position as an anointed king trumped Somerset's as Lord Protector. Because Somerset relied on the king's own regal power as the legitimizing agent of his authority, he was, ultimately, never in complete possession of the royal prerogative. In December 1547, the terms of Somerset's commission as protector were modified from Edward's achievement of majority at eighteen to the king's pleasure, which acknowledged the possibility that Edward might achieve his majority prior to his eighteenth birthday.[65] Ultimately, the invocation of Edward's own authority was capable of both bolstering the protectorate's aura of power as well as supplanting it. However, at age ten, the year he began to write his political chronicle, Edward was not yet ready to play a substantive role in any decision making process.

His kingly sovereignty nevertheless played a crucial role in the coup that toppled Somerset's protectorate. Alienated by his mishandling of the revolt, his arrogant nature, and his refusal to take counsel, John Dudley, earl of Warwick, assumed a leadership role in the *coup* which resulted in a return to the conciliar regime as mandated in Henry VIII's will. In the first week of October 1549, perceiving the Privy Council's opposition, Somerset, along with Cranmer, Secretary Petre, and Somerset's secretary, William Cecil, fled first to Hampton Court and then Windsor Castle, taking Edward with them. There, letters in Edward's name were issued calling for local musters to gather at Hampton Court, and sent to those privy councilors in London, protesting Somerset's loyalty.[66] The councilors in London, who assumed the messages came from Somerset, had no choice but to reply personally to the *king*, writing "we are grieved you should have been persuaded that we do not have the care we ought for pacifying these uproars; we are as careful as any, and shall not forget the benefits received of your father or our duties, which force us to consult and join."[67]

The Lord Mayor and the common council of London also had misgivings about the ultimate *locus* of royal authority. According to Richard Grafton, grocer, printer, and historian, when both the councilors in London *and* the king in Windsor requested men and arms, one citizen recalled the actions of the thirteenth-century Henry III, who had exacted his revenge upon the city's liberties in retaliation to earlier efforts to support the lords who had opposed him, remarking, "suche it is to enter into the wrath of a prince, as Solomon sayeth, the wrath and indignation of a prince is death."[68]

What Grafton made explicit was the belief, present in all royal minorities, that the king's subjects, from his royal councilors down to his lowliest subjects, must make decisions that contemplated not only the present, but also a future when the king would rule in his own right, and perhaps seek retribution on those who had crossed him during his minority. Richard II's savage revenge on the men who attempted to control his minority was quite well known to Tudor political society, forming the basis for a play by Shakespeare that Elizabeth I later found quite irritating. The one notable individual who seemed to have not considered the future of Edward's eventual majority was Somerset. The sordid episode of his fall from power, in which the king was exploited as a virtual royal shield between himself and the Lords in London, was perhaps the surest nail in Somerset's coffin.

THE ARTICULATE PUPPET?
NORTHUMBERLAND'S ASCENDANCY

Once the protectorate was abolished (13 October 1549), Edward's minority government returned to the conciliar regime outlined in Henry VIII's will, and remained that way for the rest of the reign. This period, the ascendancy of John Dudley, who Edward created duke of Northumberland late in 1551, witnessed Edward's integration into the further working processes of kingship. Northumberland is traditionally much maligned; engineering Somerset's trial and execution (January 1552), and expediting the king's desire to disinherit Mary and Elizabeth, Edward's statutory heirs. Later twentieth-century studies have sought to rehabilitate his career, demonstrating Northumberland's ability to cope with the wide ranging and chronic administrative problems of Edward's minority government.[69] Unlike Somerset, Northumberland was much better able to exploit Edward's gradual assumption of his royal prerogative as the legitimizing agent of his own *de facto* regency.

Northumberland and Somerset were a study in contrasts; while they had worked side by side for years under Henry VIII, the imperial ambassador accurately predicted their rivalry at the beginning of Edward's reign.[70] Northumberland certainly appeared much more concerned about Edward's personal well-being and happiness than Somerset, and cautiously allowed him the opportunity to engage in the martial activities that had been denied him under Somerset's tenure as royal guardian. Indeed, Northumberland wrapped himself around every aspect of Edward's life, controlling the household appointments, most importantly the privy chamber.[71] Northumberland realized that the surest path to control over Edward's minority government was the king's good will, exercised through the legitimate auspices of the Privy Council, which he dominated as lord president, the position Humphrey of Gloucester held during Henry VI's minority.

Northumberland's consolidation of power in early 1550 followed what Dale Hoak considered "the fiercest struggle for the powers of the crown since the Wars of the Roses" as he sacked his conservative coconspirators Wriothesley and Arundel to move unequivocally "left" toward a radical Calvinist Reformation.[72] For the remainder of the minority, Northumberland continuously weeded and replenished both privy chamber and the Privy Council with his own trusted colleagues, including Cecil, as he created the illusion that the council was governing corporately according to the terms of Henry VIII's will. Over the course of 1551 and 1552, Northumberland also attempted to create the perception that Edward was beginning to rule in his own right.

The relationship between Edward's sophisticated literary remains and the workings of Northumberland's government has always proved an inexact science. Nevertheless, Stephen Alford has suggested that Edward experienced a gradual and piecemeal integration into the functions of his government under Northumberland's ascendancy. This constituted a significant qualification to Dale Hoak's persuasive interpretation that Edward had little influence upon the policies formulated and implemented by Northumberland's regime, itself a major revision of W. K. Jordan's earlier interpretation of the teenaged Edward as on "the threshold of power."

While Edward may not have been at the forefront of formulating policy, by the fall of 1551, when he was fourteen, he had undeniably begun to take possession of certain aspects of his royal prerogative. A comparison between Edward and Richard II and Henry VI at the same ages (13 to 15), reveals a remarkably similar evolutionary process, for all of these young kings reached for the most alluring and fundamental aspect of royal power: the ability to reward. As we have seen, this became a problem for Richard II, whose *de facto* minority did not *officially* end until May 1389, when Richard was already twenty-two years of age, and announced that he had fully reached his majority. Eight years earlier, at age fourteen, elated from his quick thinking in the Peasant's Revolt of 1381, Richard had already begun to learn how to manipulate the administrative machinery of his government, to gratify his lifestyle and reward his household men and teenaged aristocratic favorites—the beginning of the long road to the Merciless Parliament of 1388. Richard II was a highly sophisticated boy-king next to Henry VI at the same age, who was already enjoying the pleasure of bestowing patronage on just about anyone with access to his teenaged ear, the long road to the financial disasters of his majority reign. Henry VI officially declared his minority over on 16 November 1436, at age sixteen, but already had begun to participate in his government the previous year.

Both Richard II and Henry VI look like underachievers compared to Edward VI, the valedictorian of English minority kings. By the time he reached his teenage years, Edward had already mastered every other aspect of kingship; appearing in public, receiving ambassadors and other distinguished foreign guests, and exhibiting a kingly persona that kept his emotions definitely in check. His knowledge of English geography was unparalleled, and his grasp of the religious, economic, and political issues his government was concerned with was exceptional. Given this, by the spring of 1551, Edward was well prepared to begin the process of learning the substantive work of a chief executive. Under the tutelage of William Petre and William Cecil, council secretaries, and William Thomas, council clerk, Edward produced a significant body of administrative memoranda.

This body of work was created simultaneously with the actual working of the Privy Council. Dale Hoak has viewed the Privy Council and the "counsel for the [e]state," which, starting in March 1552, sat weekly with Edward to debate important affairs, as separate entities, one reflecting the substantive work of government, the other, "conferences staged for the king's benefit . . . ."[73] Alford has offered an alternative interpretation; viewing the "counsel for the estate" as an outgrowth of Edward's own efforts to streamline the efficiency of the Privy Council, "for the quicker, better and more orderlie dispatch of causes," and to make the council aware of Edward's own administrative and fiscal priorities.[74] It seems reasonable to assume that the members of the Privy Council and the other men called to the "counsel for the estate," were experiencing a dress rehearsal for what council meetings might be like when the King achieved his majority, as they became acquainted with Edward's rather long laundry lists of matters he considered important.

As Edward VI made the *gradual* transition to majority king, continually writing out his ideas as he outlined the policies he wished to pursue, his councilors, constrained to keep an eye on both the present and the future, inevitably set off down that road with him. As W. K. Jordan has suggested, Northumberland recognized the inevitability of Edward's achievement of his majority, which, had he not died, could have occurred much sooner than his eighteenth birthday, as was the case with Henry VI.[75] While we know from hindsight that Edward died in July 1553, Northumberland and Edward's councilors *did not*; contemporaries recognized that Edward's political apprenticeship was a serious step toward his full majority rule. Indeed, in the last two years of his life, Edward received a state-of-the-art education in political theory and practice. If knowledge is power, Edward was a highly informed "insider" within his own minority government, with more command over what policies his government was pursuing at the age of fifteen than most of his adult predecessors *upon their accessions.*

By the fall of 1552, when he turned fifteen, Edward had developed a rather sophisticated conception of his role as king. His view of the nature of kingship constantly evolved, reflecting the highest human achievements as recounted in his thoroughly humanist educational regimen; charity, maintenance of religious and social hierarchies, education, religious conformity, defense, and domestic and foreign commerce and trade. The evolution of Edward's theories concerning the nature of his kingship reached a critical threshold in October 1552, when he composed in his own rough hand in English a list, titled "a summary of matters to be concluded," just after he returned from his "coming out" summer progress designed to present the king to his subjects as a *quasi*-majority king.[76] The "summary" revealed Edward as writing *and* thinking at the same time, characteristic of many of his treatises, including his chronicle. In several places in this document, Edward crossed out the word "my" in front of passages such as "bringing in the remnant of my debts" and substituted "the," while six lines down, Edward crossed out "my" in front of "defense." What these corrections seem to indicate is Edward's greater understanding of his relationship to both the *estate* and the *office* of kingship, as he conceptualized the corporate nature of his kingly office.[77]

As Edward reached these conclusions, Northumberland maintained the impression that Edward was an integral part of government, betraying to Cecil his impatience with Edward's progress, writing that, "I am glad that the king, on the council's advice, cut his superfluous progress, whereby the council may better attend to his affairs . . . ."[78] Like his half-sister Elizabeth, Edward VI inherited the Tudor genes for grasping economics that had by-passed Henry VIII. His "summary" paid much attention to matters of economy and commerce, of calling in his debts, and the credit of his regime. He was also concerned with education and religion.

There has been much debate concerning Edward's belief and devotion to reformed religion.[79] Foxe used all the ammunition in his exhortatory arsenal to convince us of the depth and sincerity of Edward's religiosity. Edward's piety was conventionally sincere in a decidedly unconventional period of time, but he probably also realized the political value of saintly kingship, as his court perpetuated the spectacles of leadership and power first conjured up by Henry VIII; another well-rounded Renaissance prince who was a performing king for all seasons, including the holy ones. As Edward made the transition to majority rule, he participated in visual representations that broadcast to his subjects his possession of the royal supremacy of the church, as he publicly demonstrated his high esteem for the major clerics of his reign (and future Marian martyrs), bishops Cranmer, Latimer, Ridley, and Hooper, who constituted the ultimate "think tank" for the continuing development of a Protestant Edwardian church.

In his literary remains, Edward clearly identified the relationship between education and religious, political, and social stability; his papers are filled with ideas on educating the clergy and state-imposed religious uniformity. Edward reportedly took copious notes during the sermons given at his court; as Diarmaid Macculloch has remarked, Edward's notebooks, the religious counterpart of his political chronicle, are no longer extant, which has perhaps obscured our understanding of the depth of Edward's religiosity. It is perhaps worth noting that the few reported episodes when Edward lost control of an otherwise kingly gravitas concerned religious issues; such as a possibly apocryphal tearful confrontation with Cranmer over the burning of Joan Boucher in 1550, and an emotional defense of his theological convictions in spring 1551 with his bishops, over whether Mary's household should continue to celebrate mass, in which all parties later dissolved into tears.[80]

While Edward was decidedly serious about his religious beliefs and his royal supremacy, recent historiography has emphasized the more secular interests of the teenaged king. Recently, a number of scholars have focused attention on Edward's delight in the martial aspects of kingship.[81] As Edward may have fully realized the political advantages of a widely advertised kingly religiosity, he also grasped that successful performances of *pseudo*-military exploits displaying kingly leadership also buttressed his developing royal authority. Edward's court hosted numerous tournaments and mock battles, while Edward himself participated himself in various activities, few to his personal advantage, quite unlike his father, who participated in tournaments until well into his thirties. Yet Edward made the effort, perhaps in possession of the historical knowledge that both Richard II and Henry VI, minority kings who ultimately lost their thrones, never developed the military dimensions of successful kingship.

Edward revealed his own list of priorities for the building of a well-rounded character in a letter to his friend Barnaby Fitzpatrick, the son of an Irish peer, then resident at Henri II's court in France, in December 1551, writing, "for women, as far forth as you may, avoid their company," an obvious admonition to avoid fornication, reflecting Latimer's admonitions at Lent, in 1549.[82] But Edward followed that with "apply yourself to riding, shooting, or tennis, with such honest games—not forgetting, sometimes, when you have leisure, your learning; chiefly reading the scripture."[83] This advice mirrors Edward's own developing lifestyle in his teenage years, fully integrating religious and scholarly concerns with those socializing and leisurely activities that were preparations for Edward's exercise of the wide-ranging public roles of adult kingship.

Edward also enjoyed sophisticated forms of entertainment, especially at Christmas time. The Christmas celebrations of 1551–52 featured a gentleman described as "master of the king's pastimes," and "lord of misrule," one George Ferrers, appointed to entertain the court, and creating what was, by all accounts, a particularly festive and decidedly entertaining Christmas court.[84] Edward was an active participant in the final two Christmas court revels of his reign, and clearly enjoyed the theatrical side of kingship.[85] It has frequently been explained that the 1551–52 celebrations were Northumberland's means of diverting Edward prior to Somerset's execution (23 January 1552) for allegedly plotting to overthrow Northumberland's regime.[86] However, writing to Thomas Cawarden, master of the revels on 24 November 1551, Northumberland indicated it was "the Kinges majesties plesser ys for his highness better recreation the tym of thies hollydayes to have a lord of misrule."[87] If the motivation was Northumberland's, the plan worked admirably, as Ferrers returned as "lord of misrule" next year also.

It was entirely possible, however, that Northumberland simply expedited the wishes of the king. Sydney Anglo pondered the incongruity of Ferrers, a previously close adherent of Somerset's, as "lord of misrule" at the very moment Northumberland was supposedly bent on Somerset's destruction.[88] Edward was already acquainted with Ferrers, a lawyer, soldier, poet, and historian, to whom he had previously presented an autographed copy of a history of Somerset's 1547 Scottish invasion.[89] The answer may very well have been that it was Edward's idea to appoint Ferrers, which Northumberland's constantly advertised sense of obedience and duty toward the king did not challenge.[90]

Northumberland's sense of obedience toward his king can also explain his support of the radical Protestantism that the government enshrined into statutory form in the third session of Edward's first parliament (January–April 1552), with a second Act of Uniformity, and a second Cranmer penned *Prayer Book*. Dale Hoak has argued that Northumberland's beliefs, as a loyal and obedient subject, followed those of his supreme head.[91] Once Mary's accession was an accomplished fact, he immediately switched back to the old religion. Under Edward, of course, Northumberland followed the religious predilections of his supreme head, who took his supremacy every bit as seriously as his father did. While Northumberland claimed to have followed Protestant beliefs back to the 1530s, it is worth remembering that he never openly challenged *any* of his supreme heads, from Henry VIII to Mary I.

In his work with William Cecil and William Thomas, Edward was well informed about the complexity of problems Northumberland's government faced. This leads us to a chicken or egg scenario, one that can never be resolved. On the one hand, was Edward an "articulate puppet" who was force-fed policy initiatives so he could walk into council and announce these policy initiatives as his own? This was the interpretation fashioned by A. F. Pollard a century ago, based on a French manuscript, and updated by Dale Hoak, which described Edward as "well-informed of current affairs, but persuaded . . . of the wisdom of decisions taken, as if these were recommendations the king himself should propose to council."[92]

But if Edward was not yet fully integrated into the policy making of the Privy Council, or able to get his government to support his own favored parliamentary bills, other aspects of Edward's minority kingship reflect a more expansive grasp of his royal prerogative. By the end of 1552, in a number of letters from Northumberland to Cecil are numerous references to wishing to defer to the king's will, as if Edward's assent was not necessarily assured. In an apparent row over a property exchange with princess Elizabeth, Northumberland commented, "I must appeal to the king and you whether I ever sued for it."[93] In a postscript to the same letter, Northumberland also wrote, "it is time the king's pleasure were known for the speaker of the house, that he might have secret warning as usual, the better to prepare for his preposition."[94] Later in January 1553, Northumberland wrote Cecil again with obvious concern for his standing with the king:

I perceive by your letter that the king has been moved concerning the bishop of London . . . if he [Edward] knew my care for the south as for other parts, and the hearts of us all in care for his surety and that of all his dominions, he would soon know whose care was the greatest.[95]

Perhaps at the beginning of his ascendancy, Northumberland was able to monitor and control Edward, but by the fall of 1552, as W. K. Jordan has argued, Edward had begun to develop a mind and a will of his own. There is no evidence to suggest Northumberland did anything to impede this process. Half a century ago, F. G. Emmison argued that Edward had played a crucial role in drafting memoranda relating to the reorganization of the Privy Council's work in January 1553, the result of which, had it been implemented, was to place much more direct power in the king's hands.[96] Edward also closely monitored in his chronicle, over the course of 1552, the progress made by the Revenue Commission appointed in December 1551 for the "calling in of my debts."[97] Edward was, in fact, more than a little obsessed with fiscal solvency, a predilection echoed by both his sisters during their own respective reigns.

Edward's grants of patronage also indicate a new phase of his kingship. Beginning about October 1551, grants reflecting Edward's personal wishes begin to appear in the *Acts of the Privy Council.* Not surprisingly, both Richard II and Henry VI had already begun to do exactly the same thing at that age. Small grants in the king's direct gift, generally starting around age fourteen for child monarchs, was often the primary means of a king's first use of his royal prerogative, and Edward VI probably took as much personal pleasure in authorizing his initial grants as did Richard II and Henry VI. Even Edward V, early in his brief reign, made a grant that was expedited by the authority of protector Gloucester, possibly as a means for Gloucester to build up political capital with his probably antagonistic nephew.[98]

What was probably most pleasing to Edward VI was the knowledge that he now personally possessed the authority to wield his prerogative apart from the Privy Council. This was accomplished in a stinging letter to Lord Chancellor Rich in November 1551, who had hesitated to authenticate a letter lacking the requisite conciliar signatures. Edward informed Rich, "you are not ignorant that the number of councilors does not make our authority."[99] The Privy Council itself followed up with a letter of its own to Rich, commanding him to treat the king's signature as sufficient warrant, "as was accustomed in the kinges majesties tyme last deceased."[100] Northumberland and the council's recognition of Edward's increased personal prerogative can certainly be construed as an explicit acknowledgment that the king would now personally exercise certain aspects of his majority functions.

Now in command of at least one aspect of his prerogative, Edward's initial grants were initially modest; £10 to Richard Coxe, August 1551, 100 marks for Barnaby Fitzpatrick's apparel, and the same amount for Polydore Vergil, "in way of the kinges majesties rewarde," both in November 1551."[101] Later on, grants became more substantial; for Henry Sidney a £21 annuity, while the perennial favorite Fitz-patrick gained a £150 one, both in February 1553.[102] The question of whether Edward's grants of land were the permanent acts of a majority king was seemingly resolved during Elizabeth's reign with the ruling on the "Case of the Duchy of Lancaster" (1561), which employed the theory of the king's two bodies to rule that Edward, even as a minor, fully embodied the "corporation sole" of the "body politic" of kingship, to make permanent grants of patronage under his own authority.[103]

Edward's patronage directed toward his subjects at large also was meant to be permanent. The England of today boasts of approximately a dozen Edward VI grammar schools, established in the final years of the reign, most of which simply breathed new life into schools previously attached to chantries, which had been dissolved in Edward's first parliament.[104] Augmentations commissioners such as Walter Mildmay preserved portions of this royal bounty for educational re-endowment, a policy that Edward himself greatly favored in his final years.[105] Several letters from the Privy Council in June 1552 were directed toward this purpose; one to the court of augmentations asking for certification of recently erected schools, and others to various locations appointing individual boys to various schools.[106] Nearly a year later, John Day, the future printer of John Foxe, was authorized to publish a "cathechisme" in English, a move directly related to Edward's continuing concern with education and religious conformity.[107]

The relationship between the exhortations of Edward's favored clerics, such as Nicholas Ridley, bishop of London, and Edward's own thoughts on the utility of education and the necessity of public charity, dovetailed in a striking fashion in March 1553. Grafton wrote that following Ridley's sermon, which chastised the wealthy for their lack of charity, Edward requested an immediate interview with the startled bishop, indicating his desire to hand over certain properties in his gift to the city of London, resulting in the establishment of hospitals (Christ's, St. Thomas's, Bridewell) and the Savoy, reconstituted as a "lodging for vagabonds, loiterers, and strumpets."[108] The entire episode, during which Edward may have been aware of the onset of his fatal illness, was in fact a sophisticated display of good old-fashioned Tudor royal theater; images of this scene of a beneficent young king, surrounded by grateful city officials and other notables, was reproduced continuously through the early modern period in Britain.[109] It should also be remembered that neither Northumberland nor the Privy Council had any hand in these gifts, nor did they reap any political capital, which accrued entirely to the king alone.[110]

In these facets of his kingship, Edward's majority reign had already begun by the time his fatal illness set in at the beginning of 1553.

CONCLUSION

Edward's final attempt to wield a majority prerogative is also his most famous, or rather *infamous*, as he attempted to alter the succession laid down in his father's will. In his final months, confronting his mortality as he slowly succumbed to some form of respiratory disease, Edward was concerned about the permanence of the Reformation, and the dangers to the state resulting from the possible foreign marriages of his unmarried sisters. The result was the notorious "device," a series of drafts in his own hand spread out over the first half of 1553, culminating in Edward's will, which employed royal prerogative to redirect the succession to his cousin, Lady Jane Grey, who had married Northumberland's youngest son, Guildford Dudley, in May 1553. In this instance, Northumberland may very well have simply accommodated himself to the reality of his master's desire, a symbiotic process between king and subject that Northumberland had perfected long before the spring of 1553. Despite the initial advantage, the plan failed miserably; following Edward's death (6 July 1553), Queen Mary I achieved her accession (19 July 1553) following the collapse of Jane Grey's nine-day reign.

There is another group of documents, drafted in May 1553, when Edward enjoyed a fleetingly final remission from his fatal illness, which perhaps more positively reflects the type of king Edward had become by the end of his life, as he stood on the threshold of majority kingship.[111] In his 1589 opus, *the Principall Navigations, Voyages and Discoveries of the English Nation*, Richard Hakluyt presaged the economic imperatives of the future British Empire in his acknowledgement of Edward VI's endeavors to improve England's commercial prospects, a recurrent theme in Edward's political papers.[112] Edward's knowledge of geography was well-known; in December 1551, "scientist" John Dee presented Edward with two astrological treatises.[113] In the final year and a half of his life, Edward drafted essays on the building of a "mart" in England, as he considered the advantages of such scientific studies as astronomy.[114] By the spring of 1553, Edward's interest, shared by several men the king highly esteemed, Cheke, Cecil, and Henry Sidney, coalesced in a rather naïve endeavor to discover the northeast passage to Asia. Explorers Sir Hugh Willoughby and Richard Chancellor, Sidney's protégé, set off on a voyage armed with letters, "in Latin, Greek, and divers other languages" from Edward VI, "to princes, kings, potentates inhabiting the northeast parts of the world."[115] Their mission was to explore commercial opportunities in the artic circle, as well as an alternative route to Asia, reflective of Edward's own concerns to expand England's trade network in Europe and other parts of the old world. The letters Edward purportedly wrote gave no hint of his illness; he literally announced to the far corners of the world his penultimate kingly message:

And if it be right and equity, to shew such humanitie towards all men, doubtless the same ought chiefly to be shewed to merchants, who wandering around the world search both the land and the sea, to carry such good and profitable things, as are found in their countries, to remote regions and kingdoms.[116]

To Edward, economic prosperity was just one aspect of ruling with a divine benevolence, "so that hereby not only commodities may ensue both to them and us, but also an indissoluble and perpetual league of friendship be established."[117] As did his devise for altering the succession, which failed to accomplish its purpose, Edward's letters never made it to the kings and potentates of the far northeast regions. The winter following Edward's own death, Willoughby and Chancellor froze to death in the arctic.

Even when faced with his own imminent death, Edward could meet his maker with a positive accounting of his kingship. Barely a week after his accession in 1547, Edward wrote a letter to his stepmother, Catherine Parr, concerning the goals of his reign:

For whoever here leads a virtuous life, and governs the state right, as my noble father has done, who ever promoted piety and banished ignorance, hath a most certain journey into heaven.[118]

Edward went after the pursuit of these lofty goals with conviction. It remains one of the great ironies of English history that the education and training of its last minority king far exceeded that of any of his predecessors and successors on the English throne. Edward used his royal supremacy to collaborate in the building of an English Protestant church, and focused his royal attention on streamlining the problems of administration, while fostering education, commerce, and defense. Contemporaries bewailed the catastrophic scope of their loss; Edward's death was often interpreted as the angry will of God, punishing England for its sins, by calling back a prince who offered so much hope and promise.[119]

More recently, the government of Edward's reign has been viewed as much more compatible with the Eltonian model of a privy council driven royal government which reached fruition under Elizabeth. As Hoak and Alford have noted, integrating and explaining Edward's own historical agency as king with the workings of his government provided a powerful model for legitimizing and justifying female rule under his two half sisters.[120] As the last male Tudor and minority king, Edward's reign represented the culmination of five previous efforts to confront the anomaly of a boy king, a body of precedents that has lain moribund ever since, except for those brief troubling moments in the middle of the eighteenth century. As Edward VI's death brought to a close the era of minority kings in England, however, it inaugurated the next challenge to monarchical government; the regnant queen.

NOTES

1. Portions of this chapter were presented at the annual meetings of the North American Conference on British Studies, November 2006 in Boston, Massachusetts and the Sixteenth Century Society and Conference, October 2007, in Minneapolis, Minnesota. Research funding was made possible by fellowships from Dr. Charles Harrington, Provost, and the Office of Academic Affairs at the University of North Carolina, Pembroke, and the Folger Shakespeare Library.

2. This point was made a century ago by Clements Markham, who wrote, "the result of my studies has been the conviction that the young king was by no means a cipher." See *Edward VI: An Appreciation* (London: Smith, Elder and Co., 1907), v. More recently, the late Jennifer Loach observed that in choosing between focus on Edward himself or his minority governments, the latter was the more productive course to pursue. Jennifer Loach, *Edward VI*, ed. George Bernard and Penry Williams, xiv, 39 (New Haven and London: Yale University Press, 1999).

3. For a brief discussion of the historiography of Edward VI's reign, see David Loades, "The Reign of Edward VI: An Historiographical Survey," *Historian*, 67 (2000): 22–25. For a more recent and substantive discussion, see Stephen Alford, *Kingship and Politics in the Reign of Edward VI* (Cambridge: Cambridge University Press, 2002), 5–31.

4. G. R. Elton. *The Tudor Revolution in Government* (Cambridge: Cambridge University Press, 1953). For the standard study on Tudor royal representation, see Sydney Anglo, *Spectacle Pageantry and Early Tudor Policy* (Oxford: Clarendon Press, 1969).

5. G. R. Elton, *England Under the Tudors* (New York: Barnes and Noble, 1965), 398.

6. For a succinct discussion of post-Eltonian revisionism, see John Guy, *Tudor England* (Oxford: Oxford University Press, 1988), 154–77.

7. *Letters and Papers Illustrative of the Reigns of Richard III and Henry VII*, vol. 1, ed. James Gairdner (London: Rolls Series, 1861), 233.

8. Polydorer Vergil, *The Anglica Historia of Polydore Vergil*, ed. and trans. Denys Hay (London: Royal Historical Society, 1950), 123–28. The execution of the earl of Warwick in 1399, the last direct male descendant of the Plantagenets, was a pre-condition for the marriage of prince Arthur and Catherine of Aragon. See Gairdner, ed., *Letters and Papers*, 1:113–14.

9. S. B. Chrimes, *English Constitutional Ideas in the Fifteenth Century* (London: Cambridge University Press, 1936), 32–33. For a printed version of Innocent VIII's bull see *English Historical Documents*, vol. 5, ed. C. H. Williams (London: Eyre and Spottiswoode, 1967), 445–46.

10. An abstract of Henry VII's will is found in British Library (afterward referred to as BL) additional Mss. 27402, ff. 33, and a printed version in *Letters and Papers, Foreign and Domestic, of the Reign of Henry VIII* (afterward referred to as *L&P*) 21 vols. ed. R. Brodie (London, 1862–1910) vol. 1 pt. 1, 1–3.

11. Henry VII illustrated this point to his councilors in 1501, on the eve of his daughter Margaret's marriage to James IV of Scotland, in response to their fears that Scotland may one day absorb England. Henry's reply, "the lesser is always wont for glory and honour to be adjoined to that which is very much greater," was highly prophetic. See Mortimer Levine, *Tudor Dynastic Problems 1460–1571* (London: George Allen and Unwin, 1973), 143.

12. J. S. Gunn, "The Accession of Henry VIII," *Historical Research*, 64, no. 155 (1991): 278–88.

13. Richard Grafton, *Grafton's Chronicle* (London: 1569), 951. See also J. S. Gunn, *Early Tudor Government* (London: Macmillan, 1995), 50.

14. W. H. Dunham Jr., "Henry VIII's Whole Council, 1509–1527," *English Historical Review* 59, no. 234 (May 1944): 205. Dale Hoak used the term "articulate puppet" to describe how Edward VI presented Northumberland's policies to the Privy Council as if they were his own. Dale Hoak, "Rehabilitating the duke of Northumberland: Politics and Control, 1549–1553," in *The Mid-Tudor Polity, c. 1540–1560*, ed. Jennifer Loach, Robert Tittler, 43 (Towtowa, NJ: Rowman and Littlefield, 1980).

15. For recent studies of Catherine de Medici's career, see Katherine Crawford, *Perilous Performances: Gender and Regency in Early Modern France* (Cambridge, MA: Harvard University Press, 2004), and Denis Crouzet, *Le haut coeur de Catherine de Medicis* (Paris: Albin Michel, 2005).

16. Henry VIII's first and second Acts of Succession (1534 and 1536) successively bastardized his daughters Mary and Elizabeth, and removed them from the succession.

17. For a discussion of this act, see Stanford E. Lehmberg, *The Later Parliaments of HenryVIII, 1536–1547* (Cambridge: Cambridge University Press, 1977), 20–29.

18. See R. A. Houlbrooke, "Henry VIII's Wills: A Comment," *Historical Journal* 37, no. 4 (Dec. 1994): 891–99.

19. See Dominic Mancini, *The Usurpation of Richard III*, ed. C.A.J. Armstrong (Oxford: Clarendon Press, 1936), 76–77.

20. See W.R.B. Robinson, "Princess Mary's Itinerary in the Marches of Wales 1525–1527: A Provisional Record," *Historical Research* 71, no. 175 (1998): 233–52.

21. See the preceding chapter in this volume, "The Minority of Edward V."

22. See Margaret Aston, *Lollards and Reformers: Images and Literacy in Late Medieval England* (London: Hambledon Press, 1984), 273–311. For a Tudor-era interpretation of Richard II as "spoiled," see Edward Hall, *The Union of the Two Noble Illustre Famelies of Lancastre and Yorke*, (afterward referred to as *Hall's Chronicle*) (London, 1548), A2, R1.

23. BL Add 28196. Leland also wrote a fascinating treatise of his journey. See John Leland, *John Leland's Itinerary: Travels in Tudor England*, ed. John Chandler (Stroud, Gloucestershire and Dover, New Hampshire: A. Sutton, 1993).

24. John Strype, *Ecclesiastical Memorials Relating Chiefly to Religion and the Reformation of it, and the Emergence of the Church of England under King Henry VIII, Edward VI, and Queen Mary I*, (7 vols.) (Oxford: Clarendon Press, 1822), 2, pt. 2, 483–85.

25. *Hall's Chronicle*, O1-Q1, AA1-EE3.

26. Ibid.

27. *L&P*, 1, pt. 1, 75, no. 157, which described one of the earl of Northumberland's servants saying that "my lord of Buckingham should be protector of England," in August 1509, four months after Henry VIII's accession.

28. L. B. Smith has previously argued in favor of religious motivations. See "Henry VIII and the Protestant Triumph," *American Historical Review* 71, no. 4 (July 1966): 1237–64.

29. Diarmaid Macculloch, *The Boy King: Edward VI and the Protestant Reformation* (Berkeley: University of California Press, 2002), 7.

30. For a recent interpretation regarding Henry VIII's flirtation with Protestant doctrinal change, see Roy McEntegart, "Towards an Ideological Foreign Policy: Henry VIII and Lutheran Germany," *Tudor England and its Neighbors*, ed. Susan Doran and Glenn Richardson (New York: Palgrave Macmillan, 2005), 74–105.

31. Houlbrooke, "Henry VIII's Wills," 892–93. Ives somewhat agrees with this assessment, adding that religious conformity was a secondary unifying factor for the executors. See E. W. Ives, "Henry VIII's Will: The Protectorate Provisions of 1546–1547," *Historical Journal* 37, no. 4 (1994): 901–13.

32. *Act of the Privy Council* (afterward *APC*), ed. John R. Dasent (26 vols.) (London: 1890–1907), 2: 18.

33. L. B. Smith, "The Last Will and Testament of Henry VIII: A Question of Perspective," *Journal of British Studies* 2, no. 1 (Nov. 1962): 14–27.

34. Ibid; W. K. Jordan, *Edward VI: The Young King* (Cambridge: Harvard University Press, 1968), 57–58; H. Miller, "Henry VIII's Unwritten Will: Grants of Lands and Honours in 1547," *Wealth and Power in*

Tudor England, ed. E.W. Ives et al. (London: 1978), 87–105. E. W. Ives, "Henry VIII's Will: A Forensic Conundrum," *Historical Journal* 25, no. 4 (1992): 779–804; E. W. Ives, "Henry VIII's Will: The Protectorate Provisions," 901–14; Houlbrooke, "Henry VIII's Will," 892–93.

35. For a discussion of Henry V's will, see Patrick Strong, Felicity Strong, "The Last Will and Codicils of Henry V," *English Historical Review* 96, no. 378 (January 1981): 79–102. Edward IV drew up a will in 1475, with modifications and codicils added shortly before his death; also not extant, which can only be partially reconstructed from various narrative sources. See *Collection of All the Wills Now Known to be Extant of the Kings and Queens of England* (London: Society of Antiquaries, 1780), 345–48.

36. See J. R. Roskell, "The Office and Dignity of Protector of England, with Special Reference to its Origins," *English Historical Review,* 68, no. 267 (April 1953): 193–233, and S. B. Chrimes, "The Pretensions of the Duke of Gloucester in 1422," *English Historical Review,* 45, no. 177 (January 1930): 101–3.

37. Richard, duke of York, also held the position of Lord Protector during Henry VI's incapacities during the 1450s.

38. Elizabeth I's response to a parliamentary delegation on her marriage, 1566, in *Proceedings in the Parliaments of Elizabeth I,* ed. T. E. Hartley (Leicester: Leicester University Press, 1981), 145–53.

39. Letters from Ambassador Van der Delft to Emperor Charles V, 23 and 31 January 1547. *Calendar of State Papers, Spanish,* IX, ed. Martin Hume, Royall Tyler, (London: HMSO, 1912), 4, 6–7.

40. Ives, "Henry VIII's Will: A Forensic Conundrum," 779–804.

41. The original of Edward's political chronicle is BL Cotton MSS., Nero, C, X. As W. K. Jordan has noted, scholars are much indebted to Edward VI for the clarity of his handwriting. This essay shall cite the edited version found in *The Chronicle and Political Papers of Edward VI* (afterward referred to as *Chronicle*), ed. W. K. Jordan (Ithaca: Cornell University Press, 1966).

42. Ibid.

43. Some diplomats understood the necessity of a protectorate as a means for a single head to treat with foreign governments. See *Calendar of State Papers, Venetian, 1534–1554,* ed. Rawdon Brown (London: 1873), 203 n. 480.

44. Patrick Tytler, *England Under the Reigns of Edward VI and Mary* (London: 1839), 1:169.

45. David Loades, *John Dudley, Duke of Northumberland 1504–1553* (Oxford: Clarendon Press, 1996), 87.

46. Polydore Vergil, *Polydore Vergils's English History, Comprising the Reigns of Henry VI, Edward IV, and Richard III,* ed. Henry Ellis (London: Camden Society, 1844), 1–3; *Hall's Chronicle,* O'L, R-V; and Grafton, *Chronicle,* 549. Hugh Latimer also took positive note of Humphrey, duke of Gloucester, in his 1549 Lent sermons. Hugh La-

timer, *Seven Sermons Before Edward VI*, ed. Edward Arber (London: 1869), 63–64.

47. The creation of the modern "good duke" interpretation began with A. F. Pollard, *England Under Protector Somerset* (London: Longman, Green and co., 1906), updated in Jordan, *Edward VI: the Young King*. The major revisionist work remains M. L. Bush, *The Government Policy of Protector Somerset* (Montreal: McGill-Queens University Press, 1975).

48. *APC*, 2: 15–19.

49. For the text of Cranmer's coronation speech, see John Strype, *Memorials of the Most Reverend Father in God, Thomas Cranmer* (London; Richard Chiswell, 1694), 144–45. For a recent study of Edward's coronation, see Dale Hoak, "The Coronations of Edward VI, Mary I, and Elizabeth I, and the Transformation of the Tudor Monarchy," *Westminster Abbey Reformed 1540–1650*, ed. C. S. Knighton and Richard Mortimer (Aldershot, Hants.: Ashgate, 2003), 114–50.

50. Ives, "Henry VIII's Will: A Forensic Conundrum," 793–94.

51. The Privy Council justified the coup by citing the authority of Henry VIII's will in a letter to the imperial ambassador, 11 October 1549. The National Archives (formerly the Public Record Office, afterward referred to as TNA), SP 10/9 n. 41, printed in *Calendar of State Papers, Domestic Series, of the Reign of Edward VI* (afterward referred to as *CSP*) ed. C. S. Knighton (London: HMSO, 1991), n. 411, p. 148.

52. Dale Hoak, *The King's Council in the Reign of Edward VI* (London and New York: Cambridge University Press, 1976), 55.

53. *Tudor Royal Proclamations*, Paul L. Hughes, James F. Larkin, eds. (New Haven: Yale University Press, 1964), 393.

54. See Strype, *Thomas Cranmer*, 144–45.

55. For discussions of the role of Josiah in image making for Edward VI, see Macculloch, *The Boy King*, 57–104, and Alford, *Kingship and Politics*, 100–135.

56. TNA Sp. 10/7 n. 28, printed in *CSP*, 108 n. 265.

57. Latimer, *Sermons*, 62–63.

58. John Fox[e], *Acts and Monuments* (3 vols.) (London, 1684), 2: 2.

59. G. R. Elton, *The Tudor Constitution: Documents and Commentary* (Cambridge: Cambridge University Press, 1960), 335.

60. Bush, *Protector Somerset*, 89–93.

61. *Letters of the Kings of England*, ed. James Orchard Halliwell (2 vols.) (London: Henry Colburn, 1846), 2: 30.

62. *Chronicle*, 10–11.

63. Ethan H. Shagan, "Protector Somerset and the 1549 Rebellions: New Sources and New Perspectives," *English Historical Review* 114, no. 455 (Feb. 1999): 34–63.

64. Foxe, *Acts and Monuments*, 2: 16.

65. "The Second Patent appointing Edward duke of Somerset Protector, *temp.* King Edward the Sixth; introduced by an historical review of the

various measures connected therewith." *Archaeologica* xxx (1833), cited in Hoak, *The King's Council*, 34.

66. Letters in the kings' name, from Hampton Court, to "all subjects," (Oct. 5), and from Windsor Castle, "to the bailiffs and constables of Uxbridge, Hillington, and Colham,"(Oct. 7), to render military aid. TNA SP 10/9 n. 1, SP 10/9 n. 15, *CSP* 138 n. 368, 140 n. 382.

67. Letter from Privy Council to king, 9 October 1549, TNA SP 10/9 n. 36, *CSP*, 146 n. 405.

68. Richard Grafton, *A Chronicle at Large and a Mere History of the Affaires of Englande*, 2 vols. (London, 1569), 2: 523.

69. See Barrett L. Beer, *Northumberland* (Ohio: Kent State University Press, 1973), and more recently David Loades, *Northumberland* (Oxford: Oxford University Press, 1996).

70. Letter from Ambassador Van der Delft to Mary, dowager queen of Hungary, 10 February 1547, *Calendar of State Papers, Spanish*, IX, 18.

71. Dale Hoak, "Rewriting the History of Tudor Politics and Government: The Regimes of Somerset and Northumberland," *The Journal of the Rutgers University Library* 40, no. 1: 4–13, 11.

72. For a study of Northumberland's relationship to Edward's royal court, see John Murphy, "The Illusion of Decline: The Privy Chamber, 1547–1558," *The English Court*, ed. David Starkey et al. (London and New York: Longman, 1987), 119–46.

73. Hoak, *King's Council*, 110, 120–21.

74. BL Cotton Nero C.10, f. 84, "Certain articles devised and delivered by [the] king's m[ajes]tis for the quicker, better and more orderlie dispatch of causes by his m[ajes]tis prevy counsel," Alford, *Kingship and Politics*, 162–65.

75. W. K. Jordan, *Edward VI: The Threshold of Power* (Cambridge, MA: Harvard University Press, 1970), 494.

76. BL Landsdowne 1236, f. 19. W. K. Jordan called this document "a memorandum for the council" and dated it to just prior to an underreported October 13, 1552 council meeting. See *Chronicle*, xxvii.

77. BL Landsdowne 1236, f. 19.

78. Letter from Northumberland to Cecil, 3 September 1552, TNA Sp 10/15 n. 1, *CSP* 256 n. 711.

79. The traditionalist view, Foxe's creation, of Edward's intense religiosity, has recently been questioned by Jennifer Loach. See Loach, *Edward VI*, 135–58. Diarmaid Macculloch also argued a more "balanced" view of the intensity of Edward's religious passions. See *The Boy King*, 22–35, 91–92.

80. For the Boucher episode, see John Hayward, *The Life and Raigne of King Edward the Sixth*, ed. Barrett Beer (Kent, OH: Kent State University Press, 1993), 37. For a discussion of the Mary episode, see Macculloch, *The Boy King*, 36–39.

81. See Loach, *Edward VI*, 135–58. In his chronicle, Edward became fascinated with the career of the imperial sailor Andrea Doria, who was en-

gaged in fighting infidels in North Africa. See *Chronicle*, 42, 45–47, 65–66.

82. Gilbert Burnet, *Bishop Burnet's History of the Reformation of the Church of England*, (London: Richard Priestly, 1820), 3:244.

83. Printed in Halliwell, *Letters*, 48–49.

84. *Documents Relating to the Revels at Court in the Time of King Edward VI and Queen Mary* (The Losely Manuscripts), ed. A. Feuillerat ((London: David Nutt, 1914), 26.

85. Suzanne Westfall, "The Boy Who Would be King: Court Revels of King Edward VI, 1547–1553," *Comparative Drama*, 35 (Fall 2001–Winter 2002):272–90.

86. Grafton, *Chronicle*, 2: 526–27.

87. Folger Shakespeare Library L. B. 257.

88. See Anglo, *Spectacle Pageantry*, 306. Also William Patten, "The Expedition into Scotland in 1547," in *An English Garner: Tudor Tracts, 1532–1558* (Westminster: Archibald Constable, 1903), 97.

89. John Berteville, *Recit de l'expedition en Ecosse l'an et de la battayle de Muscleburgh* (Edinburgh, 1825).

90. Perhaps the most striking piece of evidence of Northumberland's elevated sense of duty toward Edward VI was a letter written to William Cecil, 7 December 1552, in which the duke recalled the fate of his father, Edmund Dudley, "though my father, after his master was dead, died for doing his master's commands, I will serve without fear, seeking god's glory, and his highness's surety." TNA 10/15 no. 66., printed in *CSP*, 279–80.

91. Hoak, "Rehabilitating the Duke of Northumberland," 45.

92. A. F. Pollard, *The Political History of England, 1547–1603* (London: Longmans, Green and Co., 1910), 60; Hoak, "Rehabilitating the Duke of Northumberland," 29–51.

93. Northumberland to Cecil, 3 January 1553, TNA SP 10/18 n. 6, *CSP*, 288 n. 804.

94. Ibid.

95. TNA SP 10/18 n. 9, *CPS*, 290 n. 809.

96. F. G. Emmison, "A Plan of Edward VI and Secretary Petre for Reorganizing the Privy Council's Work, 1552–1553," *Bulletin of the Institute for Historical Research*, 31 (1958): 203–10.

97. *Chronicle*, 102. See also J. D. Alsop, "The Revenue Commission of 1552," *The Historical Journal*, 22 (September 1979): 511–33.

98. Paul Murray Kendall, *Richard the Third* (New York: W.W. Norton and Co., 1955), 216.

99. TNA SP 10/13, n. 55, *CSP*, 206 n. 555.

100. *APC*, 3: 411, 416.

101. *APC*, 3: 247, 387–88.

102. *Calendar of the Patent Rolls, Edward VI, vol. v, A.D. 1547–1553*, (afterward referred to as *CPR*), (London: 1926), 3, 8.

103. See Marie Axton, *The Queen's Two Bodies: Drama and the Elizabethan Succession* (London: Royal Historical Society, 1977), 12–17.

104. For instance, letters patent issued 20 March 1553, created a grammar school at Grantham out of the "late chantry Trinity." *CPR*, 35–36. See also W. K. Jordan, *Philanthropy in England 1480–1660* (London: Routledge, 2006), 156, 239, 287.

105. See Stanford Lehmberg, *Sir Walter Mildmay and Tudor Government* (Austin: University of Texas Press, 1964), 20–26.

106. *APC*, 3: 68, 78.

107. *CPR*, 43.

108. Grafton, *Chronicle*, 530–31. Grafton later served as "Treasurer General of the Royal Hospitals of King Edward VI's Foundation." J. A. Kingdon, *Richard Grafton: Citizen and Grocer of London* (London: Rixon and Arnold, 1901), 55.

109. BL 14/cap 3, table 24, plate VI. Printers of the Society of Antiquaries 1785, "crowned and enthroned Edward VI giving the charter of Bridewell to lord mayor Sir George Barnes and the alderman of the city, April 10, 1553."

110. Grafton's description of these events has confused modern historians: as Grafton went from describing Somerset's execution (22 January 1552) immediately to Edward's interview with Ridley. See Grafton, *Chronicle*, 530–31. However, the patent for the grants, which begins with the statement, "touched by the miserable state of the orphaned, aged, and sick poor . . . ," was issued 26 June 1553, two months after the event, *CPR*, v. v, 1547–53, 283–85.

111. 7 May 1553, letter from W. Petre to Sir W. Cecil, "the king is well amended, and that so apparently, as continuing to keep himself close a few days longer, his majesty shall be able to take the air." *Historical Manuscripts Commission, Calendar of the Manuscripts of the Marquis of Salisbury*, p. I (London: Eyre and Spottiswoode, 1883), 121 n. 448. Northumberland also wrote to Cecil the same day with the news of Edward's remission, Strype, *Ecclesiastical Memorials*, 2: 2, 505–6.

112. A recent brief analysis of Hakluyt's work is found in Peter Ackroyd, *Albion: The Origins of the English Imagination* (New York: Nan. A Talese, 2002), 282–83.

113. Charlotte Fell Smith, *John Dee* (London: Constable and co., 1907), 13.

114. BL Add Mss. 4724, Cotton MSS Nero, C, x, 85 ff., printed in Jordan; *Chronicle*, 168–75.

115. Richard Hakluyt, *Hakluyt's Collection of the Early Voyages, Travels, and Discoveries of the English Nation* (5 vols.), vol. 1 (London: Evens, McKinley, Priestly, 1809), 256–58.

116. Ibid.

117. Ibid.

118. Halliwell, *Letters*, 2: 25.

119. For instance, see William Baldwin, *Beware the Cat and the Funerals of King Edward the Sixth*, ed. William P. Holden (New London, CT: Connecticut College, 1963), 68–69.

120. See Hoak, "Coronations," 114–51; Alford, *Kingship*, 175–207.

WOE TO THEE, O LAND?
SOME FINAL THOUGHTS

Charles Beem

". . . and thy princes eat in the morning."

Ecclesiastes, 10:16.

The continued existence of the British monarchy can be explained by a multiplicity of factors, one of which is its extraordinary historical flexibility. As R. A. Griffiths has suggested, over the long march of English history, royal minorities offered an early yet substantial contribution to the erection of a conceptual model for the subsequent development of constitutional monarchy, in which a democratically elected parliament governs Britain in the name of a duly consecrated monarch, whose royal personage embodies the nation's sovereignty. Much of this has to do with the employment of political fictions, one of the more enduring features emergent in the big picture of the historical evolution of the monarchy. Today, Queen Elizabeth II possesses awesome temporal and spiritual power which she does not personally exercise, a form of suspended belief first conjured up for the benefit of both nine-year-old Henry III and the magnates and prelates responsible for his government in 1216. Two centuries later, to the political nation of 1422, the accession of nine-month-old Henry VI sharply brought into focus the theoretical relationship between the king as a flesh and blood individual *and* as an undying institution inhabiting distinct private and public spaces both simultaneously and indivisibly.

These conceptual thresholds in turn provided a powerful impetus for the continued development of English kingship over the course of the later middle ages and the early modern period. Further down the long road of English history, the modern monarchy has evolved into an "exquisite fiction," a form of perennial minority status. While the constitution does not formally recognize that Elizabeth II no longer wields the prerogative of her medieval and early modern predecessors, her undying *persona publica* remains indivisible from the sovereignty of the state. In this sense, the conceptual flexibility that made Henry III's 1216 accession a reality can readily be identified as a significant moment in British history.

Successful kingship throughout English history, minority and otherwise, depended upon what Christian Hillen has termed "consent," the consultative and consensual process between king and subjects that began long before Magna Carta. The continuing negotiation of the relationship between kings and subjects, the centerpiece of which was the medieval and early modern evolution of parliament within the fabric of English political life, is a central theme of the collective history of English royal minorities. Yet to consult and to consent also implied responsibility; to summon the "woe to thee" quote was not so much a criticism of minority kingship as it was expressing an obligation on the part of the king's subjects to lend their support to the underage king, and, ideally, guide him down the proper path to a successful majority kingship.

Alongside the need for consent and support was the drive for consensus between political factions, in attempts to create collective responsibility for negotiating minority reigns, much like the twentieth-century coalition war cabinets of David Lloyd George and Winston Churchill. This was the driving political logic behind the most successful of English royal minorities; which, like fighting in world wars, were always considered to be extraordinary circumstances that required the utmost in non-partisan unity. The minority king's achievement of his majority was the obvious goal; which required a successful minority reign. As Machiavelli wrote on the first page of *The Prince*, kingdoms only needed to maintain their established institutions and create *ad hoc* policies to suit the political circumstances of the moment in order to remain viable, the recipe for success under Henry III, Henry VI, and the early years of Richard II's minority. Only when the drive for consensus took a back seat to personal gain, as happened during the reign of Edward V, did this minority reign amount to failure.

The bedrock of "consensus" was undoubtedly Magna Carta, the historical significance of which, as Frank Wiswall explained, does not date from the reign of John, who received papal absolution from observing its tenets, but from the minority of Henry III, in which baronial consensus caused an underage king to ratify not once but several times what eventually emerged as the cornerstone of the English constitution. The history of royal minorities, in fact, supplied a number of red-letter dates for the now discarded Whig interpretation of history, which viewed the entirety of English history as an unstoppable progression toward parliamentary democracy. Yet, as Wiswall has demonstrated, Henry III's minority also represented the apex of papal power and influence in England, which provided early key support for the reconfirmations of Magna Carta, wielding the spiritual sword to help establish the legitimacy of thirteenth-century minority successions not just in England.

The judicious and restrained exercise of temporal power was also critical to the success of Henry III's minority regime. The collective responsibility displayed by the baronage, unmatched in the history of other thirteenth-century European royal minorities, set a high bar for disinterested administration that was never fully matched in five subsequent royal minorities. At the same time, the person of the king was absolutely necessary to provide legitimacy for the actions of his minority government; witness the youthful king's personal presence at Rockingham Castle in 1220, critical for the resumption of royal custody, an act mirrored three and a half centuries later by Edward VI's emphatic letter to the Devonshire rebels of 1549, commanding them in his name to cease and desist in their treason. In both cases, the ultimate locus of royal power rested unambiguously within the bosom of the underage king, a fact never lost on the men who staffed minority regimes, with the notable exception of Edward Seymour, duke of Somerset.

Because he was fourteen when he became king in 1327, following the constitutional trauma of his father's deposition, Edward III's minority bequeathed different yet equally durable precedents, as Edward III was recognized as a king fully vested in both the estate as well as the office; there was no thought to revive Marshal's position of *Rector Regni et Regnum*, nor indeed was there any individual who conceivably could fill Marshal's shoes. Instead, the real winner here, in the long term, was parliament; presiding over the negotiation of a royal deposition and the accession of a fourteen-year-old king; and providing the consent of the community of the realm for these momentous events.

As the minority progressed, however, *de jure* fiction mingled uneasily with de facto reality. While a minority council was duly appointed in parliament, and initially began to perform its mandate, there subsequently was a decided lack of motivation or organization to provide substance for the engines of consensus, while Queen Isabella and her paramour, Roger de Mortimer, failed to exercise either fiscal or foreign policy restraint. Nevertheless, as James Bothwell has shown, the entire epoch of Edward II's final years and Edward III's minority and early majority reign displays striking administrative continuity, as Edward III made the smoothest of transitions to a long and momentous majority reign, once Mortimer was sacrificed and dowager queen Isabella was rusticated.

Richard II seemingly represented the ultimate triumph of primogeniture, succeeding Edward III at the age of ten even though he had three adult royal uncles quite capable of ruling without the employment of political fictions. The form and function of his de facto minority was remarkably similar to the *model* of 1327, the crucial difference here is that the council appointed in parliament continued to perform its functions, as both John of Gaunt and Richard's mother, the dowager princess of Wales, used their preeminent positions to secure stability without the need for even a de facto regency, allowing consensus to emerge.

As Gwilym Dodd has argued, Gaunt's exclusion from membership on the continual councils implied no diminution of his power and influence, which was employed to complement, not compete with, the "fiction" of Richard II's status as a minor. Dodd further suggested that Richard might have been better served by a Gaunt regency that might have implanted a sense of discipline within a youthful king who was spared the rod, to forever bear the historical cross of youthful incompetence. Indeed, if the causes of Richard's deposition were to be found in his minority experience, then sixteenth-century Tudor apologists such as Edward Hall were perfectly entitled to comprehend a succeeding eighty-three-year dynastic nightmare, commencing with the murder of the deposed but still anointed Richard 1400, the curse of the House of Lancaster, and the probable murder of the innocent Edward V by the wicked usurper Richard III in 1483, which fractured the House of York, a situation only resolved by Henry Tudor's victory at Bosworth.

To early fifteenth-century observers, however, the early years of Richard's de facto minority experience provided an effective and positive model for the political nation following Henry V's unexpected death in August 1422. However, the accession of an infant made the fiction of adult rule established by Edward III and perpetuated by Richard II implausible, requiring a further refinement of the current state of political theory regarding the estate and office of king. As the Lords explained it to Humphrey duke of Gloucester in 1428, Henry VI was fully vested in the estate and office of kingship since the moment of his accession; since he was unable to maintain his estate and wield his office personally because of his tender years, it was both the lords in parliament's right and duty to provide continuity for the execution of the royal office until such time as the king entered into his majority. Indeed, Henry VI's long, corporate style minority government had the potential for more significant ramifications for the development of English kingship than any other minority either before or after it in time, had not Henry VI failed so miserably during his majority reign. The creation of the office of Lord Protector of England, originally created as a symbolic but powerless face saving device for Gloucester, later evolved into an occasional but formidable vice-regal position for nearly two centuries, until the regicide Oliver Cromwell finally rendered the position untenable in the seventeenth century.

While Henry VI's minority experience represented the apex of collective stability, this powerful precedent dissolved as factionalism destroyed Edward V's reign as it fractured the house of York. Indeed, it was precedents derived from Henry VI's minority that provided the political logic behind the Wydeville decision to crown Edward as quickly as possible, as Michael Hicks has made abundantly clear. For the succeeding house of Tudor, all positive precedents derived from previous royal minorities were filtered through the lens of Richard III's violent usurpation of the throne.

Indeed, if the first two Tudor kings believed their own propaganda, the history of English royal minorities was central to their understanding of their kingdom's recent history. Henry VIII could hardly bank on the appearance of "coherent principles of collective noble responsibility," which had failed so miserably in 1483. Instead, Henry called upon parliament, his great partner in the jurisdictional phase of the English Reformation, to grant him the statutory authority to create his own version of minority consensus and stability, which was based squarely upon the corporate models of Richard II and Henry VI's minority regimes, and vested in the only recently emergent Privy Council, a striking example of the intersection of medieval precedent with the modernizing trends of the Tudor state.

As Edward VI's minority commenced, parliament's unique relationship with minority regimes reached a further level of development, as statute law emerged as the form in which Reformation religious policy was implemented. Indeed, both Mary's Counter-Reformation legislation and Elizabeth's reestablishment of an independent Anglican church followed the model laid down during Edward's minority, as did the Privy Council driven executive, formulated during Northumberland's ascendancy, which reached its developmental fruition under Elizabeth.

Indeed, the Tudor minority seemingly represented a remarkable break with the medieval minority past. Or did it? As the anonymous writer of the "Notes concerning the minority of a king" manuscript noted, according to the political theory behind the precedent of 1429, and the motivation for a swift coronation in 1483, the crowning of the underage king obviated the need for a lord protector in 1547, as the fiction of adult rule could then commence once Edward VI was crowned. The eighteenth-century mind, more comfortable with a rigidly defined constitution than their mid-Tudor counterparts, was evidently not sure whether Somerset's appointment as Protector was reflective of medieval precedent, or an early modern break with the past. Nevertheless, writing in the twilight of the eighteenth-century Whig oligarchy, the author drew the obvious parallels that were later integrated into the venerable but now discredited Whig interpretation of history: Henry III's reconfirmations of Magna Carta, the lords in parliament's ability to thwart duke Humphrey's pretensions in 1428, and Edward VI's providential participation in the building of an English Protestant Church.

The collective impact of English minority reigns also finds a home in more recent historiographical trends. In the introduction to their volume entitled *Tudor England and Its Neighbors,* historians Susan Doran and Glenn Richardson suggested that Tudor foreign policy was formulated as ad hoc "crisis management" responses to immediate situations, rather than long-term formulations that pointed toward the inevitable march of political modernity. A similar conclusion might be drawn from the history of English royal minorities. As all the preceding chapters attest, no real permanent constitutional mechanisms were ever put into place to prescribe the form and function of a minority government. Nevertheless, with the single exception of Edward V's failed reign, English royal minorities were symptomatic of quantum leaps in the political importance and relevance of corporate administrative structures; inner, greater, and privy councils, and the increased scope and competency of parliament as a legislative and advisory body, developments which represent the greatest collective legacy of English minority reigns.

INDEX